AF477852

Andrei Sharov

Andrei Sharov

SKIRA

Art Director
Marcello Francone

Design
Luigi Fiore

Editorial Coordination
Vincenza Russo

Editing
Anna Albano

Iconographical Research
Paola Lamanna

First published in Italy in 2016 by
Skira Editore S.p.A.
Palazzo Casati Stampa
via Torino 61
20123 Milano
Italy
www.skira.net

Printed and bound in Italy. First edition

ISBN: 978-88-572-2879-2

Distributed in USA, Canada, Central & South
America by Rizzoli International Publications,
Inc., 300 Park Avenue South, New York, NY
10010, USA.
Distributed elsewhere in the world by
Thames and Hudson Ltd., 181A High
Holborn, London WC1V 7QX, United
Kingdom.

Photo Credits
© 2016. Digital Image The Museum
of Modern Art, New York / Scala, Firenze:
p. 96 bottom
© 2016. Foto Fine Art Images / Heritage
Images / Scala, Firenze: p. 98
© 2016. Foto Scala, Firenze: p. 96 top
© 2016. Tate, London / Foto Scala, Firenze:
p. 118
© National Gallery London / Art Resource,
NY: p. 95 bottom
© RMN-Grand Palais / Art Resource, NY:
p. 101
© RMN-Grand Palais / René-Gabriel Ojéda /
Art Resource, NY: p. 102 right
© RMN-Réunion des Musées Nationaux /
distr. Alinari, Firenze: p. 116 left
© RMN / Thierry Le Mage / Réunion des
Musées Nationaux / distr. Alinari: p. 95 top
© Städtische Galerie im Lenbachhaus:
p. 99 top
Bridgeman Images / Alinari: p. 117 right
Bridgeman-Giraudon / Art Resource, NY:
p. 102 left
HIP / Art Resource, NY: p. 106 bottom
HIP / Art Resource, NY: p. 112 bottom
HIP / Art Resource, NY: p. 97
Iberfoto / Archivi Alinari: p. 116 right
Scala / Art Resource, NY: p. 99, bottom right

Editors
Paola Gribaudo
Agniya Mirgorodskaya

Curators
Vasily Klyukin
Oksana Salamatina

Producers
Andrey Srtukov
Olga Sorokina
Marc Ivasilevitch
Victoria Lukyanenko
Alex Shakhsuvarov

Contents

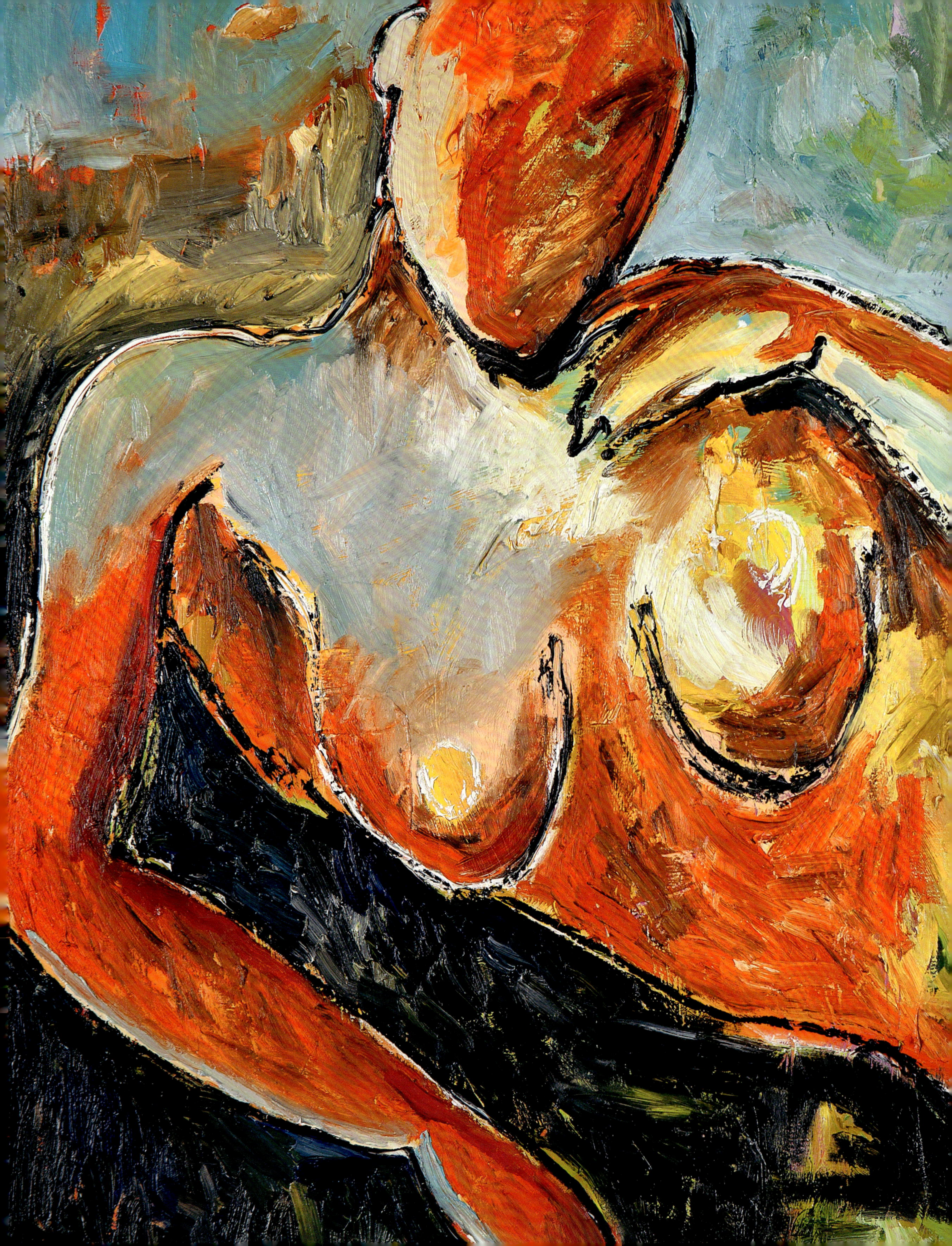

At Home in the World

Lilly Wei

Lilly Wei is a New York-based art critic, art writer and independent curator.

Reclining No. 3 (detail), 2012

Andrei Sharov is a multidisciplinary Russian artist of international repute whose projects have taken him all over the world. Like countless artists before him, including such illustrious compatriots as Mikhail Vrubel, Kazimir Malevich, Aleksandr Rodchenko and Liubov Popova as well as others such as Picasso who famously collaborated with Sergei Diaghilev and the Ballets Russes, Andrei Sharov is enthralled by theater and dance and is a celebrated designer of costumes and stage sets. Commissioned by Renault, he designed a Formula One racecar for Fernando Alonso, acclaimed as the most beautiful automobile at the Grand Prix of Turkey in 2006. He is a couturier of great originality and flair, his interest in fashion of longstanding. In addition, Sharov is a photographer, particularly interested in portraits that investigate the inner life of their sitters. He is also a painter of note, his temperament inevitably leads him toward the expressionistic, dramatic and extravagant—a hallmark of all his projects—and toward increasingly brilliant, combustible hues.

His vivid, often high-contrast paintings can be rough as well as fluid, driven by his love of the pigment's materiality, by its sensuousness and versatility. His paintings crackle with energy, at times brimming over with an emotionality uncannily produced by color and brushstroke. Because Sharov works across disciplines, even though they might overlap, he does not want to belong to any particular group of artists, preferring the independence of an outsider. And he is always willing to take creative risks, open to new stimuli supported by a vast archive of historical sources.

Sharov was born in Moscow in 1966. He studied at the Moscow Institute of Technology, graduating with a degree in fashion design in 1987. He has always wanted to be an artist; for him there were never any other possibilities. He studied painting and drawing privately at first, encouraged by his parents, although his father was a physicist and his mother a mathematician. He continued to study fine arts at the Moscow Institute, even while pursuing a degree in fashion. His influences are many but artists to whom he feels particularly close include Vrubel, Gustav Klimt, Vincent van Gogh, Willem de Kooning, Andy Warhol, and Jean-Michel Basquiat. Sharov, like several of these artists, values spontaneity. He does not use preliminary sketches and prefers to make his paintings in one session as one prolonged, continuous burst of energy, similar to the processes of Zen masters, capturing the forces of the moment.

Sharov maintains a large studio in Moscow but also has one in Monaco and in other European art centers such as Paris and Amsterdam, as the need and inclination arise. He says he finds it invigorating to work in different studios; they give him fresh impetus. He also prefers to work without interruption and when in work mode, he shuts his studio doors for complete privacy, so engrossed that he loses track of time, he says. His medium at the moment is oil, but he has also experimented with less traditional materials, some of which have been highly toxic to work with, if also very beautiful.

Sharov's first acknowledged painting was *Big Paunch with Ear and Eye* (Bolshepuzui Uhoglaz, p. 8) from 1987, which depicts a satiric, cartoonish figure

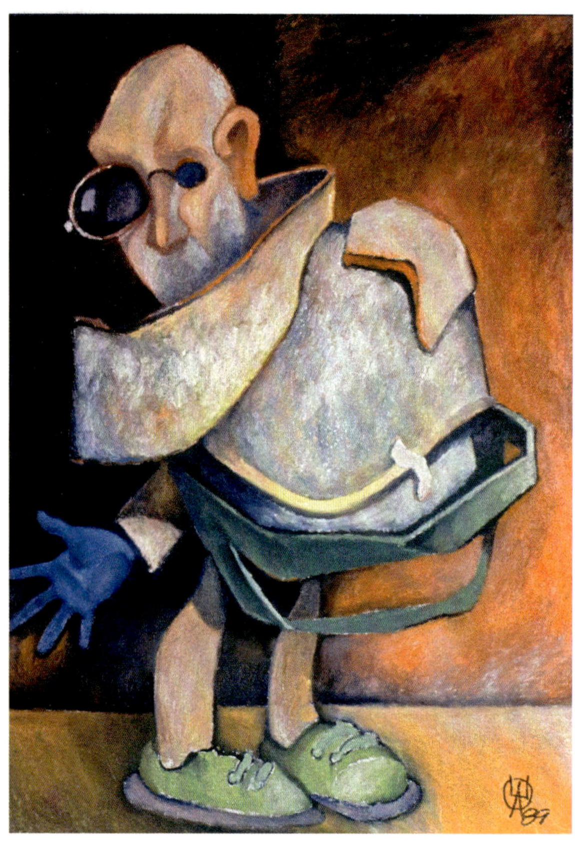

with sociopolitical implications. In this painting, it can be seen that he has always been a colorist, his insistent, staccato brushwork already in evidence, already assured. He is a painter of abstracted figurative forms, his subjects often based on portraits, still lifes, interiors, and combinations of these genres which he sometimes presents as assemblages of sorts, his palette a full spectrum, with red a favorite hue, the star of his color repertoire.

In his painted portraits as in his photographs, he is deeply engaged by states of feelings, embodied as much through the treatment of the paint as through facial expression. One portrait is that of a girl with an abundance of soft brown hair and a lushly brushed red hat that recalls Modigliani in the pure oval of the face, the extended line of the nose. The eyes are cast down, the mouth omitted, her thoughts enigmatic. But it is the richly textured, tremulous markings that bear the burden of expression, and the picture is all the more compelling because of sensitive brushwork.

Sharov likes to re-work the same themes, reconfiguring them to explore other meanings, other readings, each ultimately unique. Some of his recent paintings have appropriated famous nudes, such as Ingres' *Grande Odalisque* (p. 95), translating the smooth elegance and sumptuous details of the Neoclassical masterpiece into flickered strokes of paint and bold, jarring patches of colors that convey not only Sharov's personal intensity and restlessness but also the agitated tempo and dissonances that characterize current culture. The head of Sharpov's pink and white nude, *Old Courtesan (Nude Woman Reclining on a Sofa)*, 2012 (pp. 12–13), is set off by a crimson ground like a profane halo. She is holding a turquoise fan, a cloud of bright, yolk-colored yellow nearby increasing the voltage, the interior presented as a mélange of brash patterns that is the antithesis of the cool, knowing unflappability of the Ingres. Sharov's nude is sexier, heated, more intimate, much more Miami or Las Vegas than nineteenth-century Paris.

Another nude figure is also based on Ingres, on the *Grande Baigneuse*, her voluptuous back to us, transformed by Sharov into a slimmer, more modish woman configured to today's standards, half sheathed in a lipstick red that clashes sharply with the burgundy daubed next to it. Whether this form is nude or not is uncertain visually, although the title is *Nude Woman in a Red Chair*, 2012 (p. 92). Spotlighted, she is seated on the arm of a couch, perhaps in a club, emerging from the velvety dimness of the background, looking far more sexually challenging than Ingres' rather chaste nude. Another painting portrays a male figure, a black man, a hipster, wearing sunglasses and a coolie-like hat, his arms folded, hands yellow and orange, encircled by a lightening strip of red that seems to charge him with energy. He leans out of a painterly ground that is reminiscent of a Clyfford Still, the American Abstract Expressionist of magnificently jagged force fields. Sharov likes to play with narrative intention and to find unexpected associations.

Other nude figures evoke a relationship with the Impressionists and Post-Impressionists, the Fauves and Matisse, their riotous colors reappearing in these paintings, the application of pigment verging on the pointillist at times, the tossed strokes of color displaying Sharov's considerable talent for absorbing and transforming. One nude, holding a towel before her, seems solarized, garbed in electrified hues that suggest a futuristic body suit, the towel to preserve her modesty made redundant. Another nude, reclining, seems almost sculpted by small quick hammer strokes of blistered paint, the colors the crimson orange, turquoise blue and sunny yellow that he often uses, enhanced by violets and lavenders, deep and pale greens in the field behind. The figure's pose is awkward, but it makes her pres-

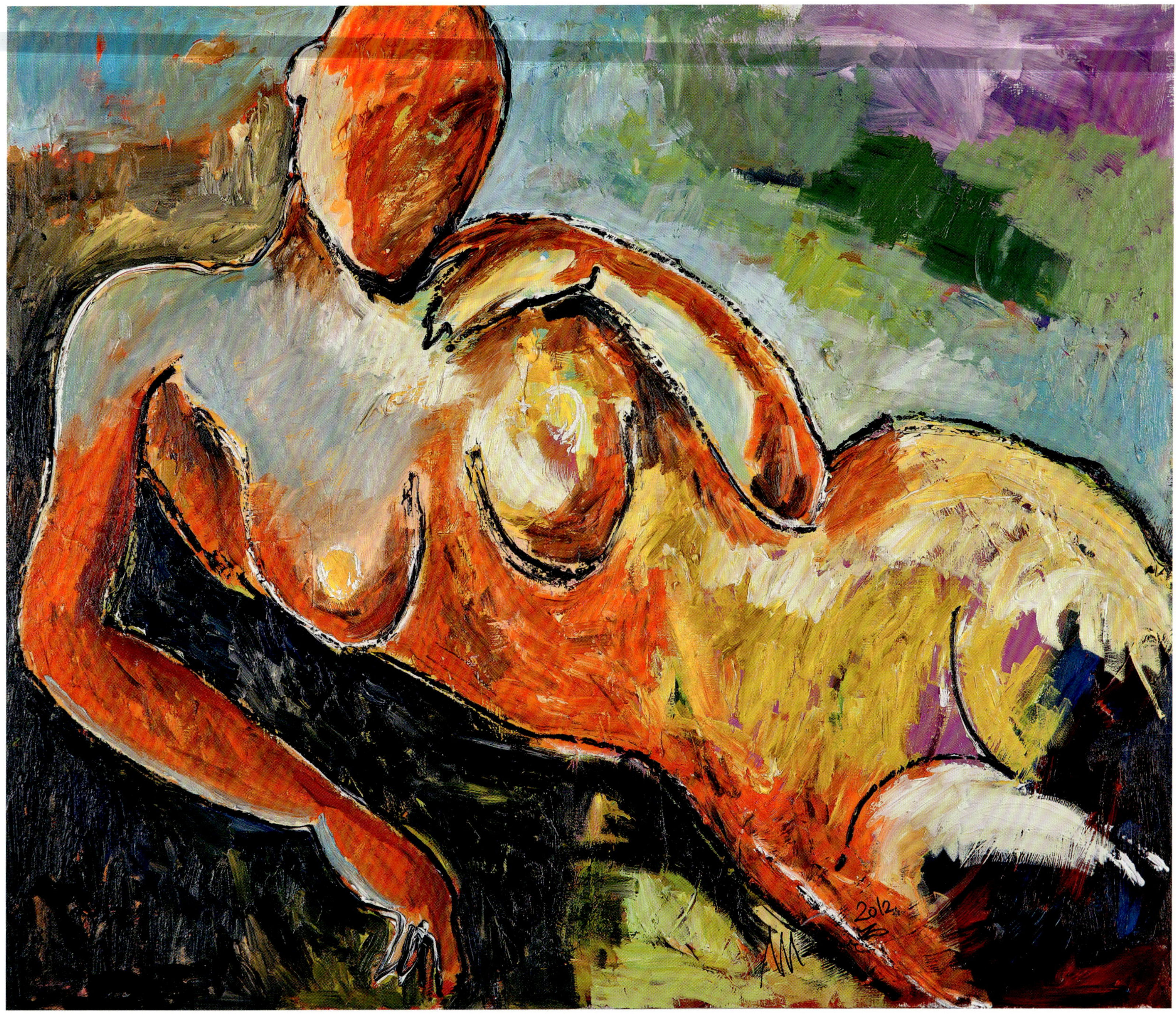

Reclining No. 3, 2012
oil on canvas, 100 x 120 cm
V. Klyukin Collection

ence all the more powerful, all the more felt. Another female nude is more graceful, her body delicately curved, but the flesh is flagellated by thick punctuations of white, yellow, and earth-colored marks, accented by reds, pinks, a touch of green and blue, stretched out, floating in a dark void. A lovely still life of a pastel bowl of pears seen close-up, on the other hand, while equally flickered by paint, is more refined in effect with a whiff of danger, presenting a fragile-appearing surface that suggests crystal on the verge of shattering.

Andrei Sharov is constantly searching for ways to expand his vision and create more complex work, to extend the limits of what he knows in order to enrich his art, pushing beyond his familiar boundaries in order to make himself increasingly cosmopolitan, an ardent chronicler of today's fast-paced, always changing world.

WOMAN

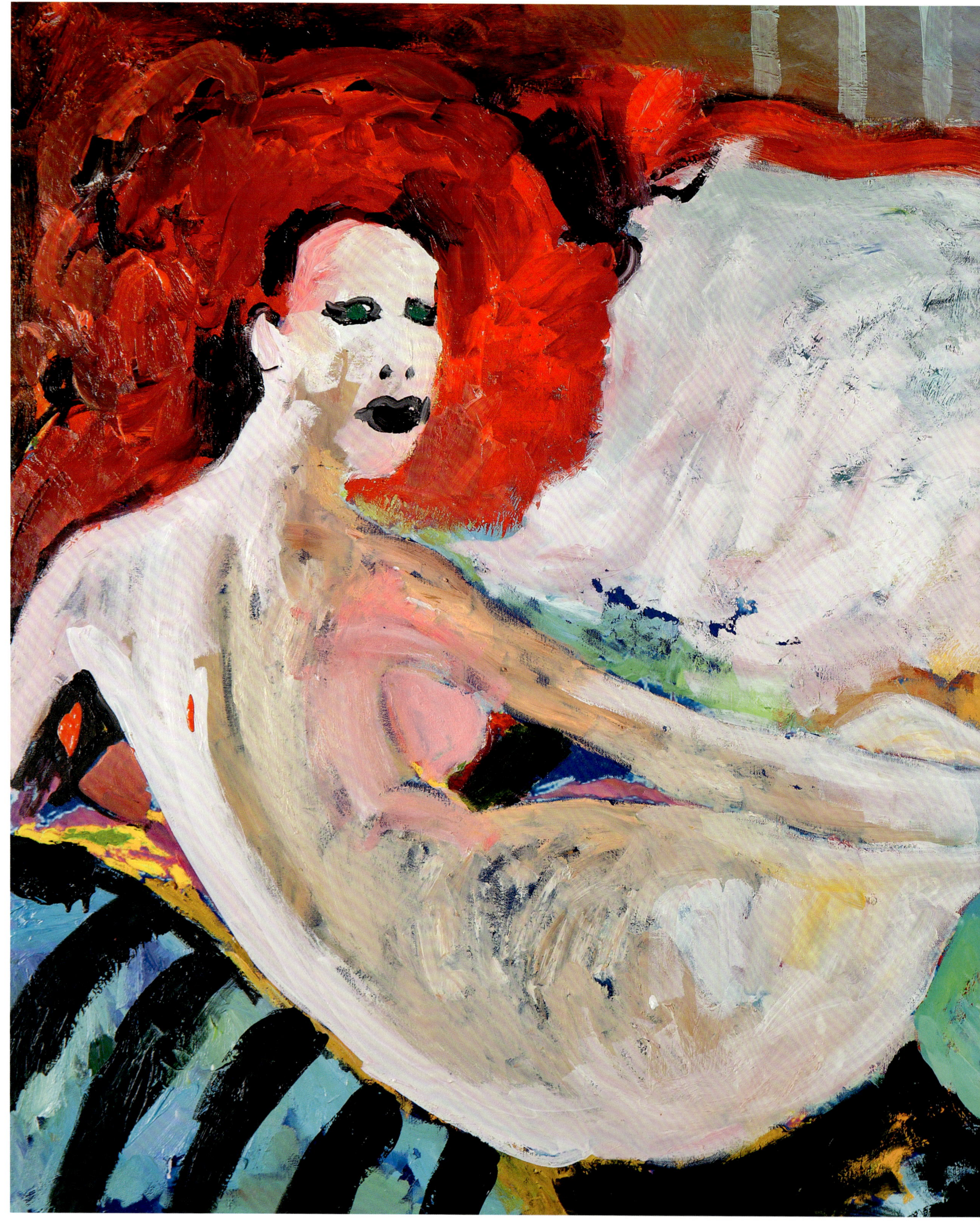

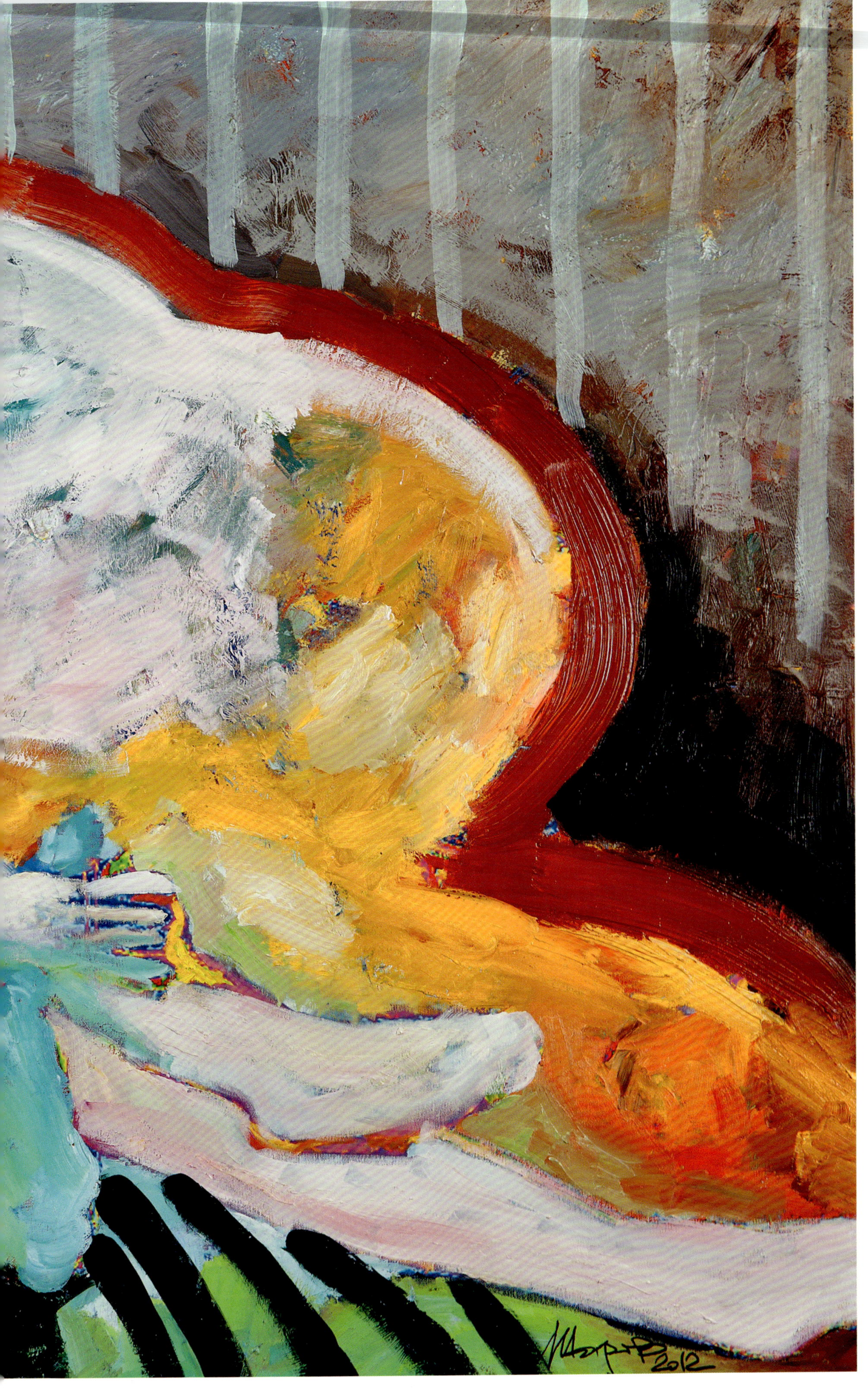

Old Courtesan, 2012
oil on canvas, 100 x 150 cm

Nude in Pink, 2014
oil on canvas, 100 x 120 cm
Private collection

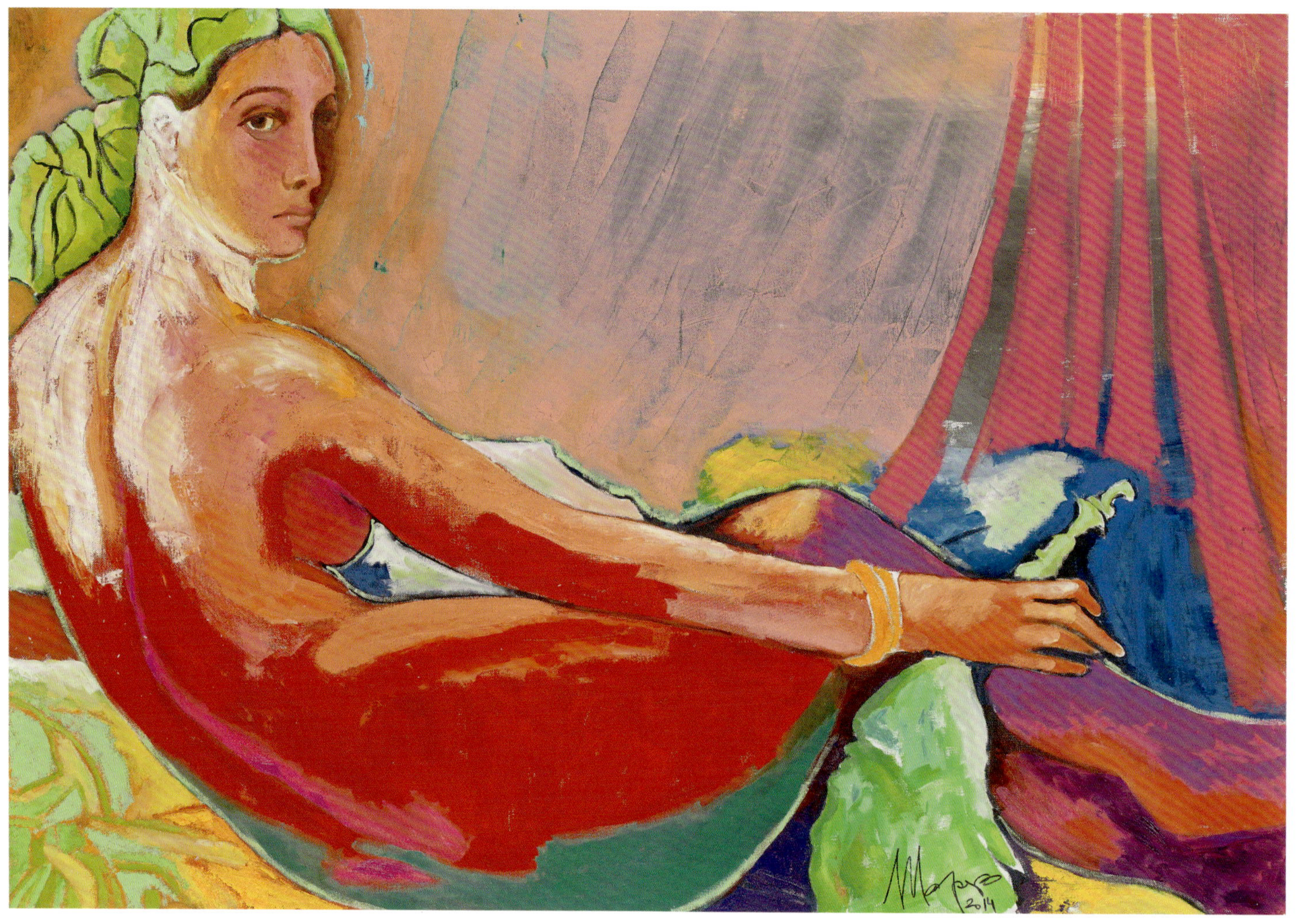

Reclining Nude in Magenta, 2014
oil on canvas, 88.58 x 145.25 cm
Private collection
Courtesy of the artist and Salamatina
Gallery, New York, Atlanta

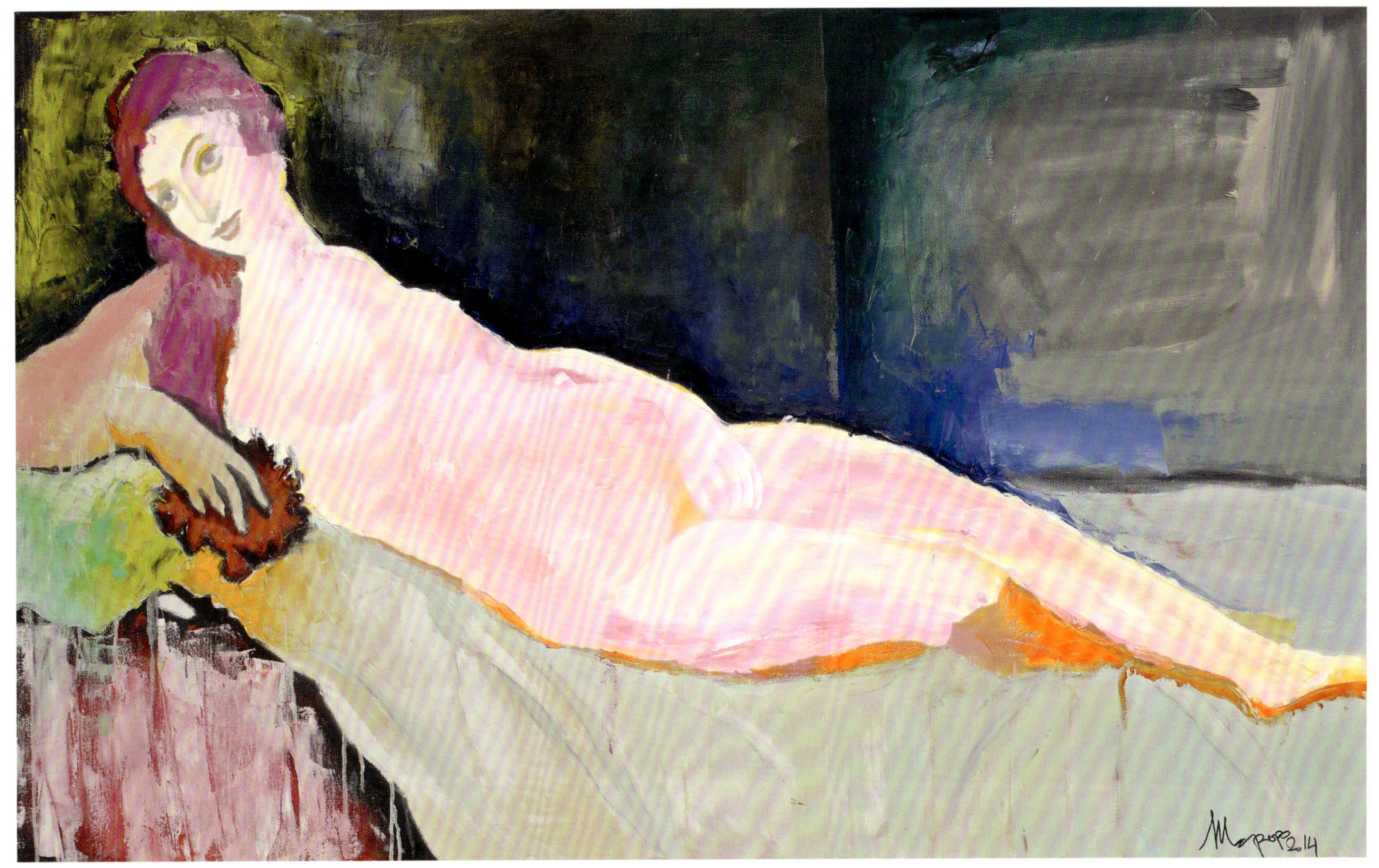

Reclining Nude, Head Resting
on Right Arm, 2012
oil on canvas, 100 x 150 cm
Courtesy Nassau County Museum of Art
(NCMA), Roslyn, New York

Nude in the Sunlight, 2012
oil on canvas, 90 x 60 cm
V. Klyukin Collection

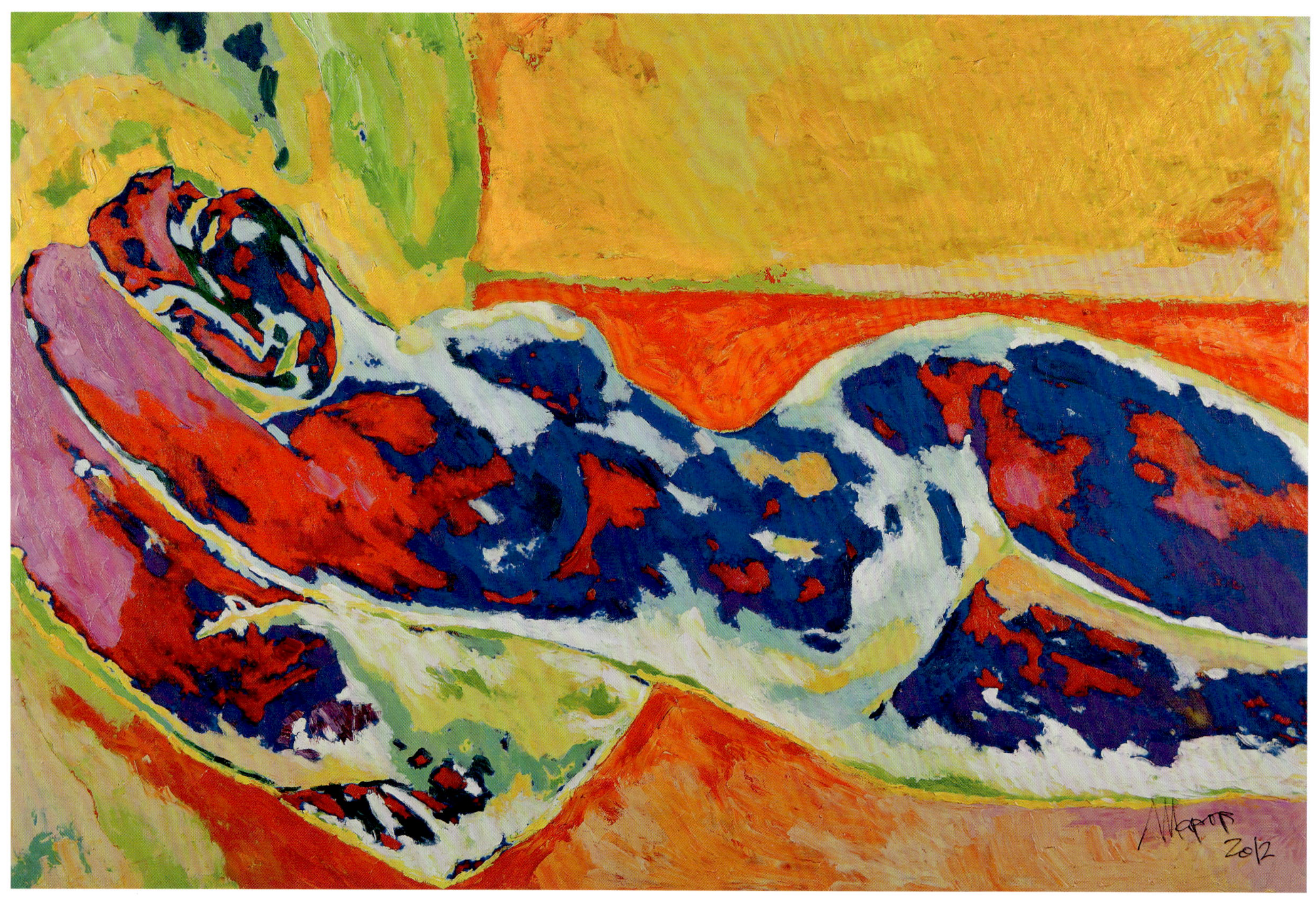

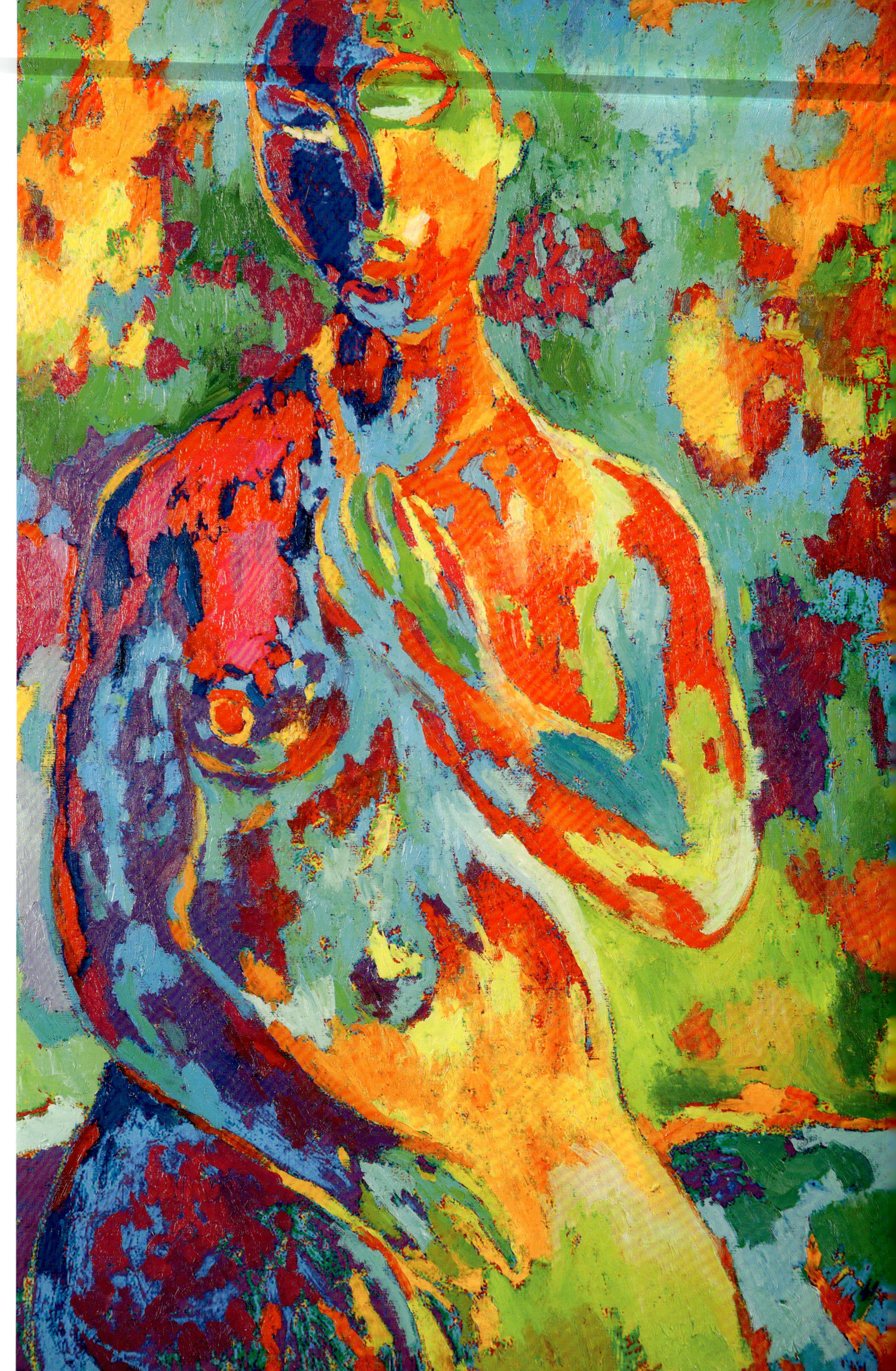

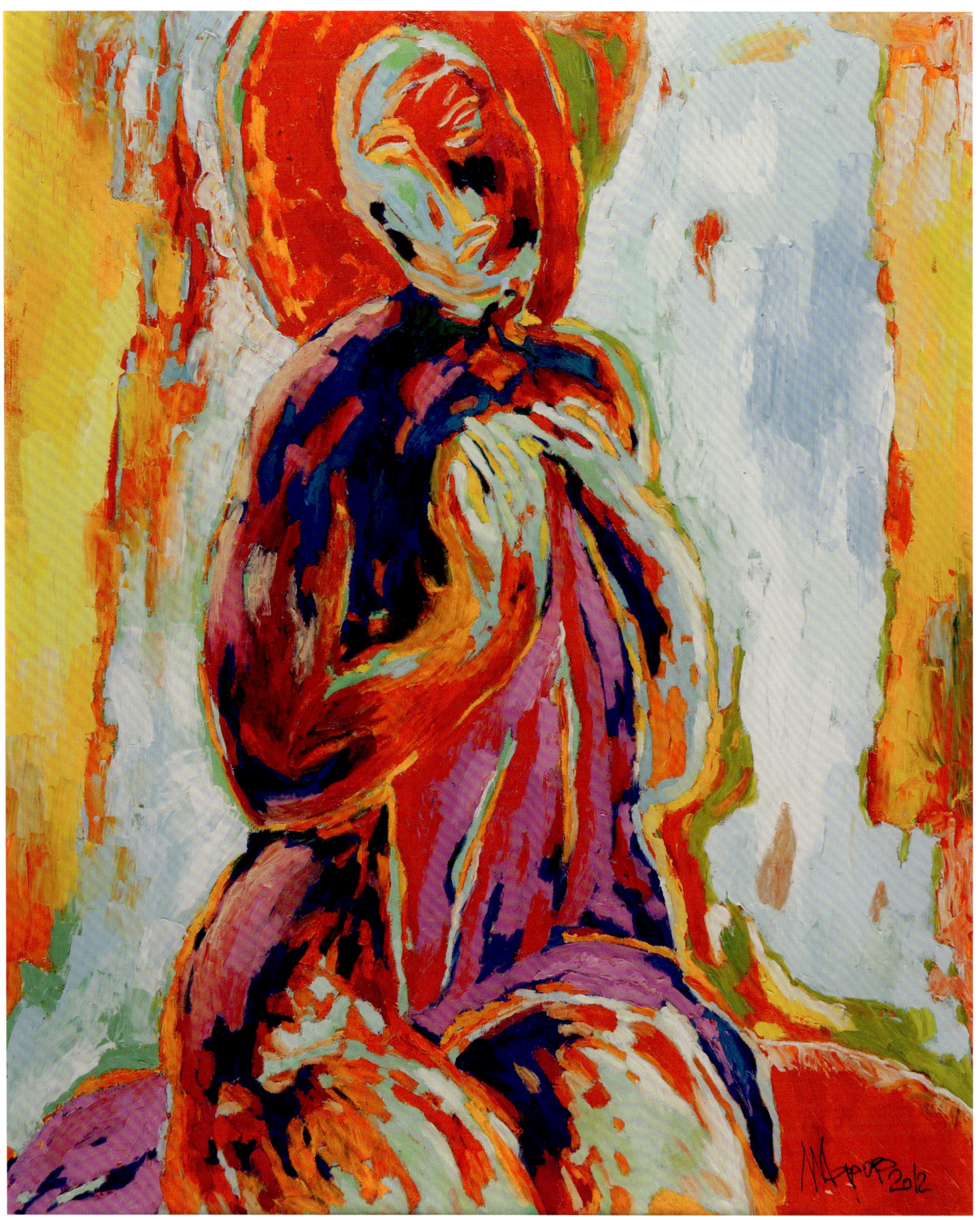

Nude with Towel, 2012
oil on canvas, 120 x 100 cm
V. Klyukin Collection

Homage to de Kooning, 2016
oil on canvas, 120 x 100 cm
Courtesy The Heckscher Museum
of Art, Huntington, New York

Pages 20–21
In the Sun, 2016
oil on canvas, 120 x 190 cm
V. Klyukin Collection

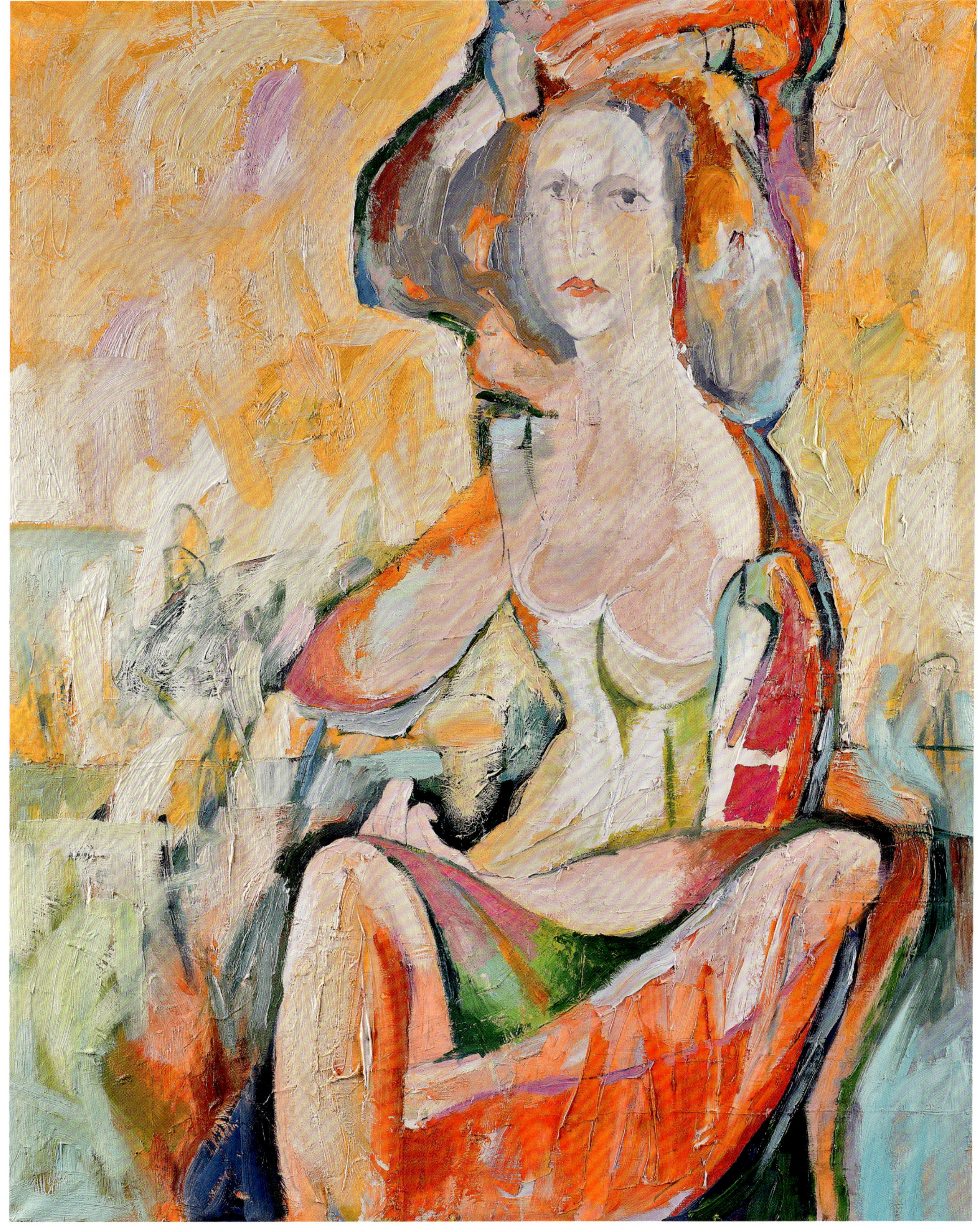

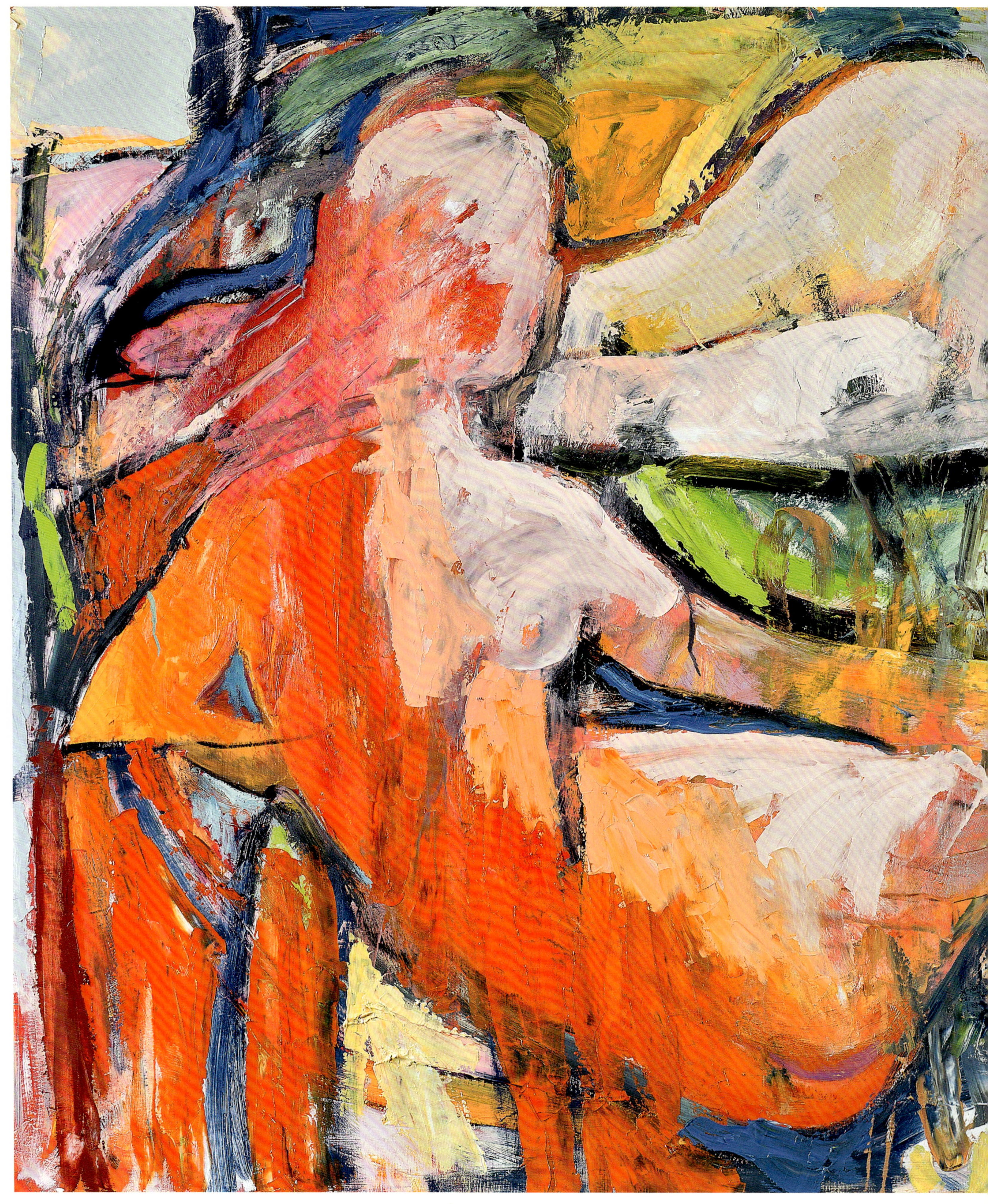

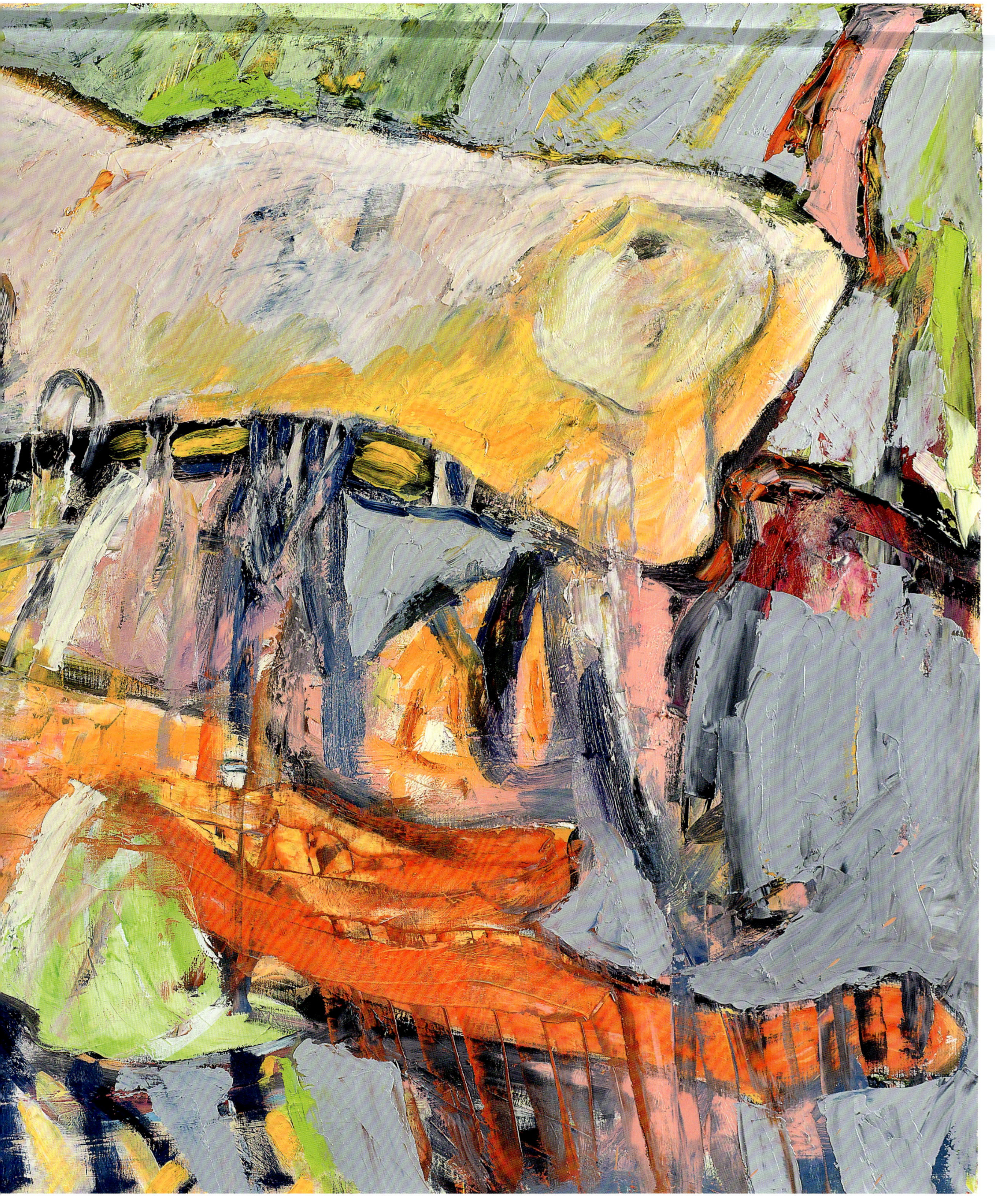

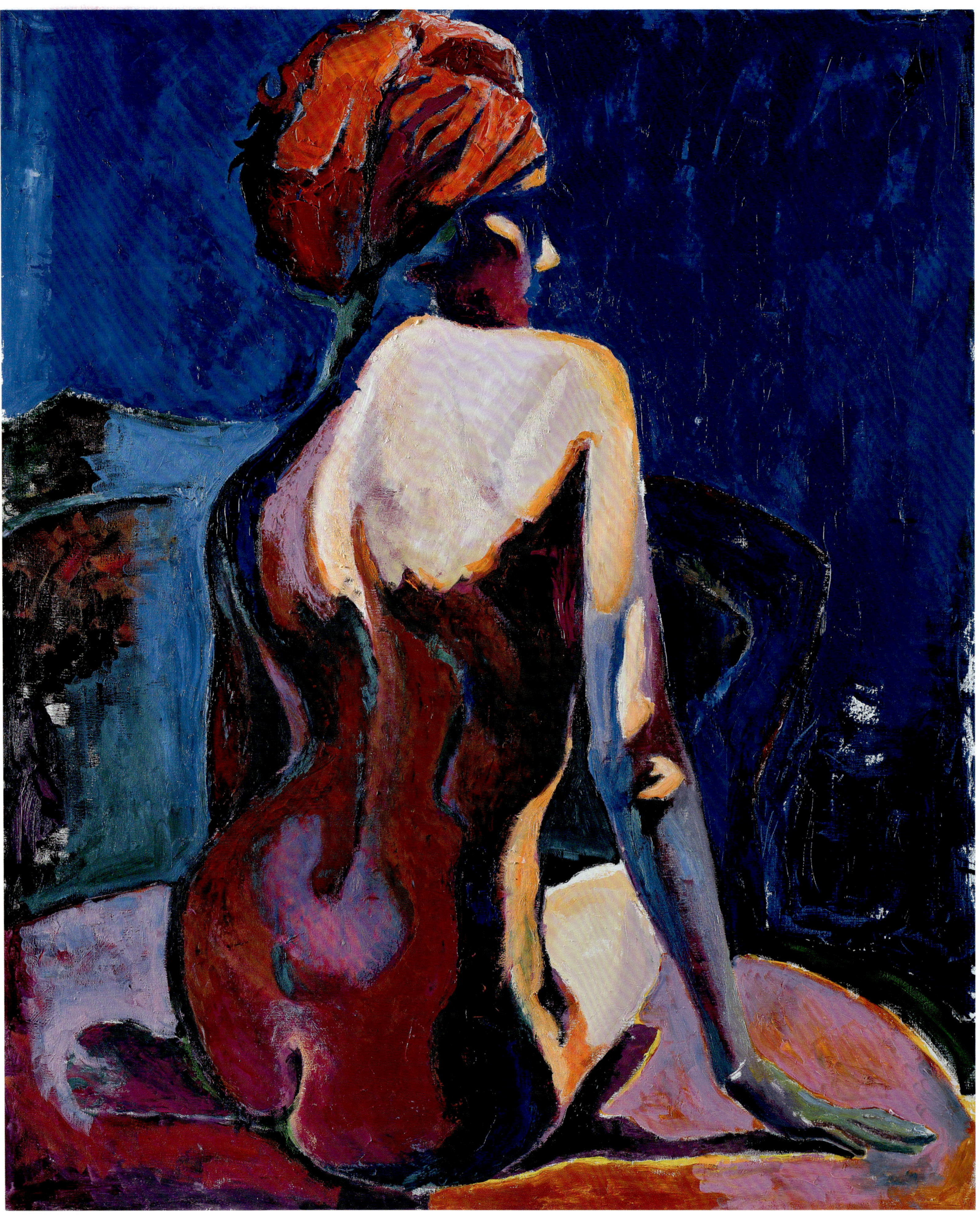

Nocturnal, 2015
oil on canvas, 120 x 100 cm
Alex and Victoria Shahsuvarov
Collection

Flora, 2012
oil on canvas, 150 x 100 cm
Private collection

Page 24
Back, *ZH1* Series, 2014
oil on canvas, 120 x 100 cm
V. Klyukin Collection

Page 25
Back, *ZH1* Series, 2016
oil on canvas, 120 x 100 cm
Property of the artist
Courtesy of the artist
and Salamatina Gallery,
New York, Atlanta

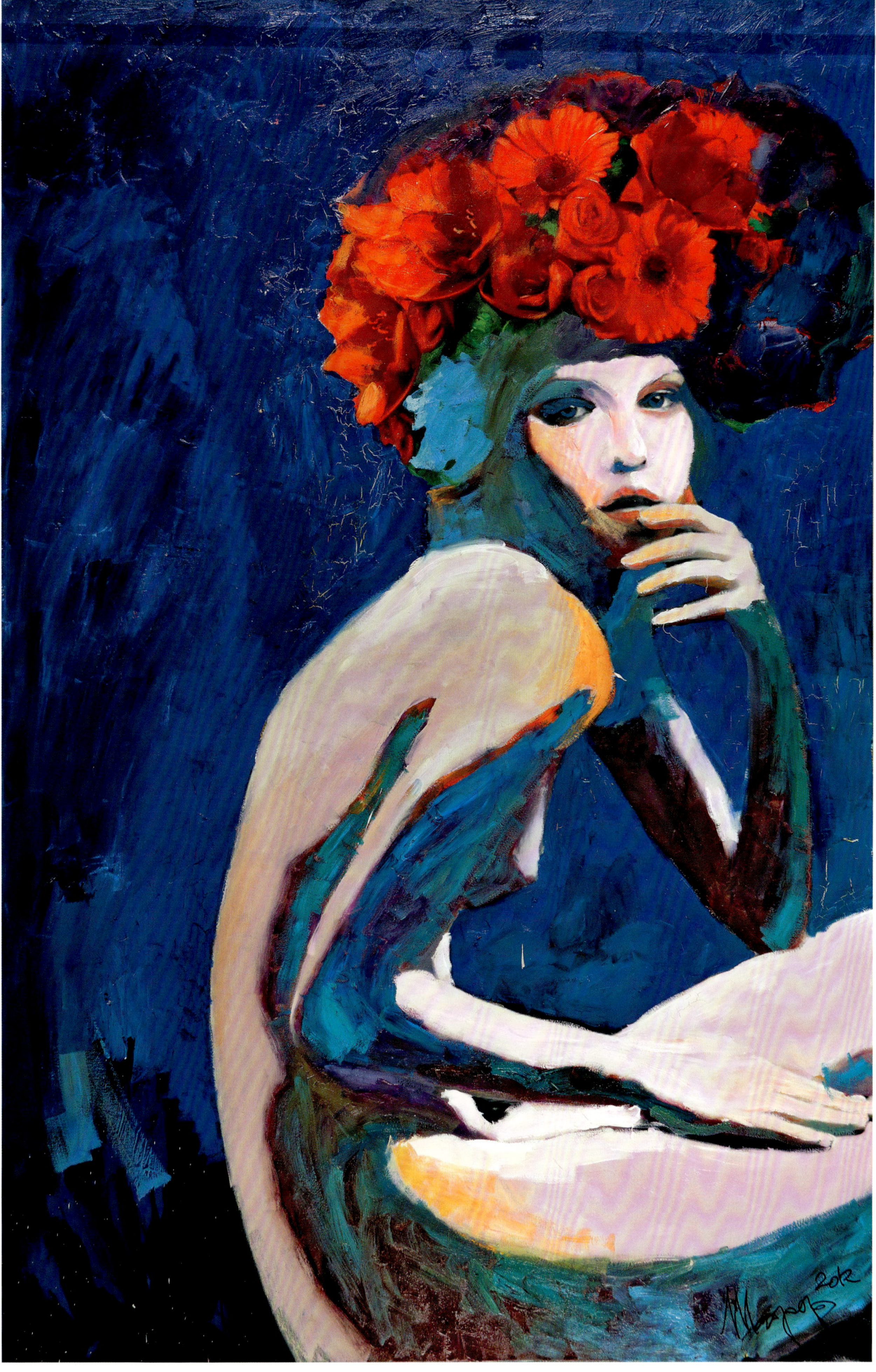

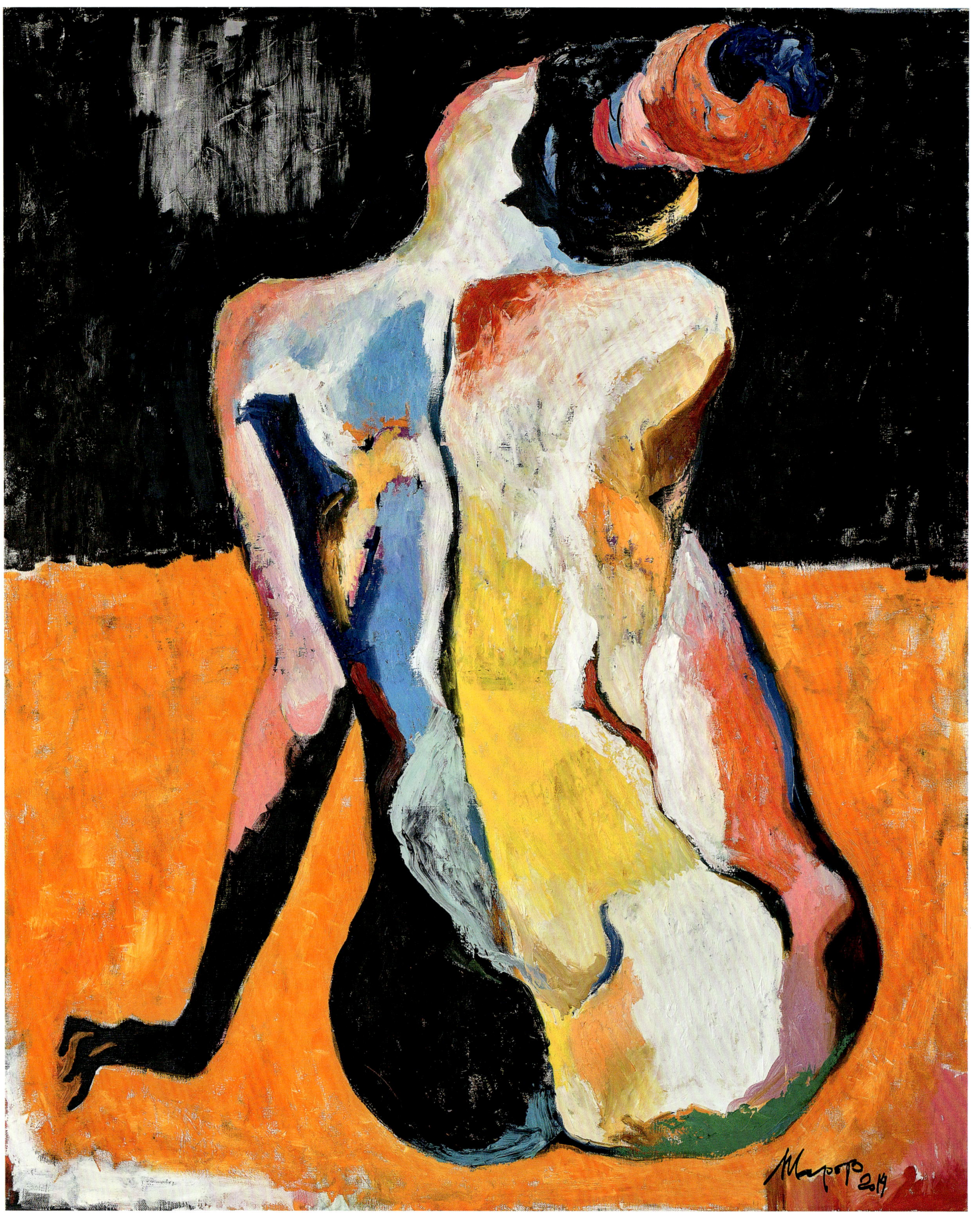

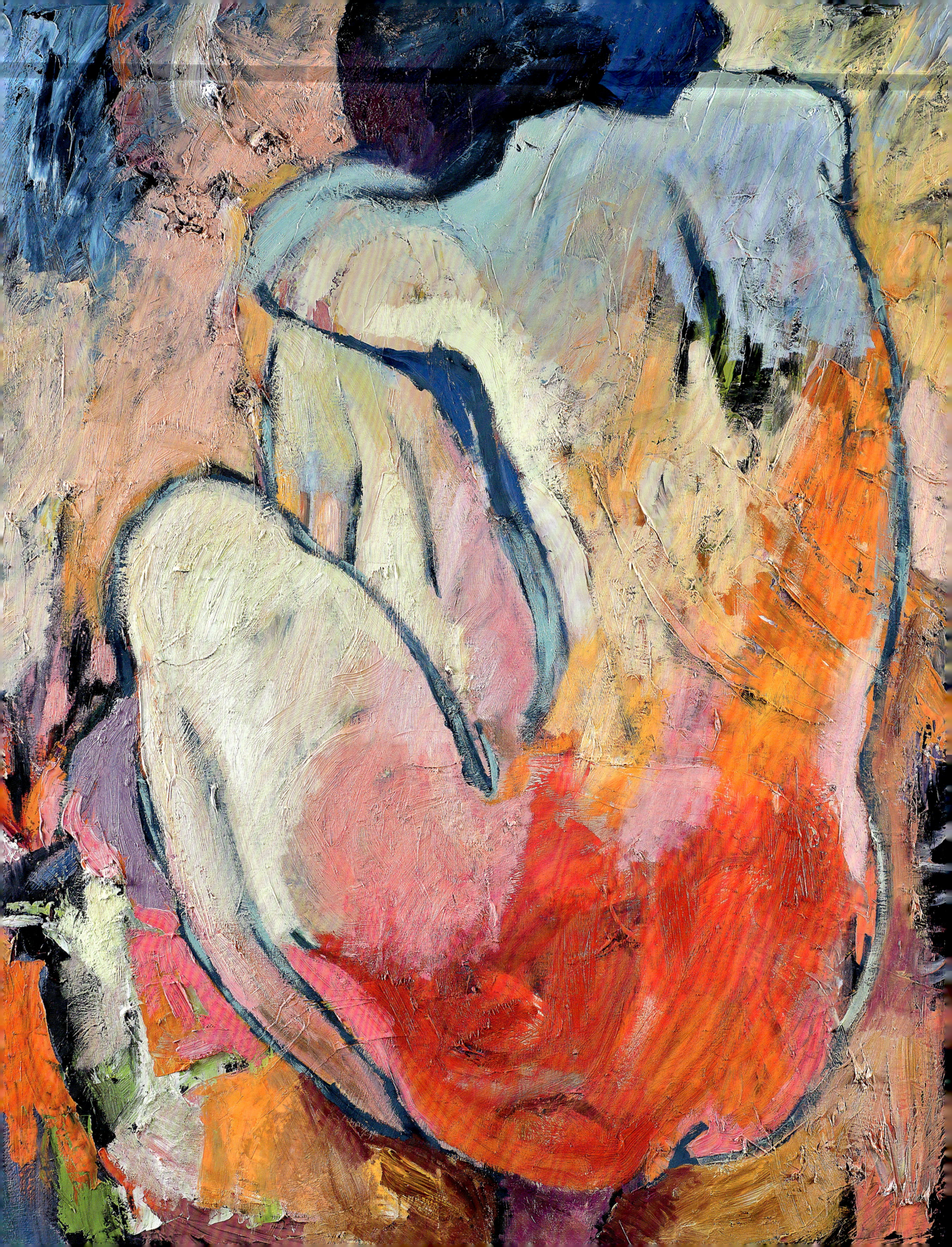

Seated No. 2, 2015
oil on canvas, 60 x 90 cm
V. Klyukin Collection

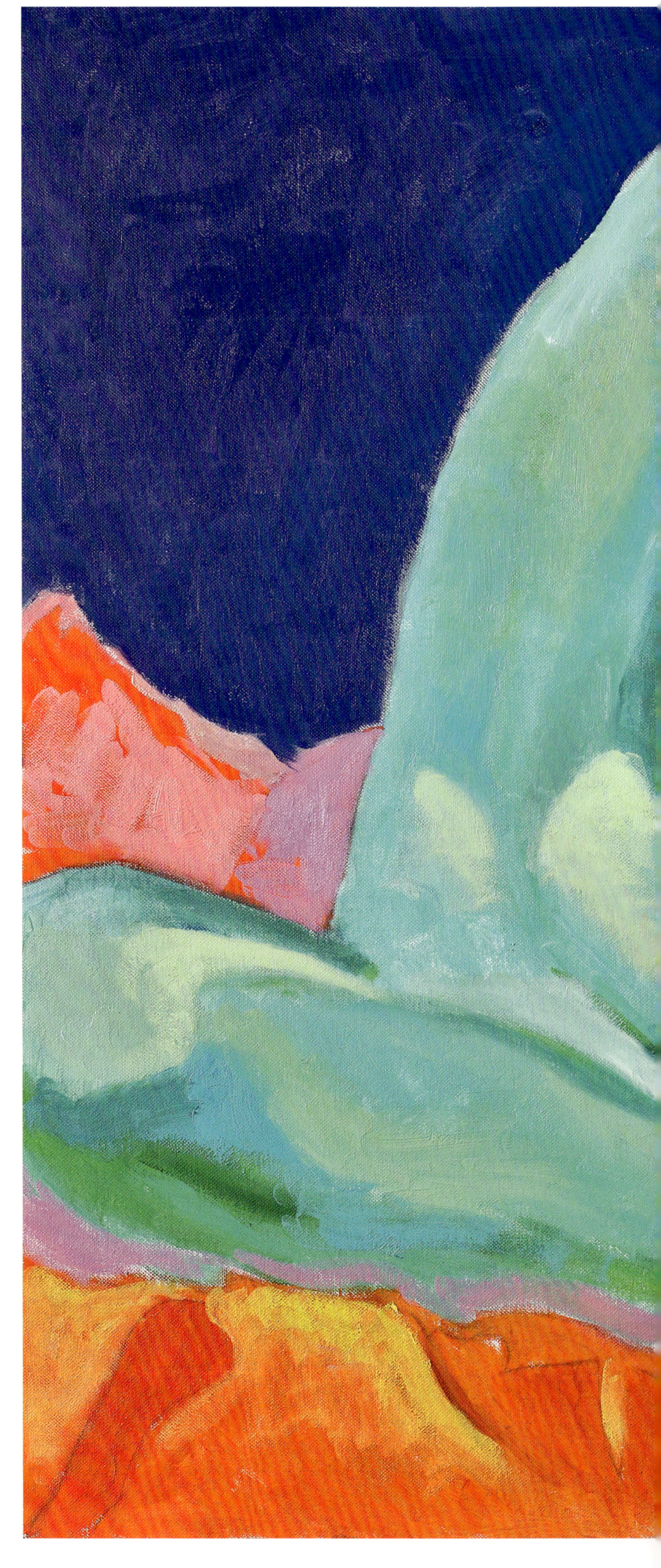

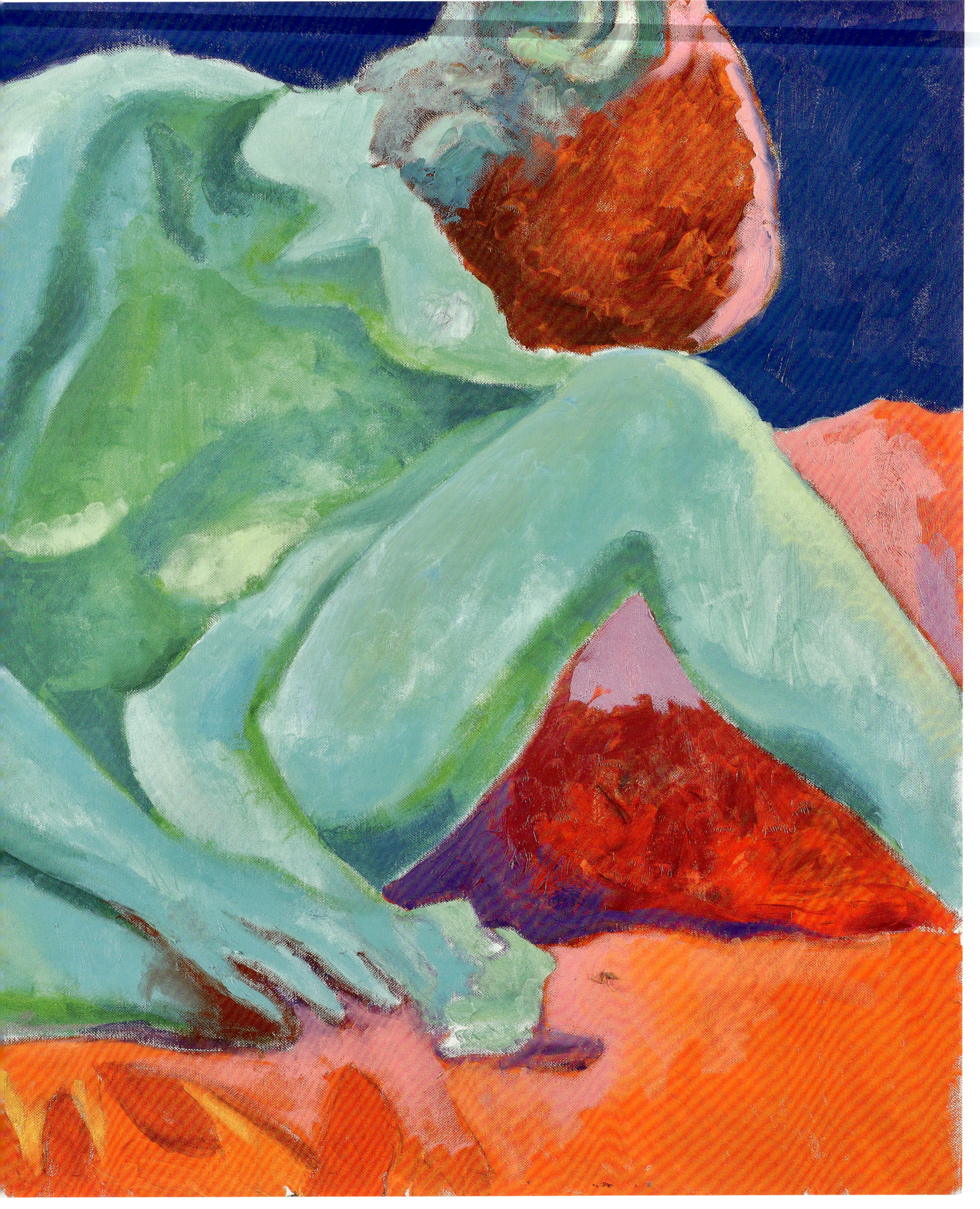

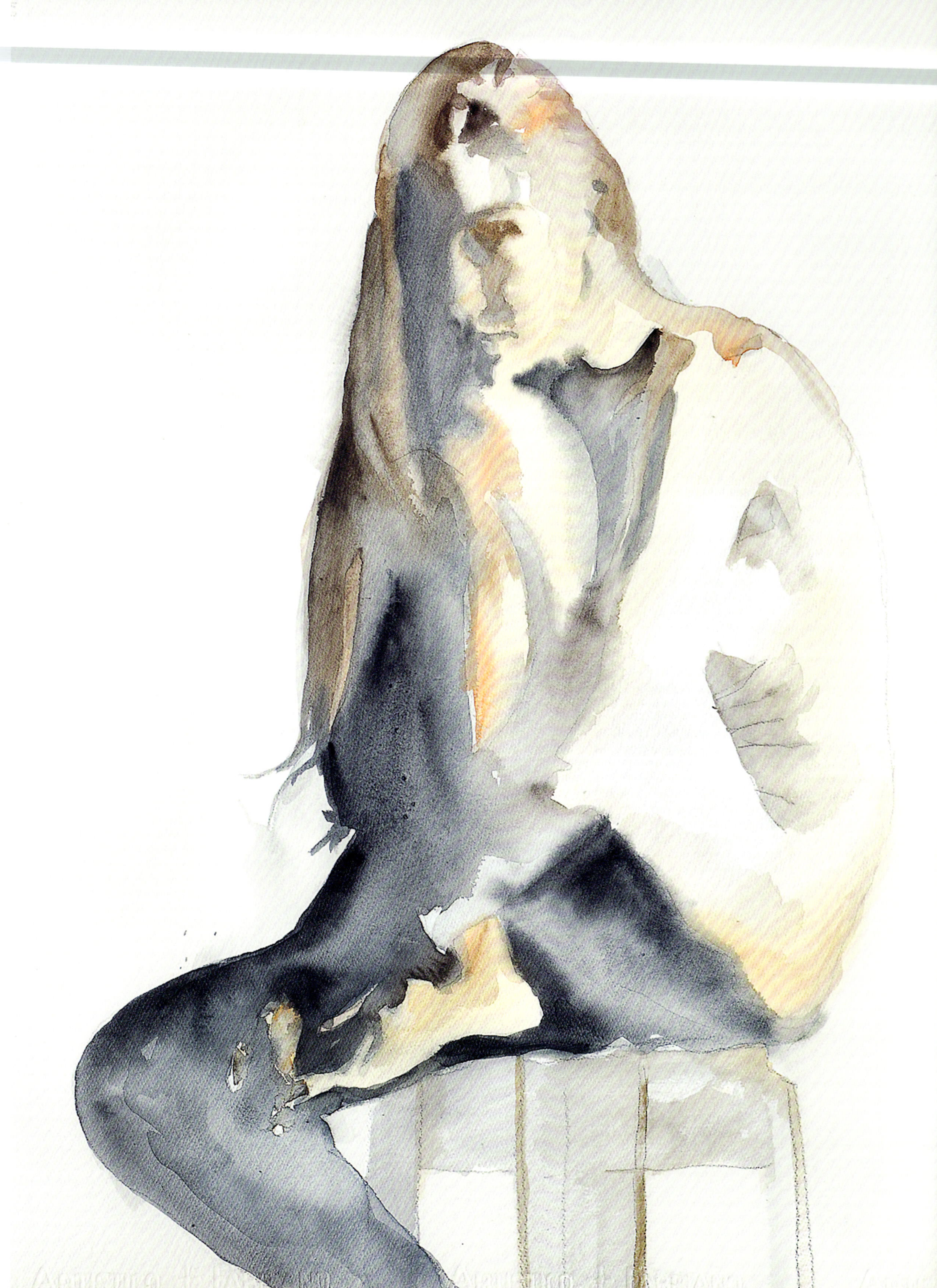

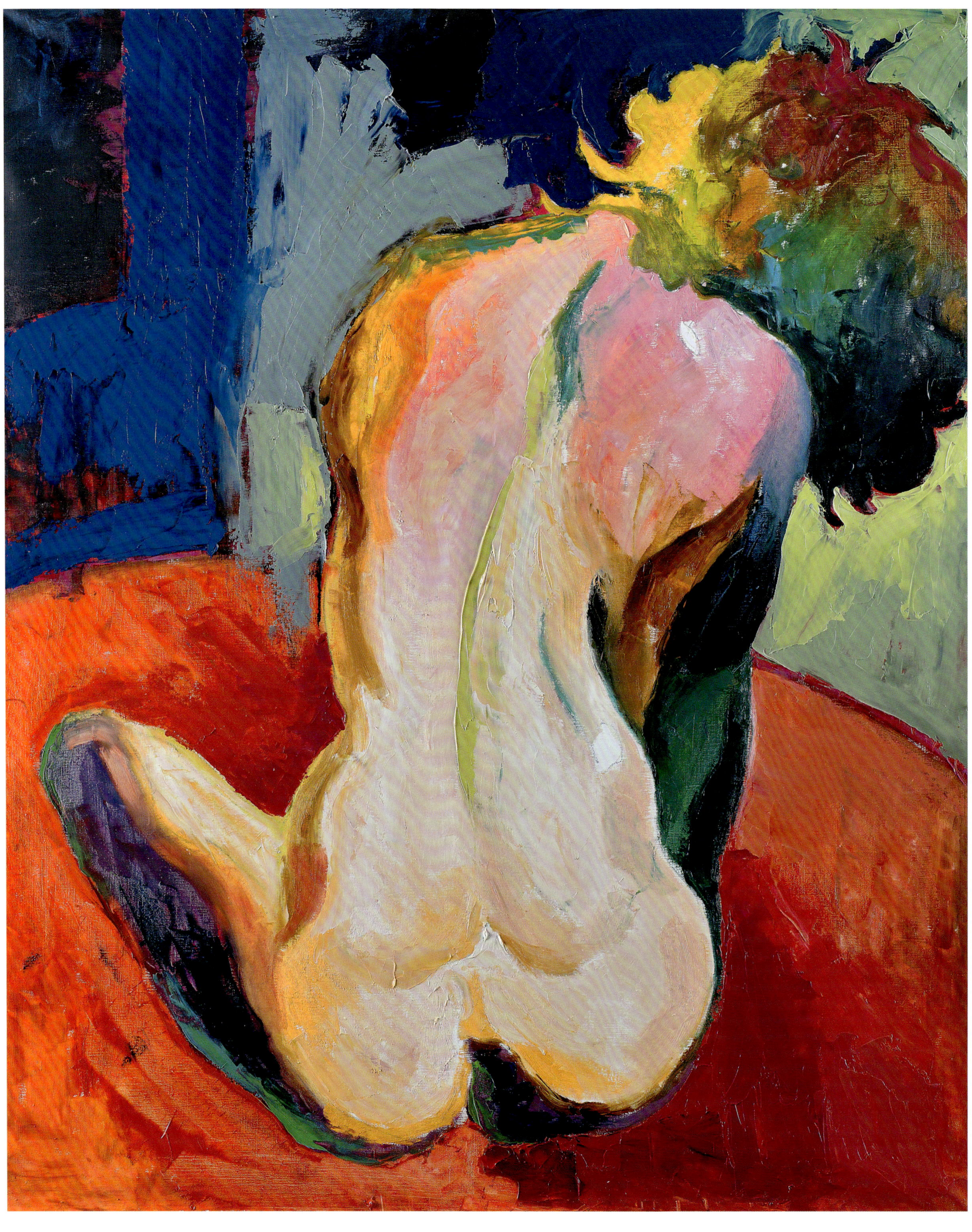

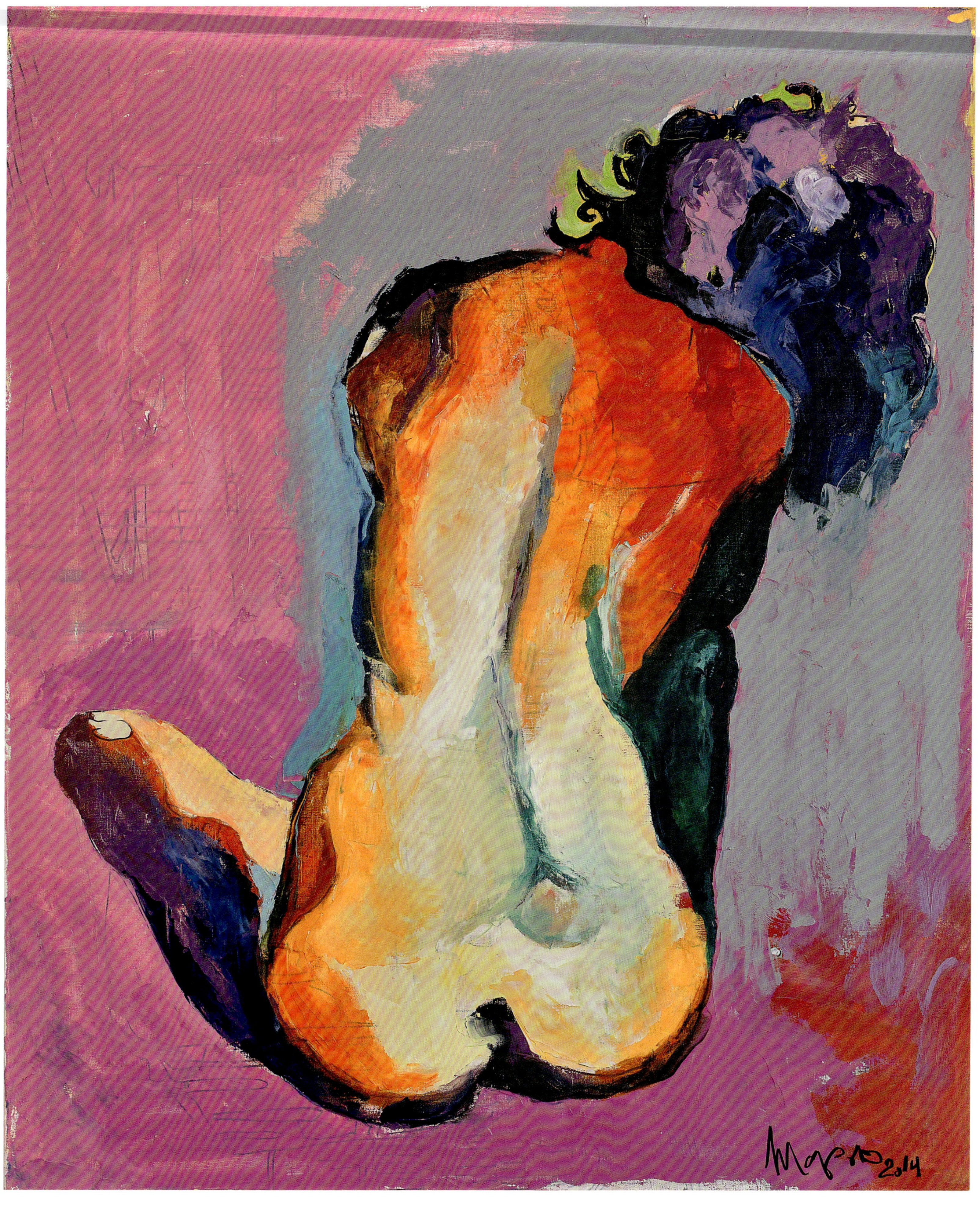

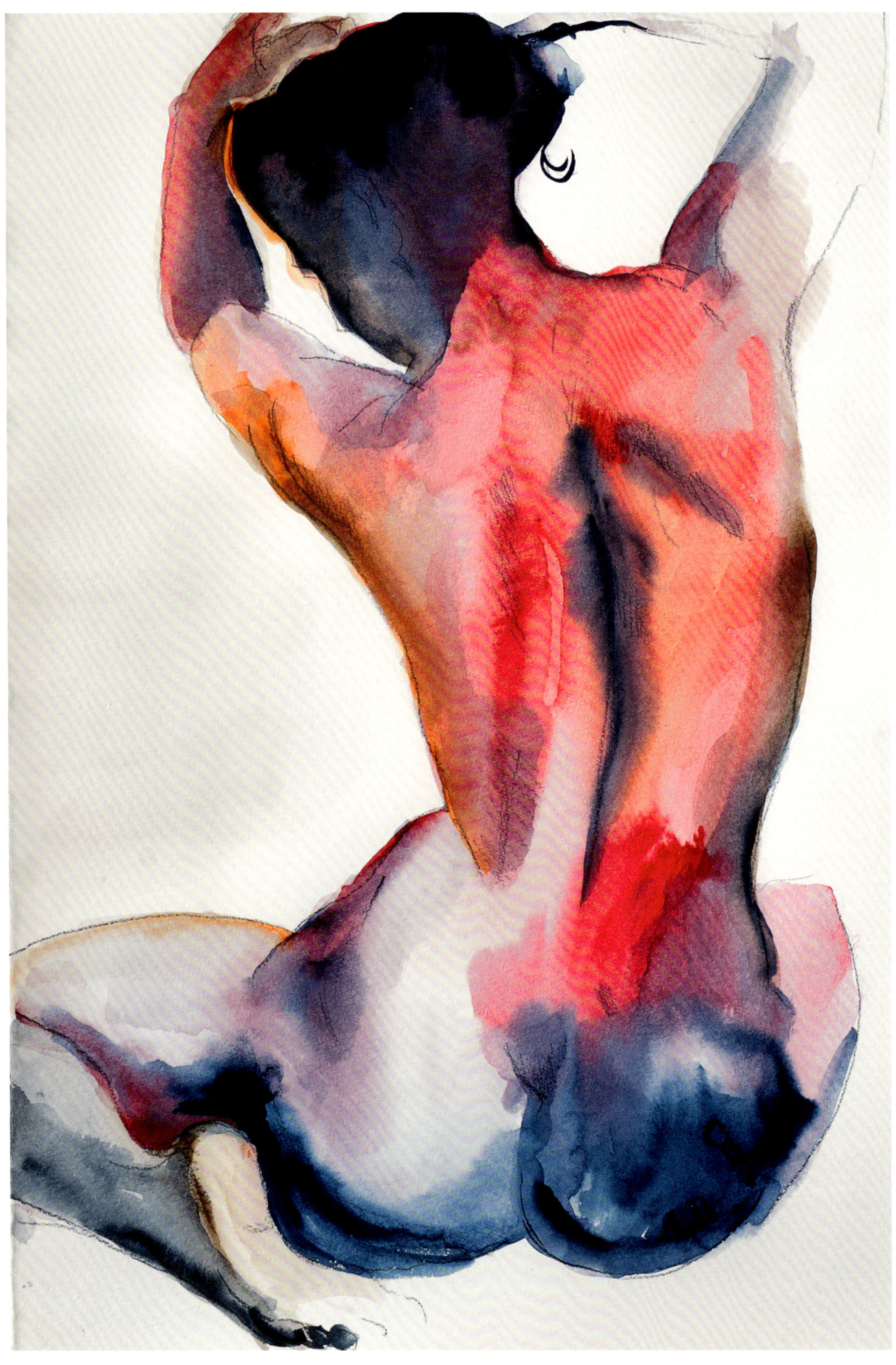

Back, ZH1 Series, 2014
watercolor, 57 x 38.5 cm
Private collection

Back, ZH1 Series, 2014
watercolor, 39.5 x 29.5 cm
K. Nersesov Collection

Page 34
Back, Zh1 Series, 2014,
oil on canvas, 150 x 120 cm
K. Nersesov Collection

Page 35
Back, Zh1 Series, 2015
oil on canvas, 120 x 100 cm
I. Sosin Collection

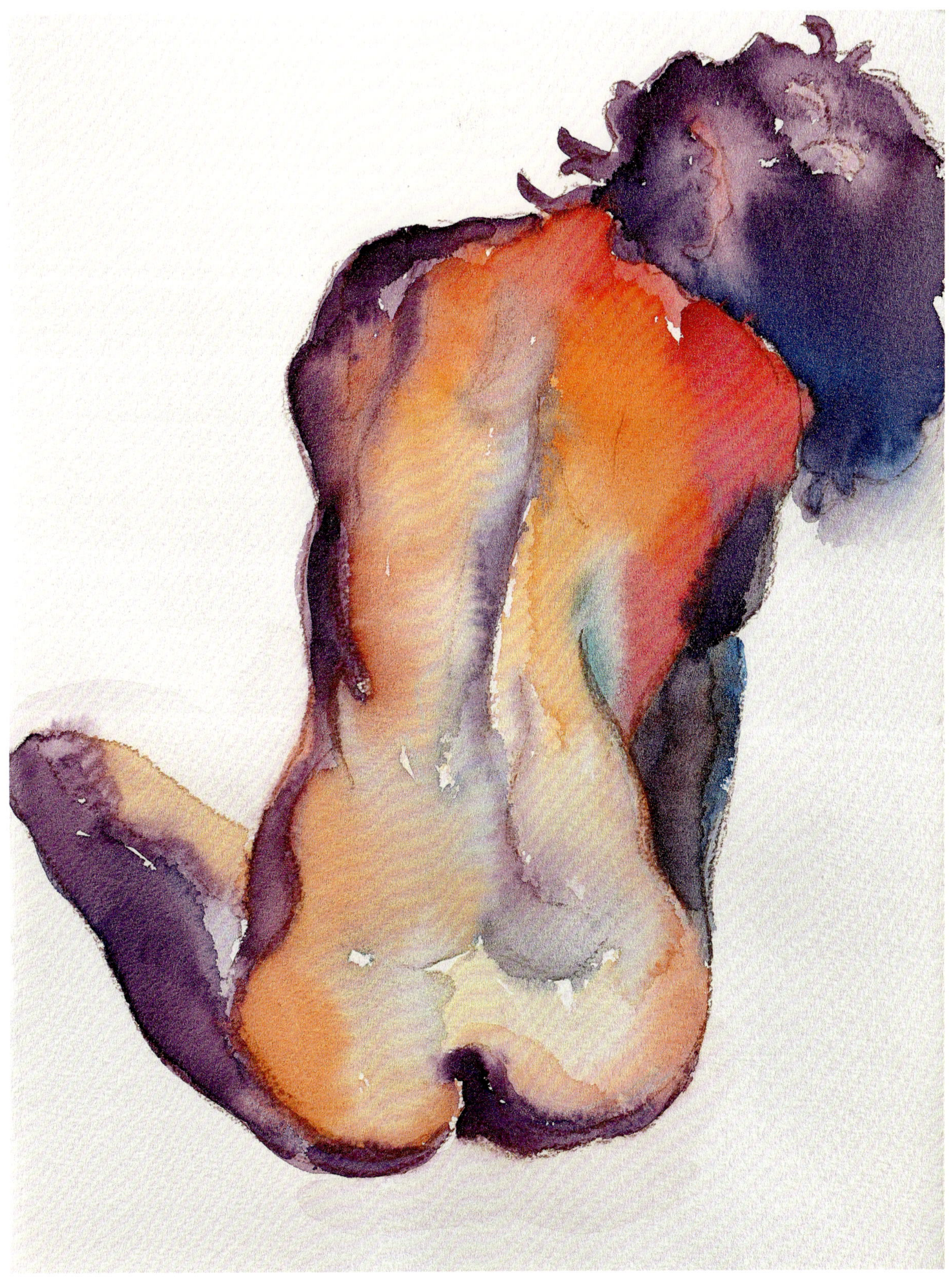

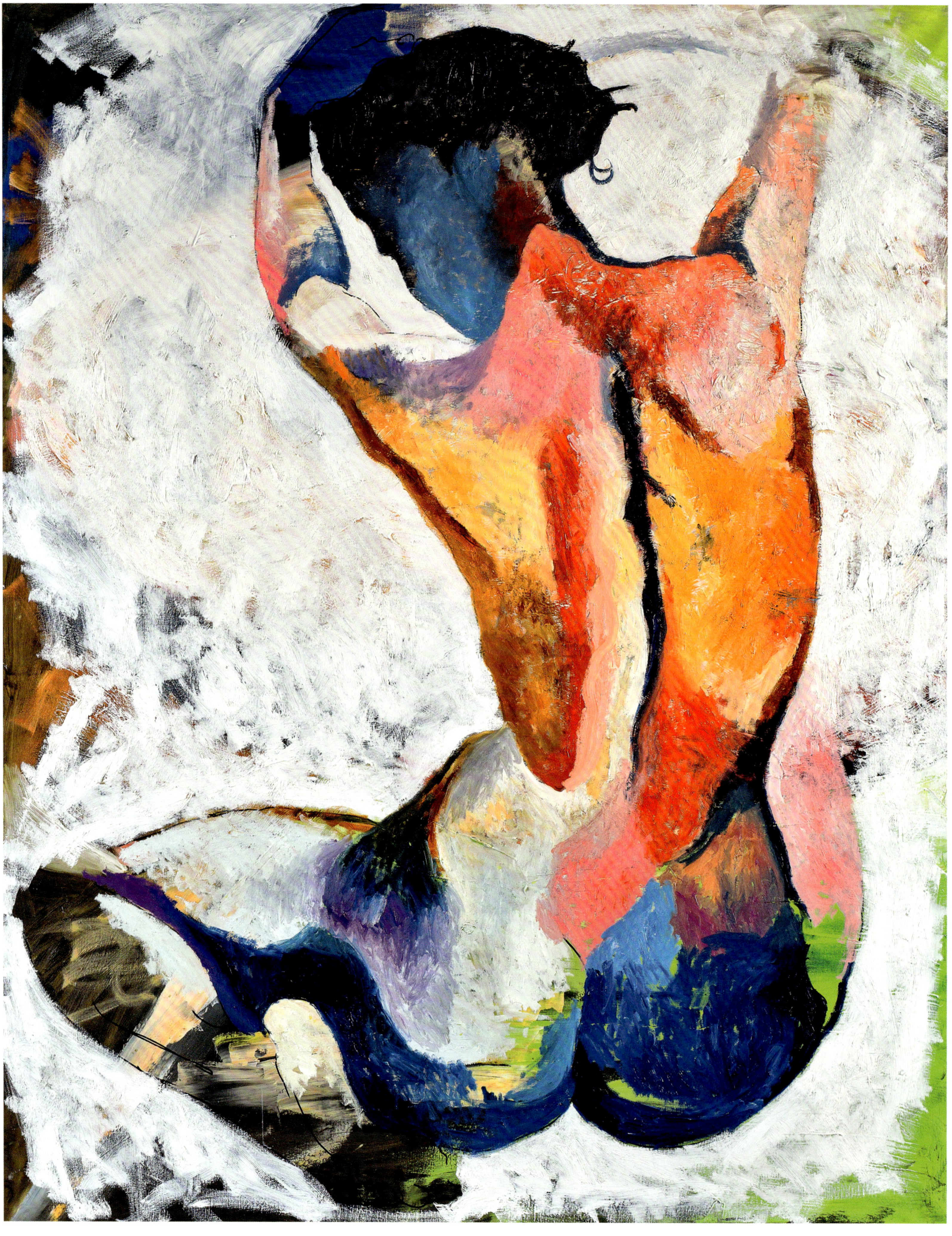

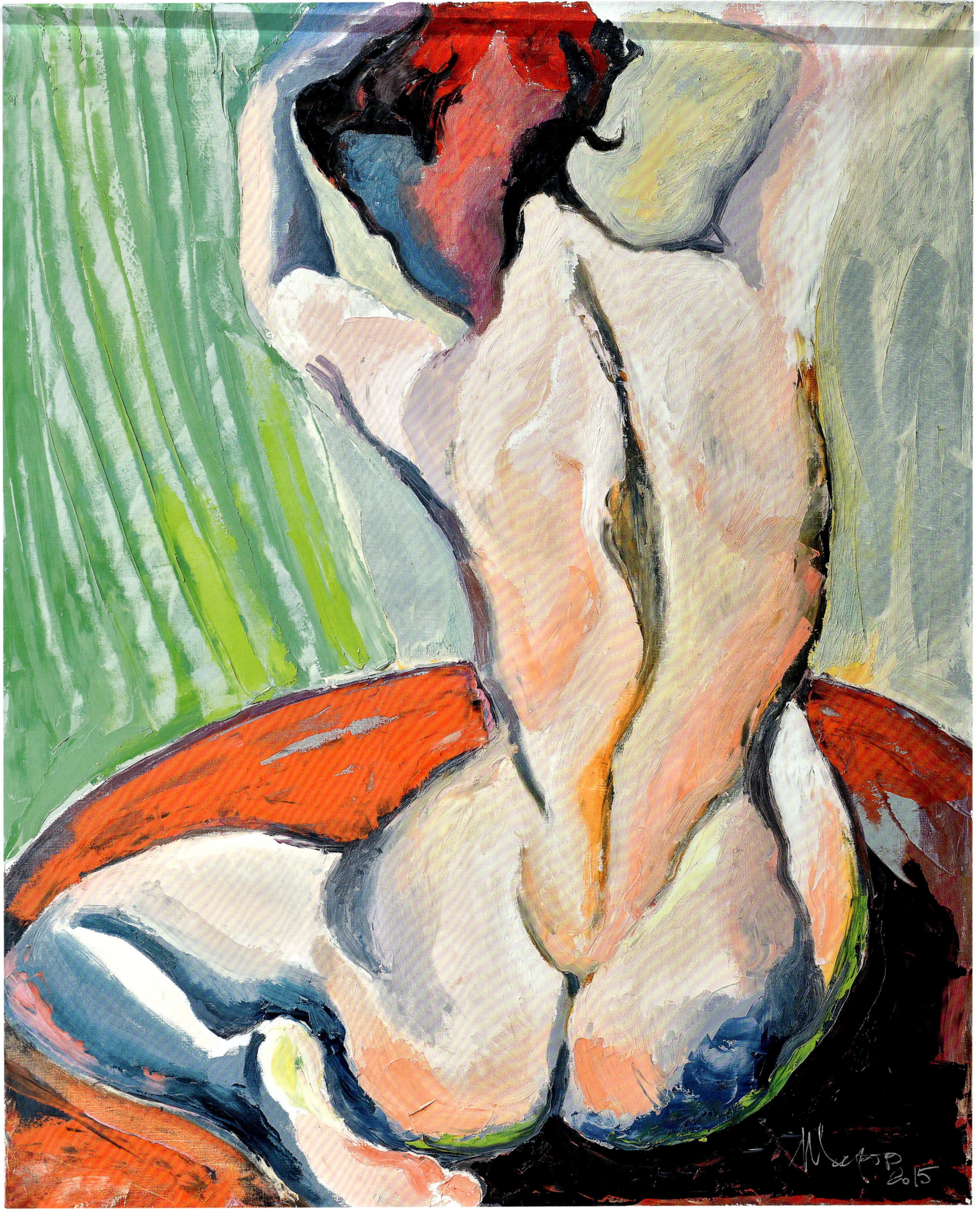

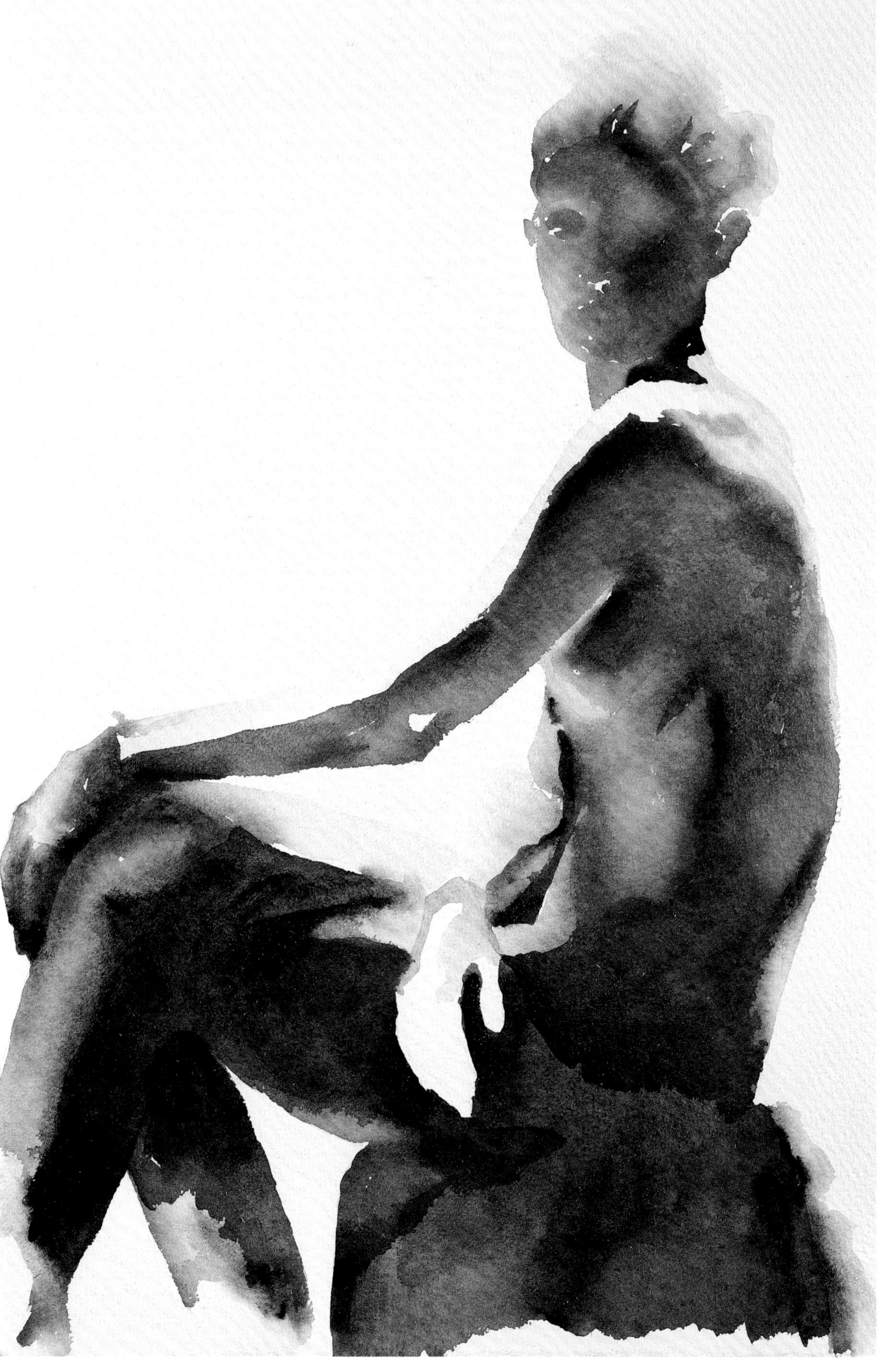

Lightshade 11, ZH2 Series, 2014
watercolor, 58.5 x 38.5 cm
V. Klyukin Collection

Lightshade, ZH2 Series, 2014
watercolor, 58.5 x 38.5 cm
Private collection

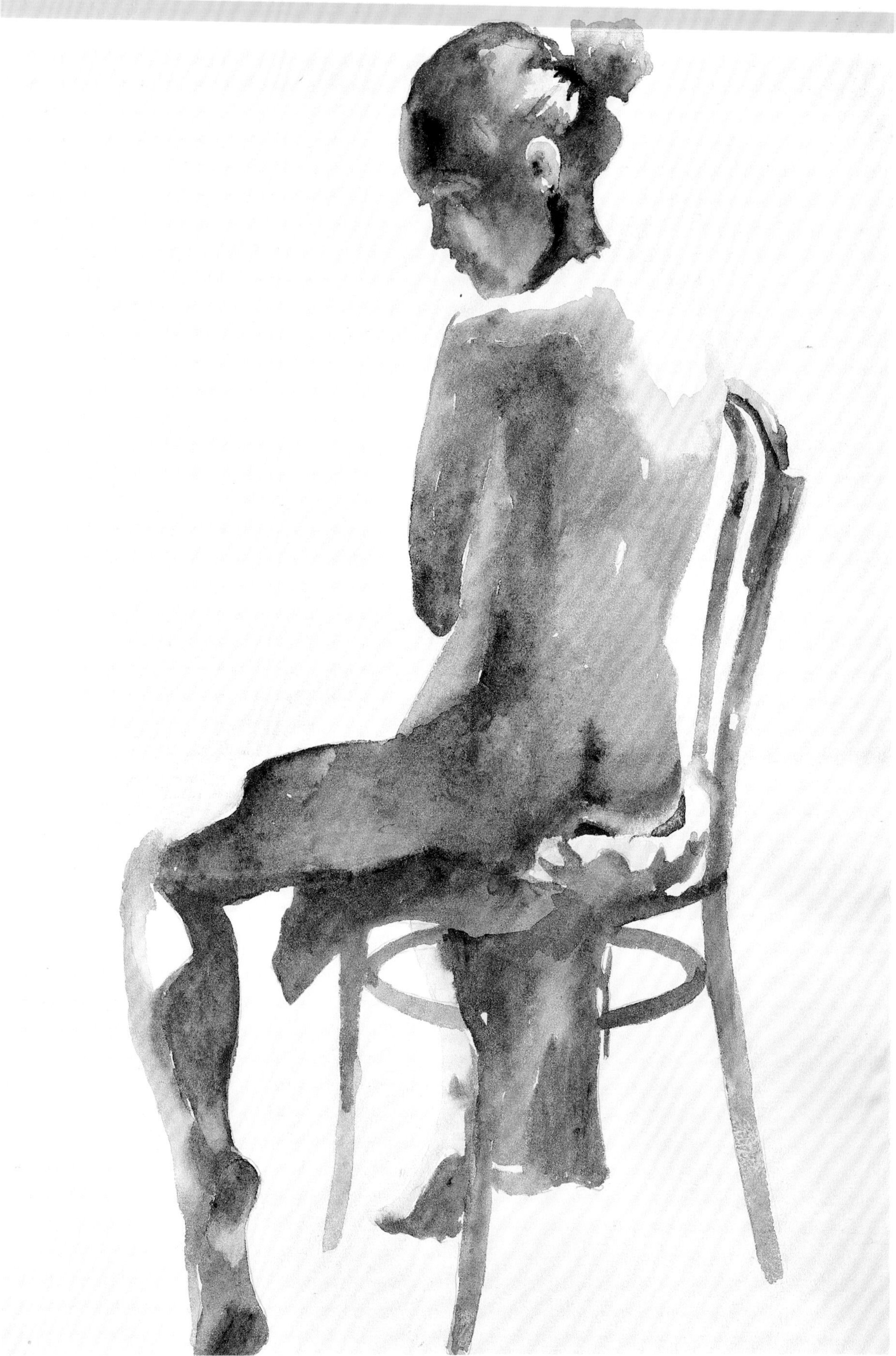

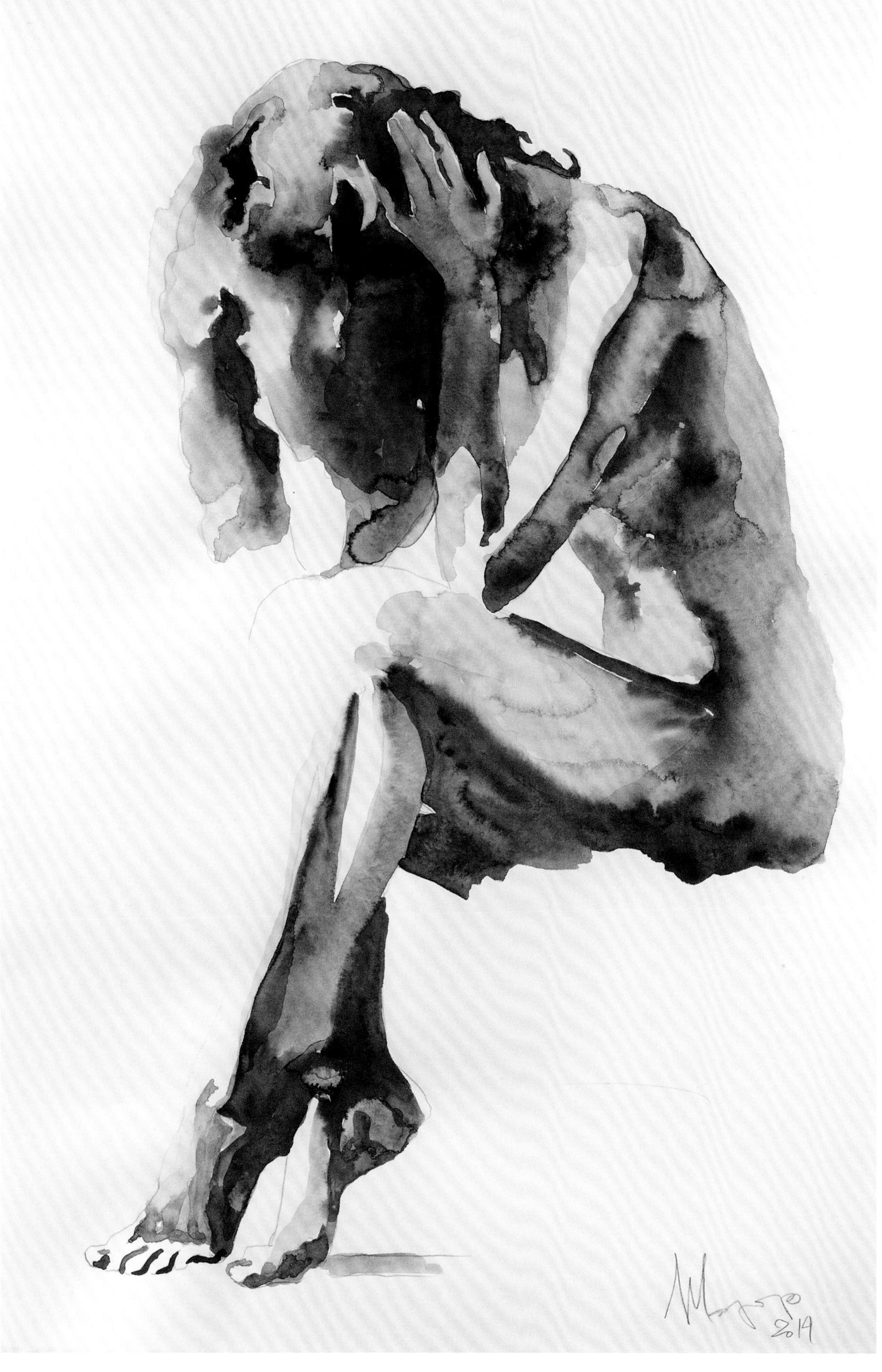

Lightshade, ZH2 Series, 2014
watercolor, 58.5 x 38.5 cm
Private collection

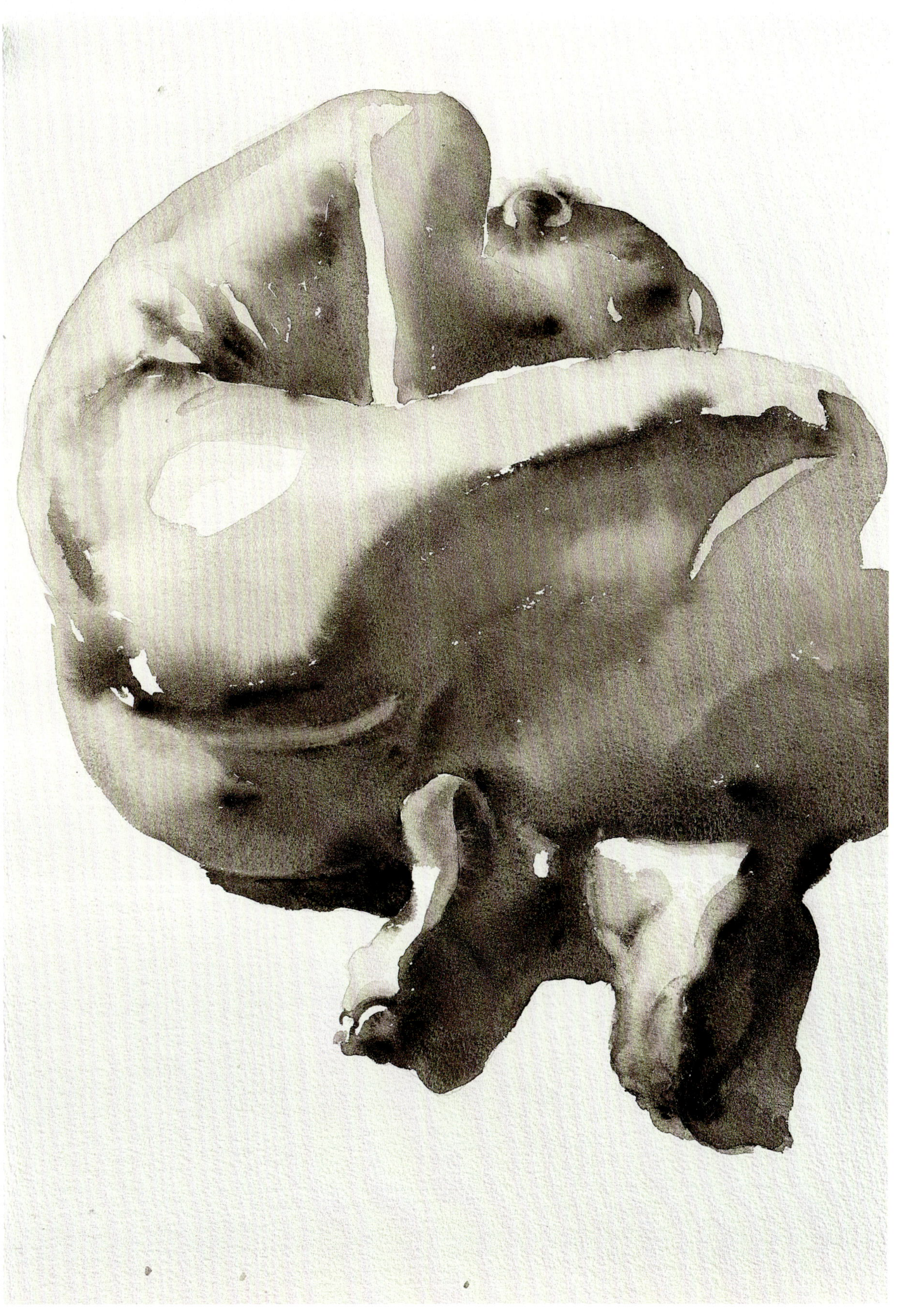

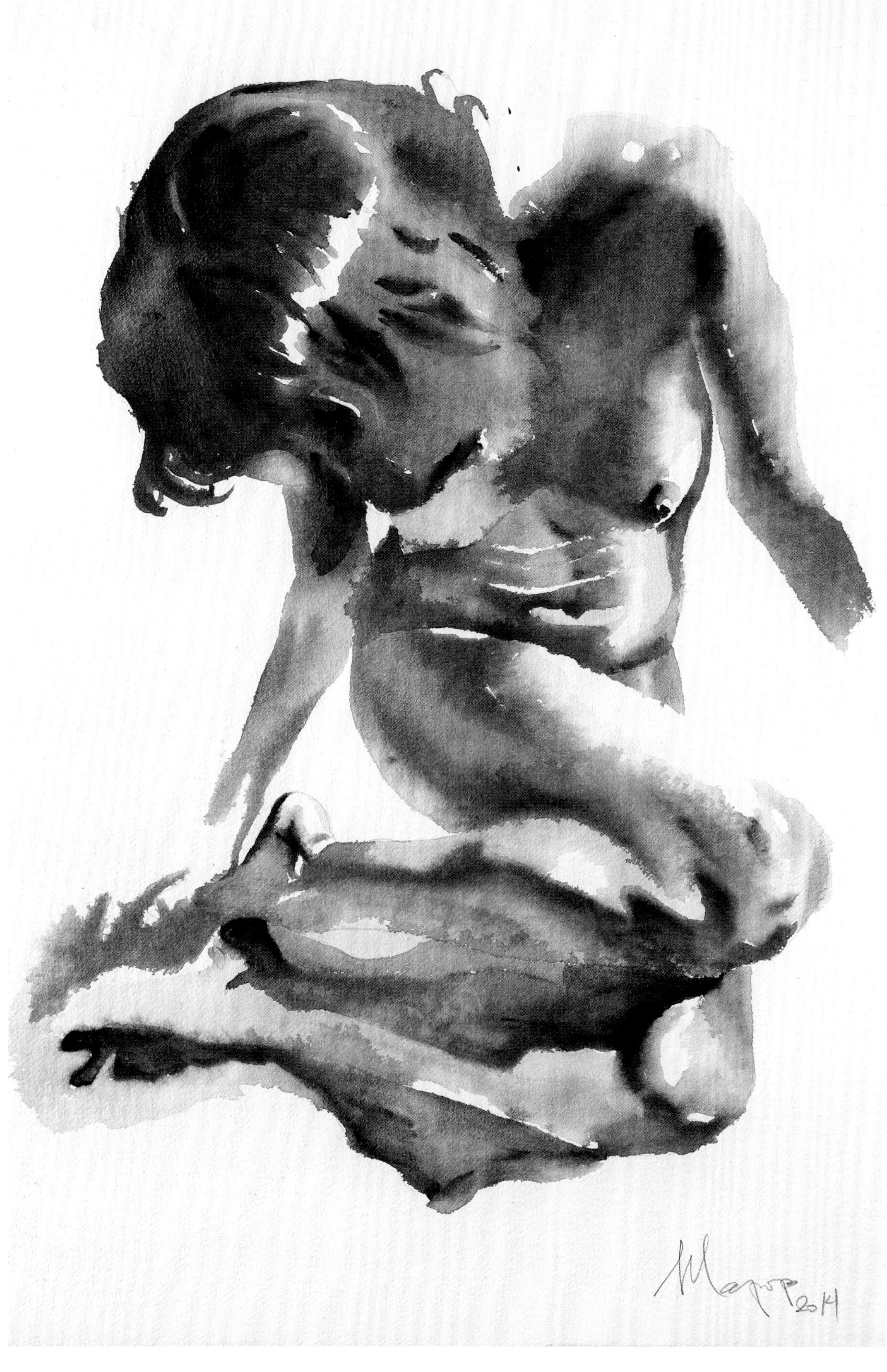

Lightshade 5, ZH2 Series, 2014
watercolor, 58.5 x 38.5 cm
Private collection

Lara, 2014
watercolor, oil on canvas, 58.5 x 38.5 cm
D. Groysman Collection

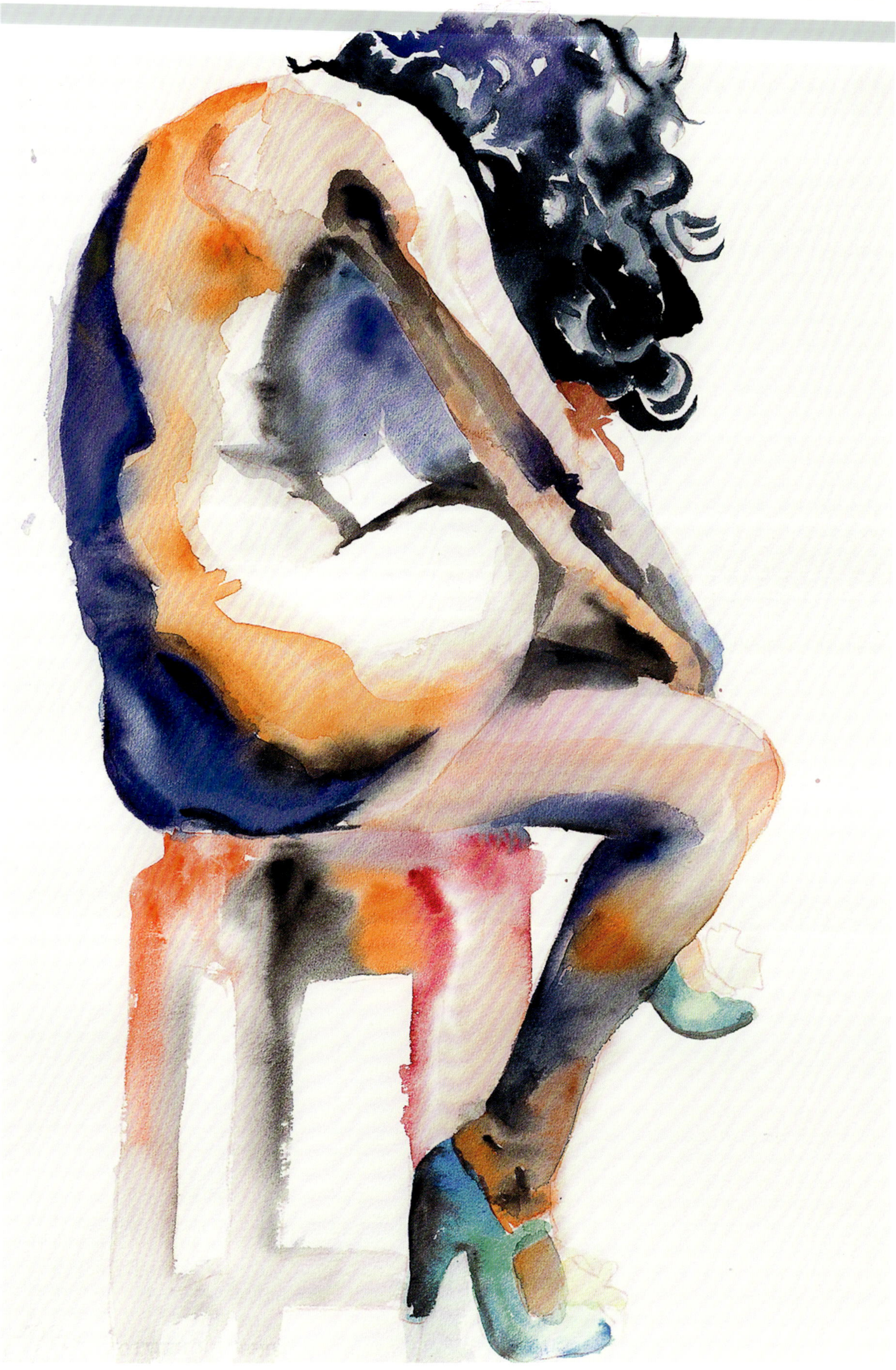

Untitled No. 1-4, 2016
watercolor, 36,5 x 30 cm
Courtesy of the artist and Salamatina
Gallery, New York, Atlanta

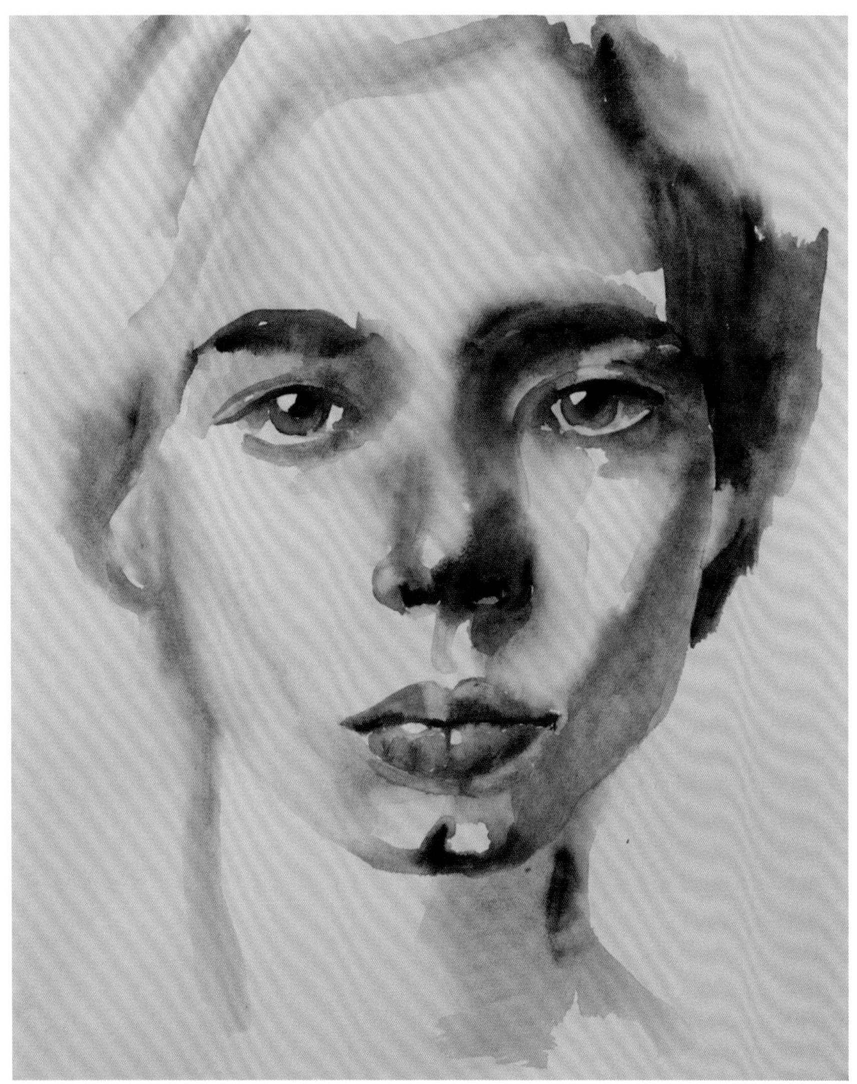
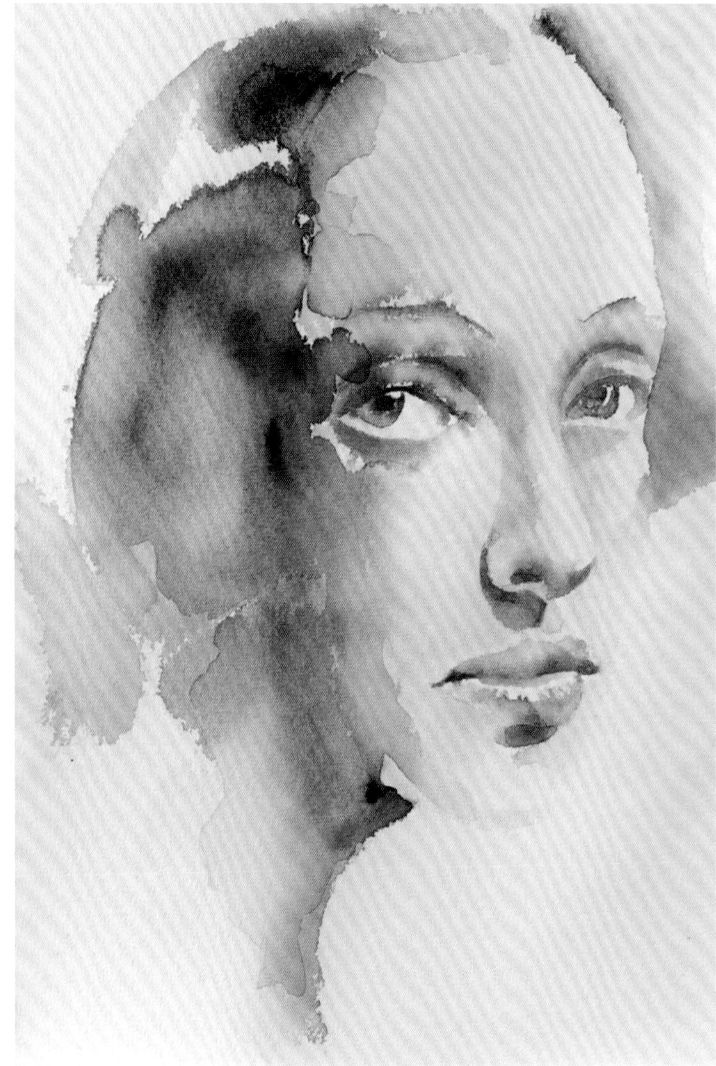

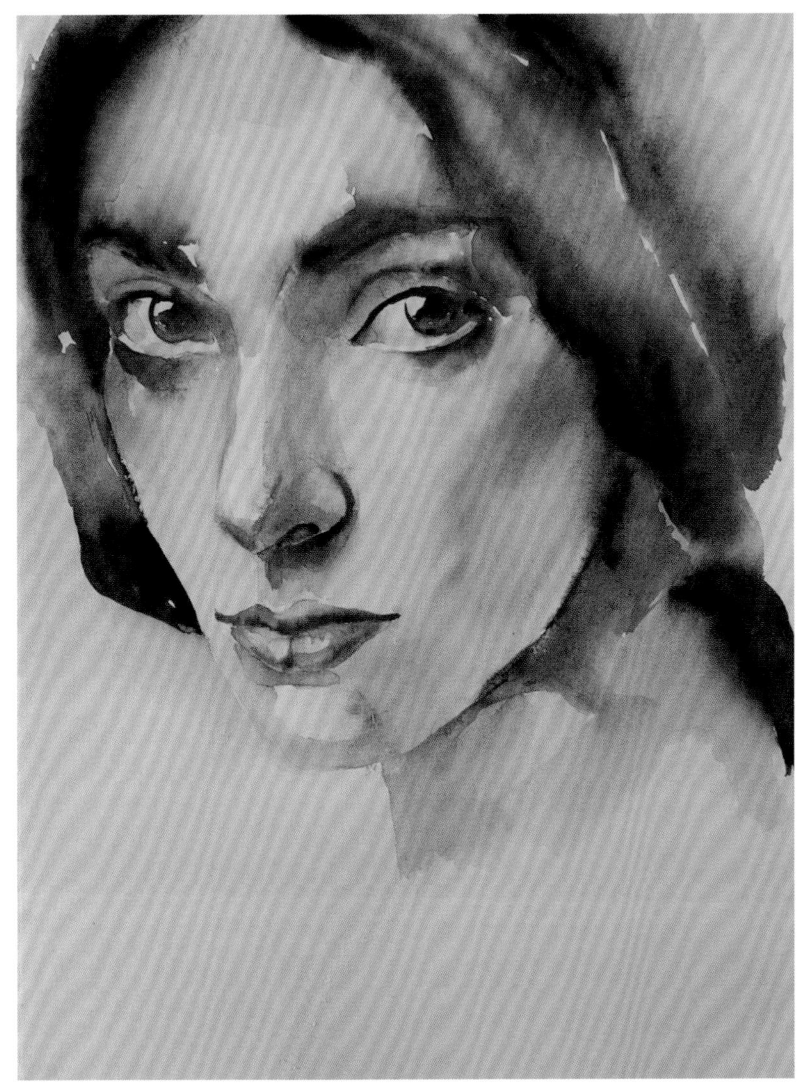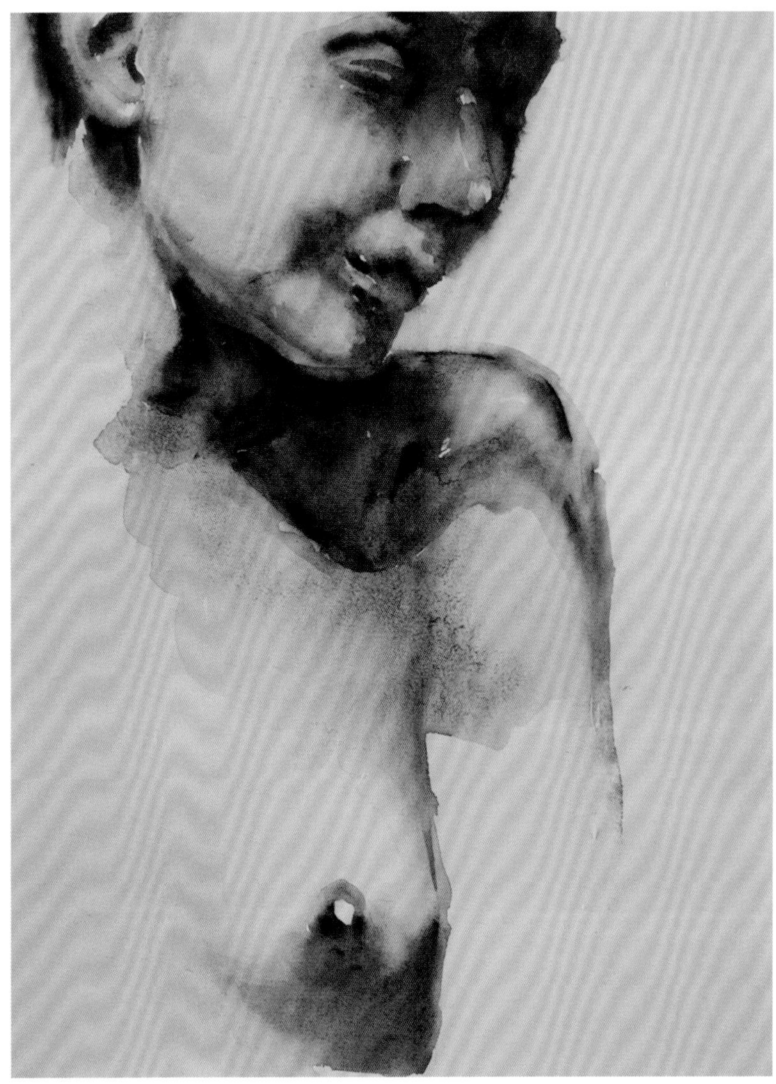

PORTRAITS

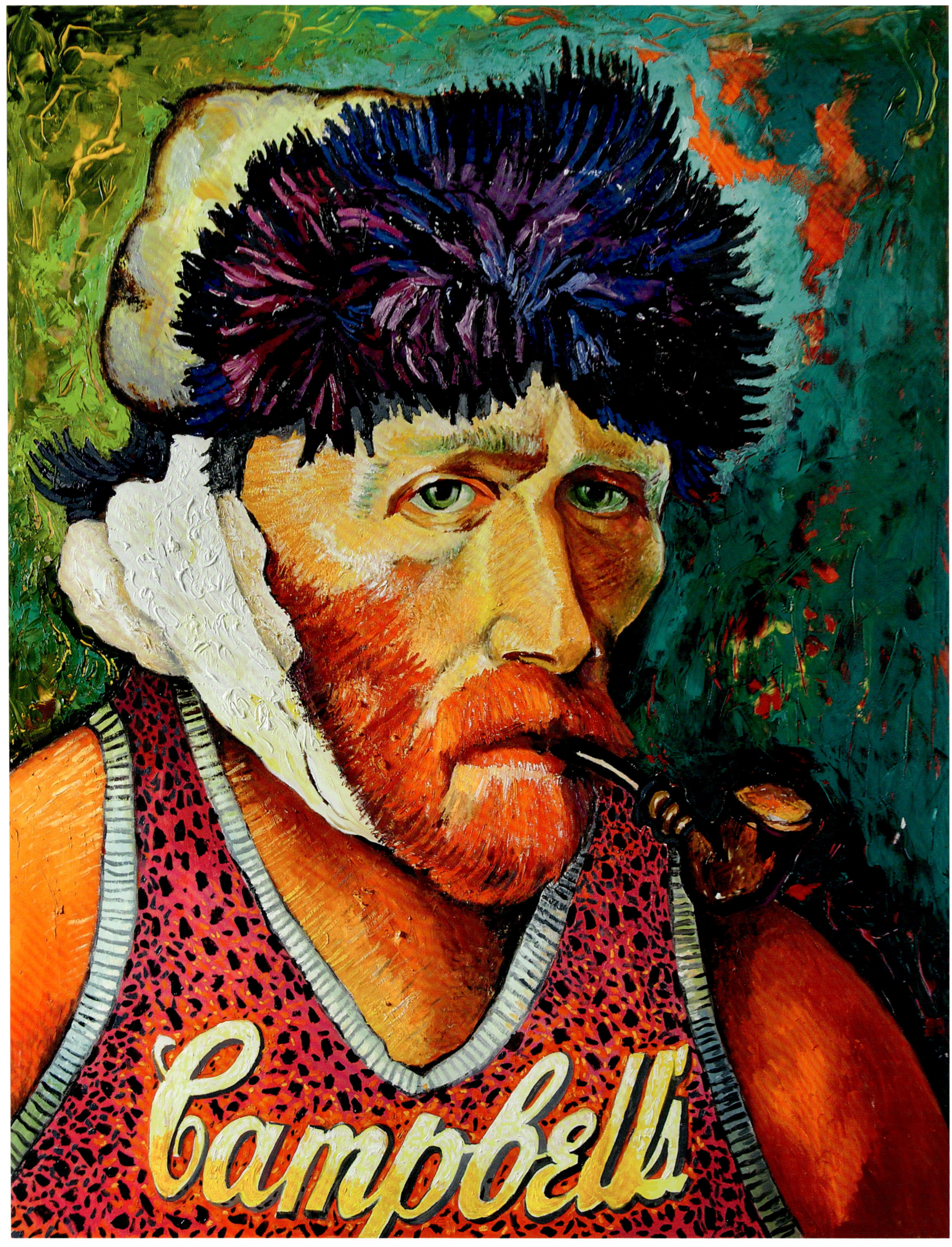
Campbell's

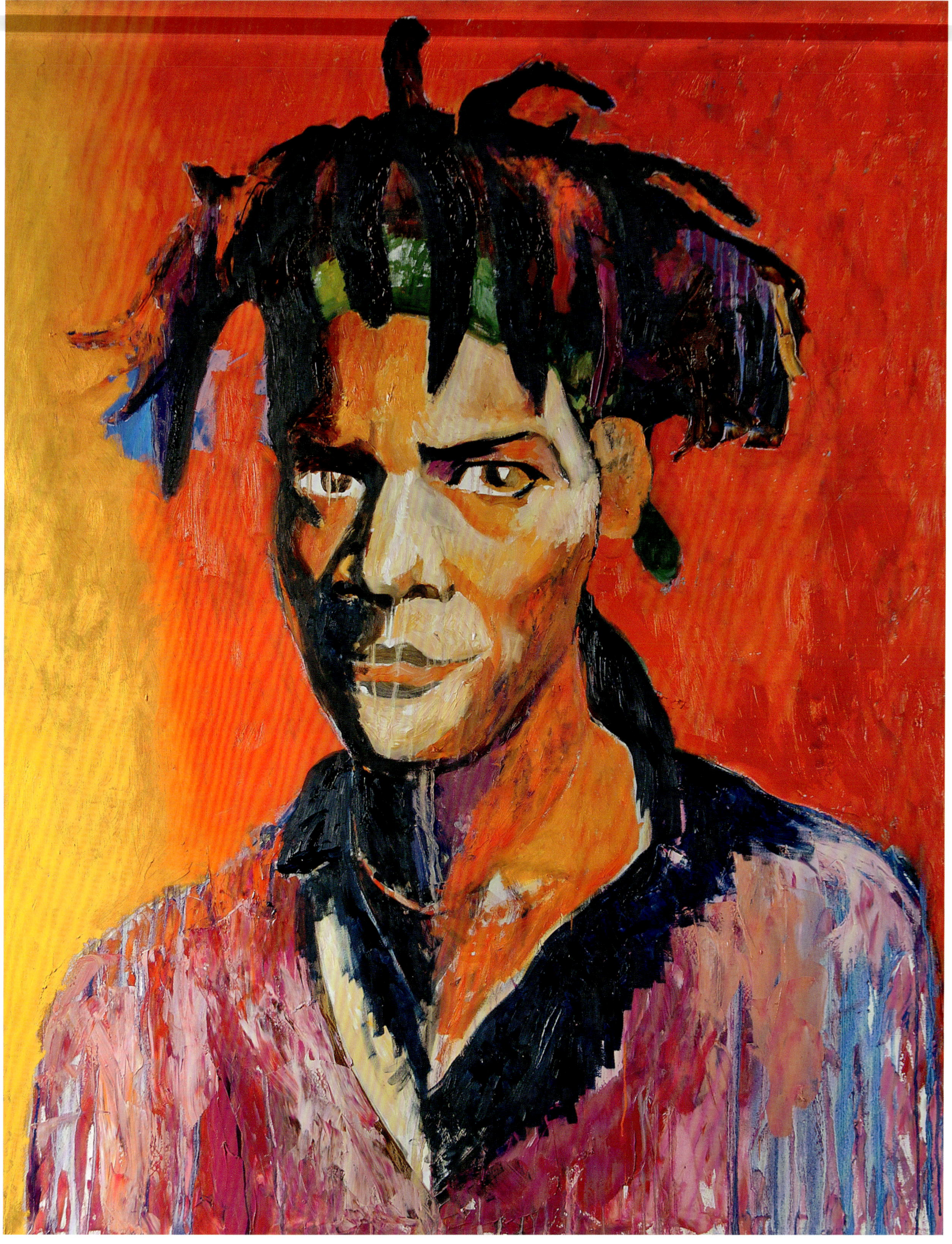

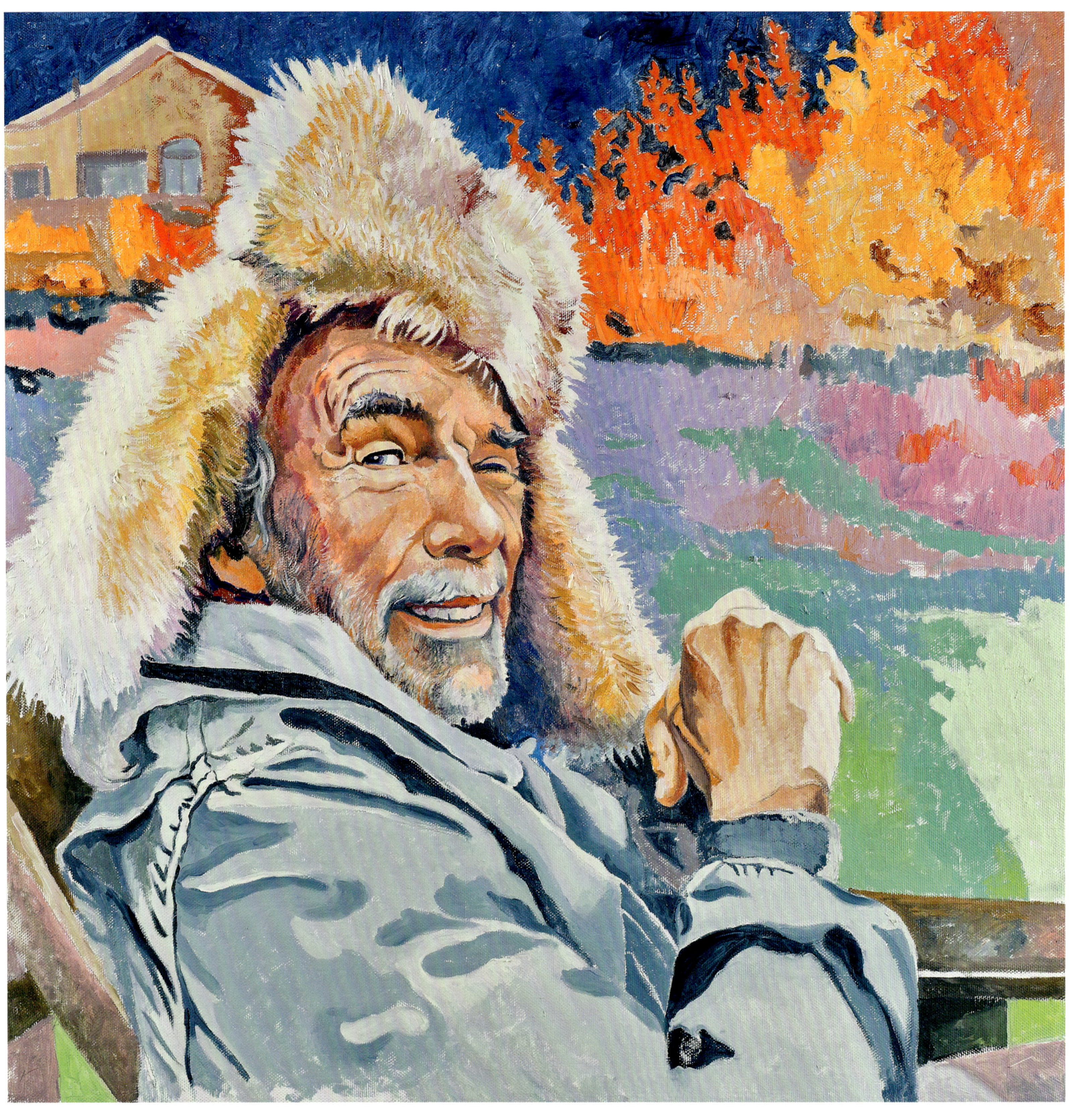

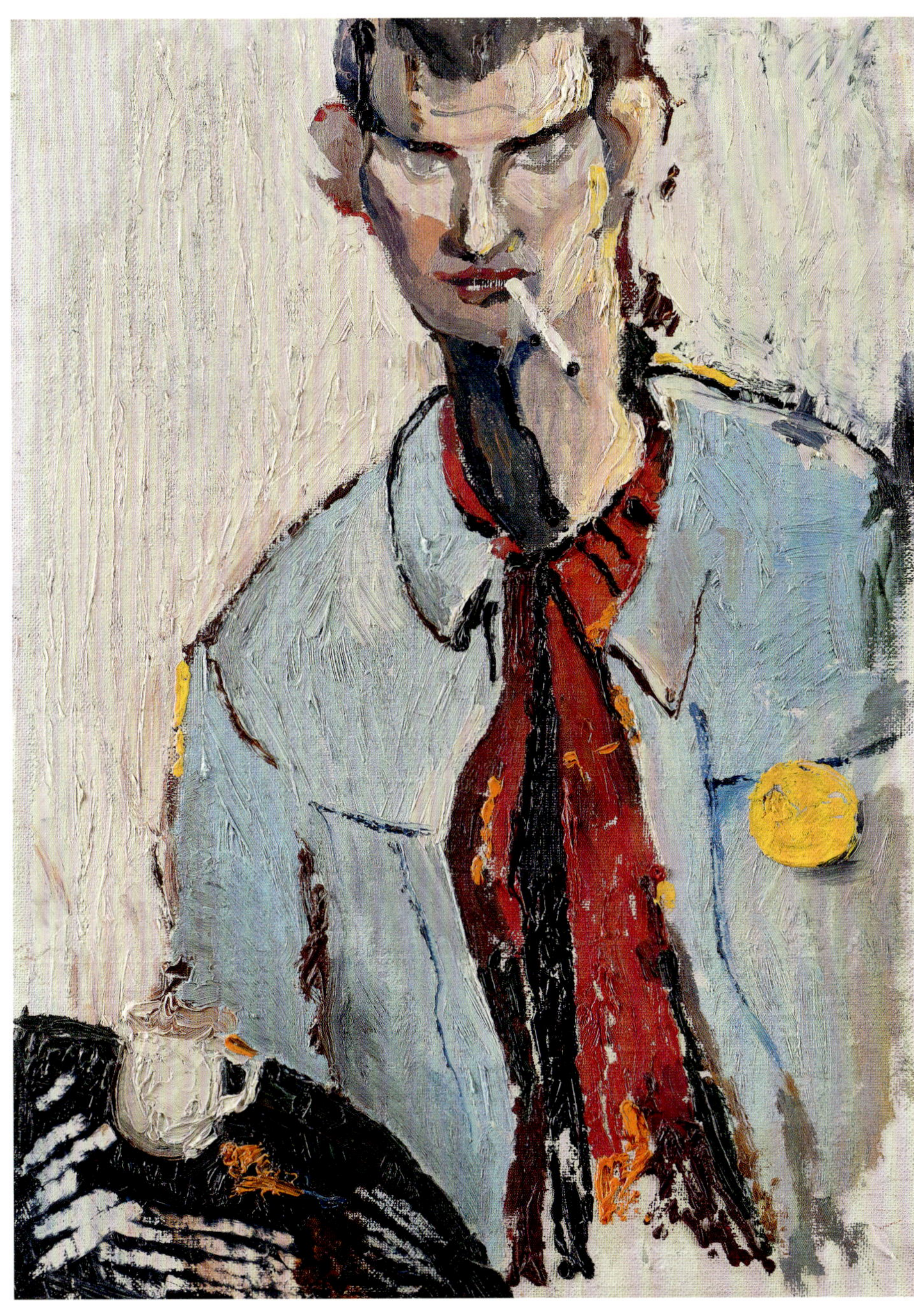

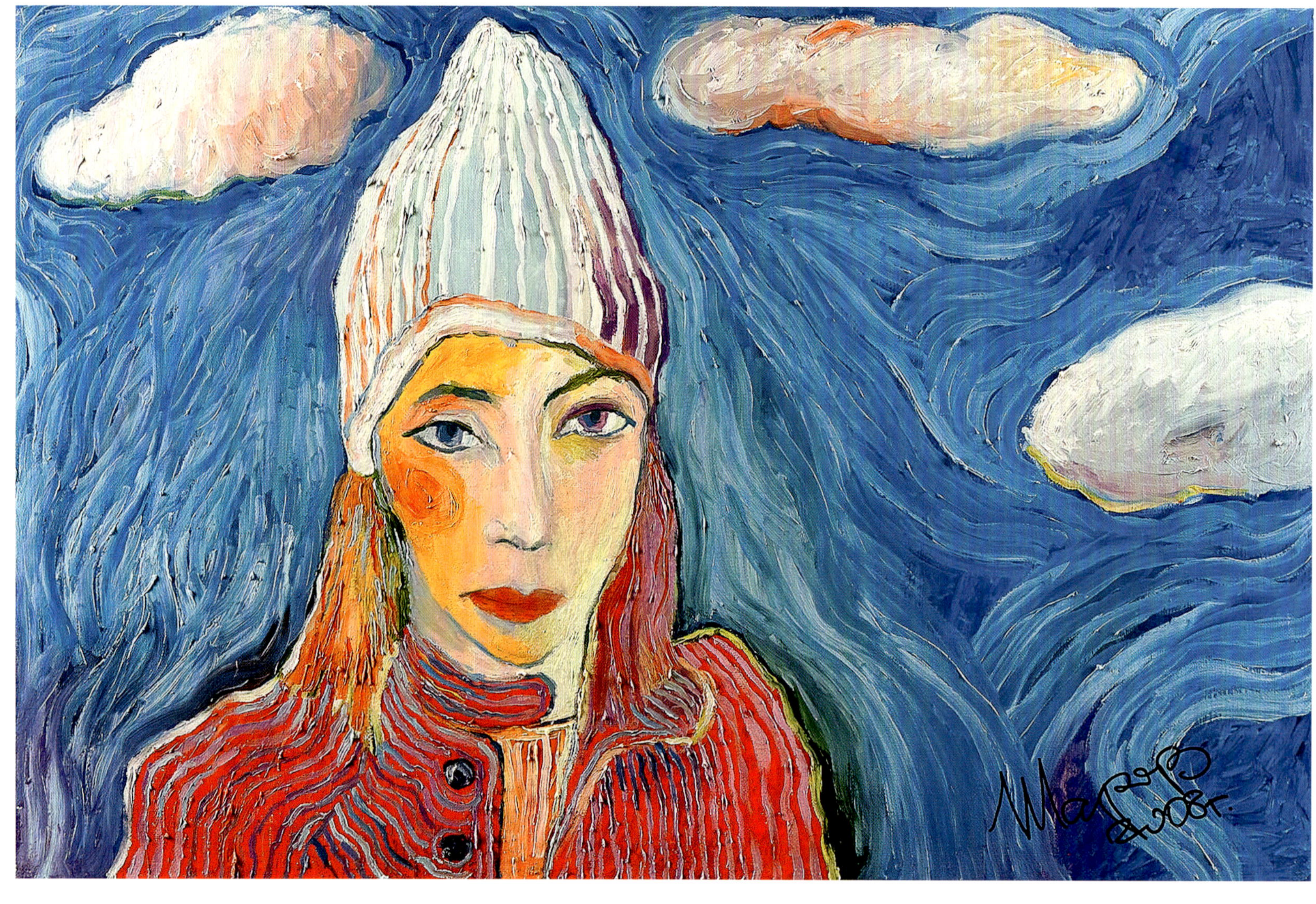

Portrait of Taisiya, 2008
oil on canvas, 40 x 60 cm
Property of the artist
Courtesy of the artist and Salamatina
Gallery, New York, Atlanta

Portrait No. 3, 2015
oil on canvas, 100 x 80 cm
V. Klyukin Collection

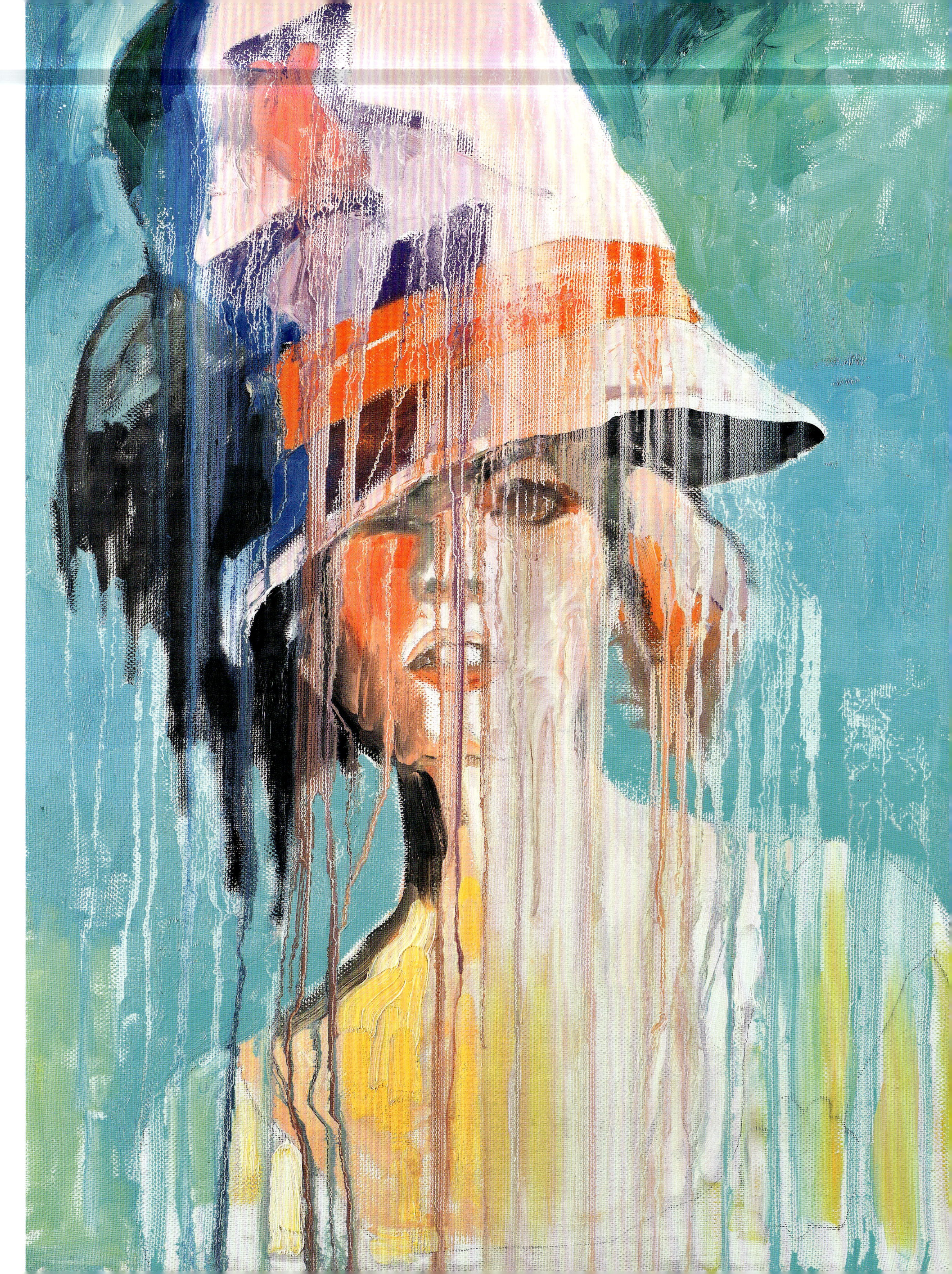

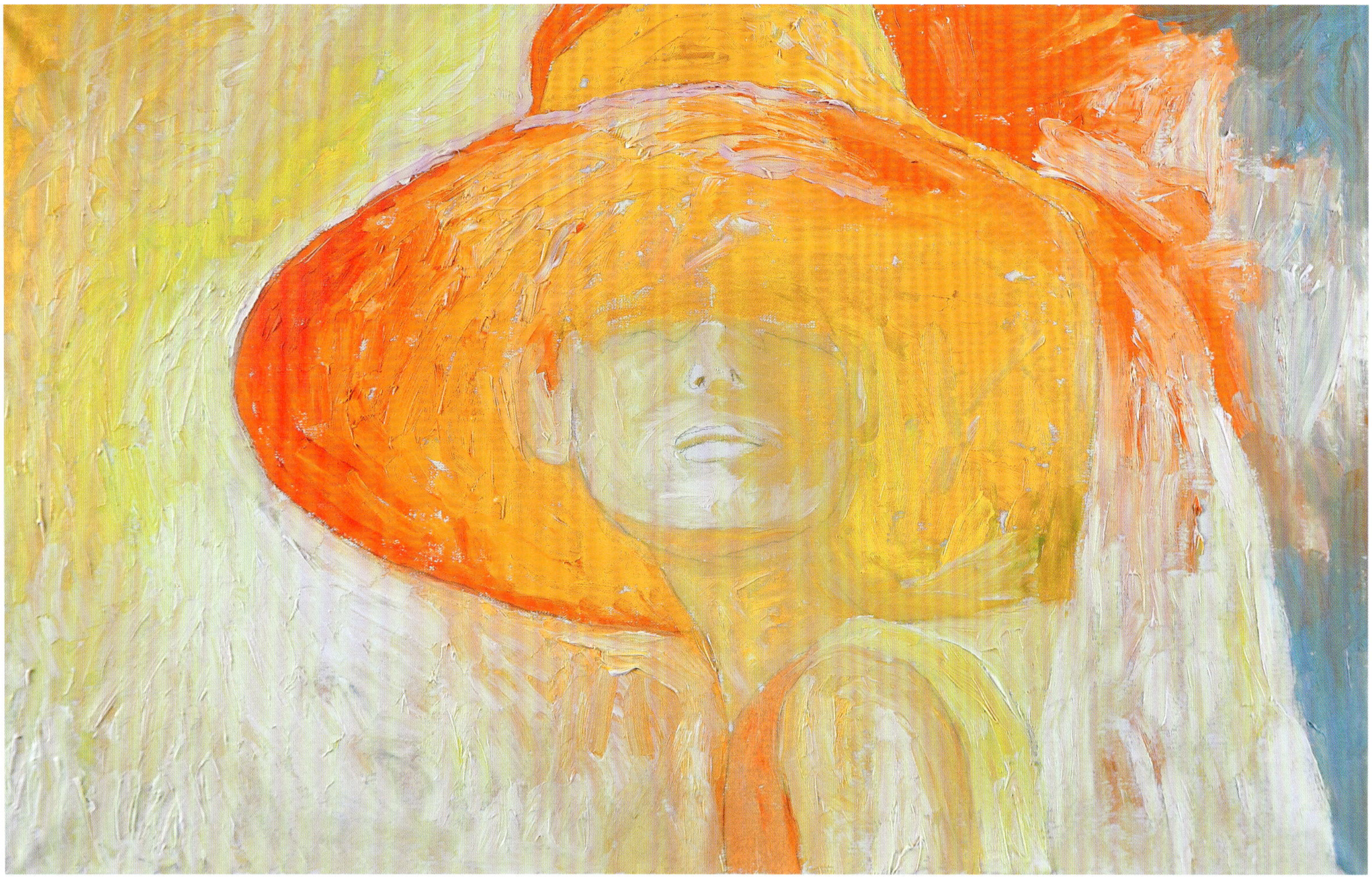

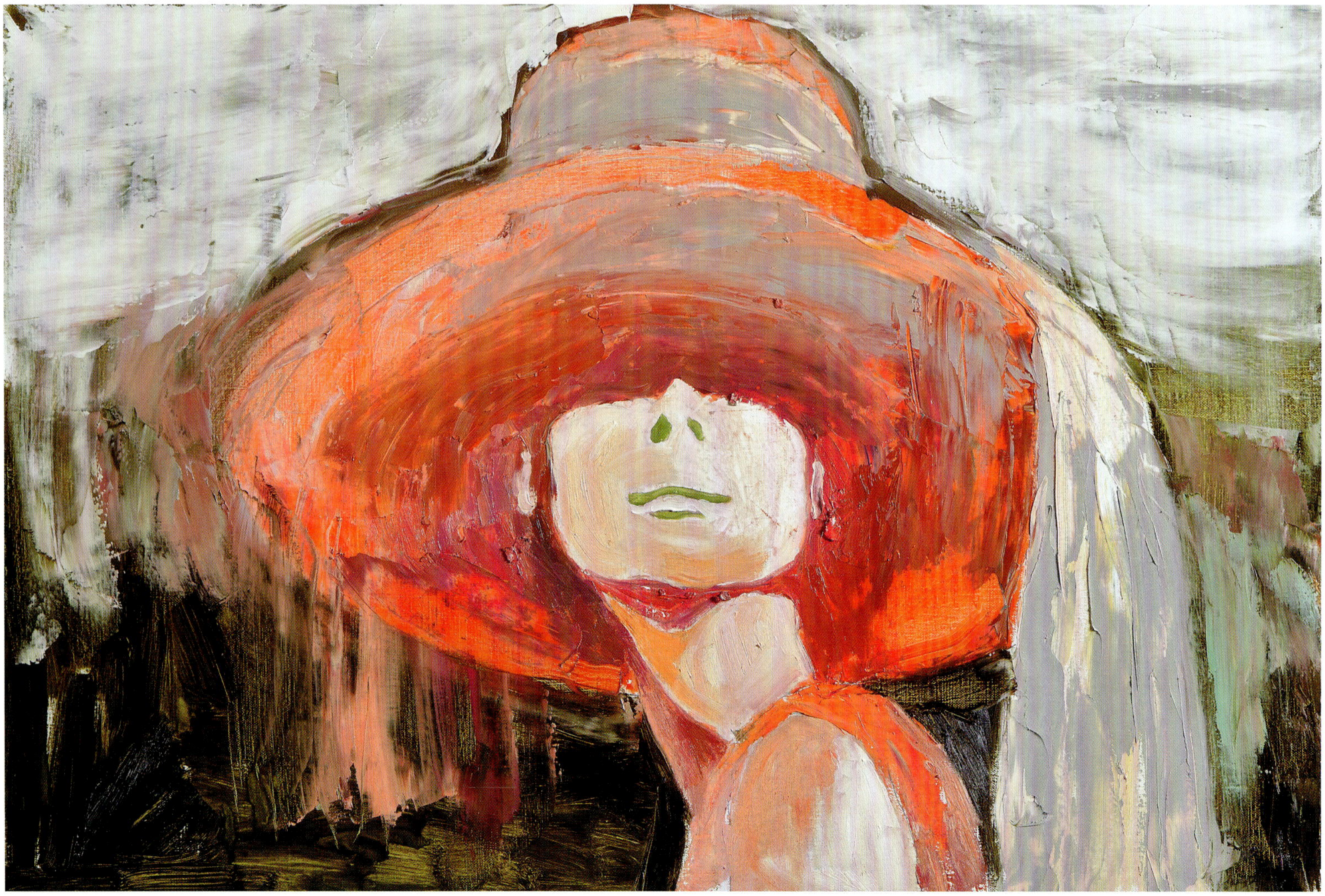

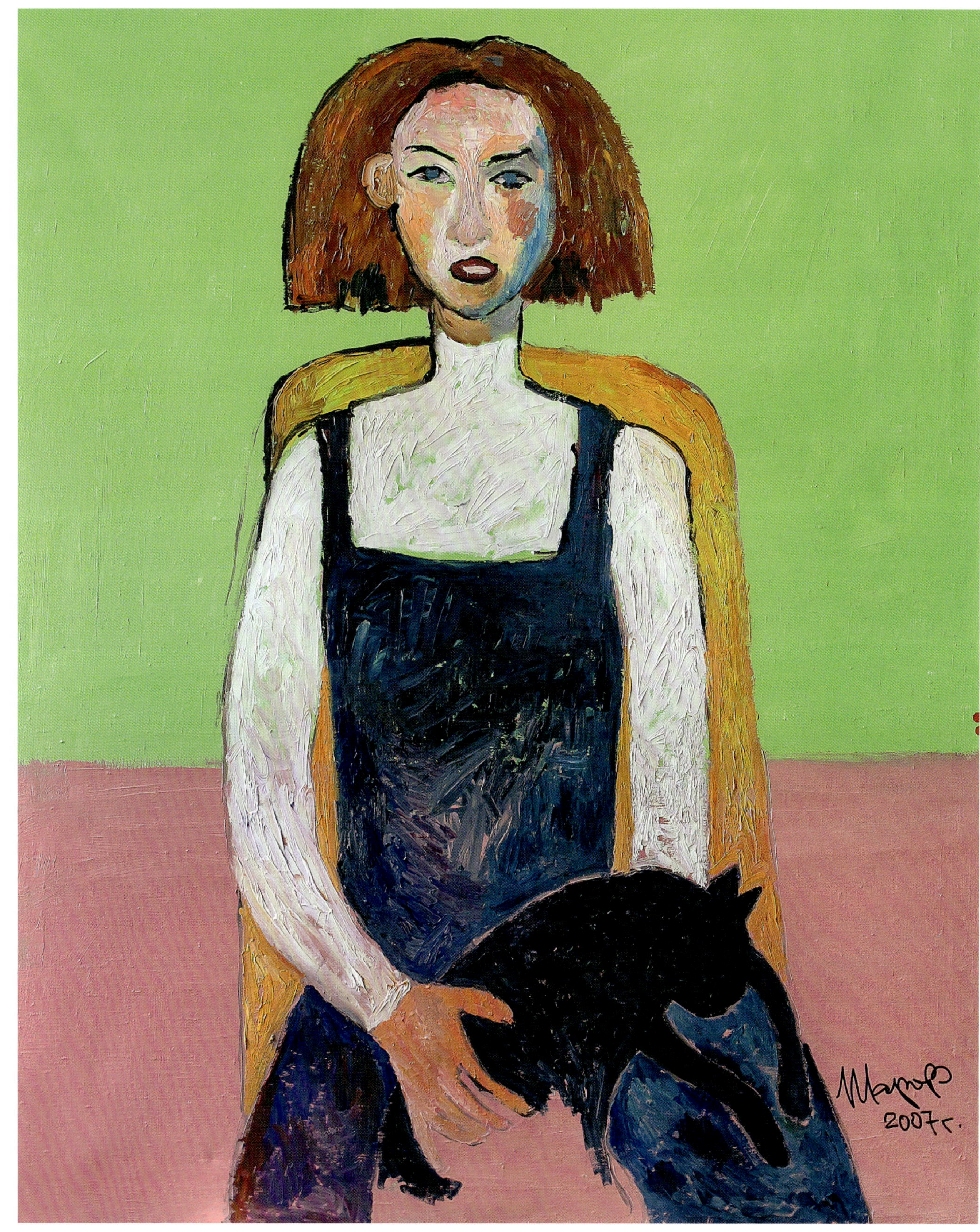

Audrey, 2012
oil on canvas, 120 x 100 cm
Property of the artist
Courtesy of the artist and Salamatina
Gallery, New York, Atlanta

Audrey, 2012
oil on canvas, 60 x 80 cm
Property of Nadezhda and Katherine
Solzhenytsin

Portrait of a Girl with a Cat, 2007
oil on canvas, 120 x 100 cm
T. Melnikova Collection

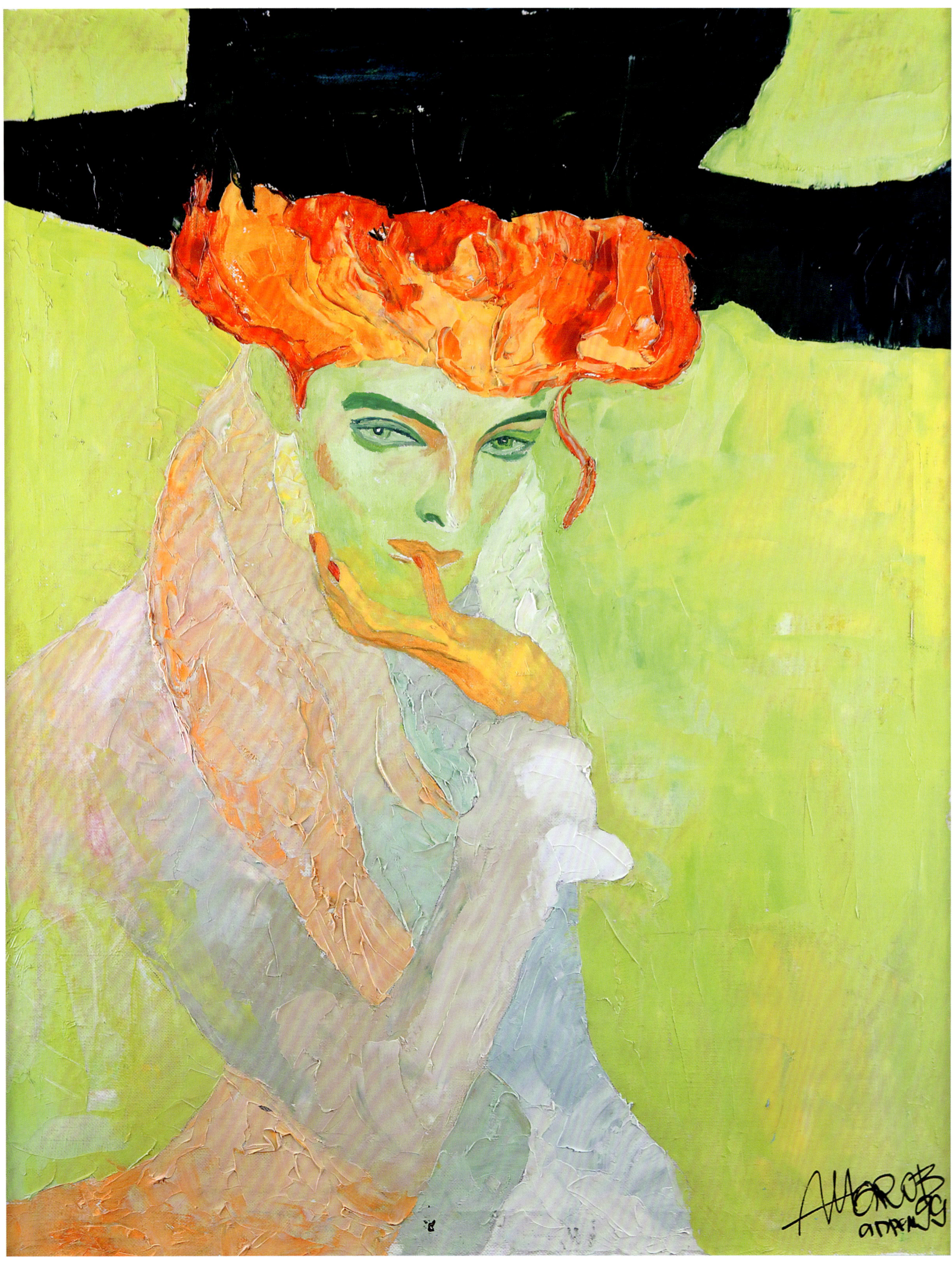

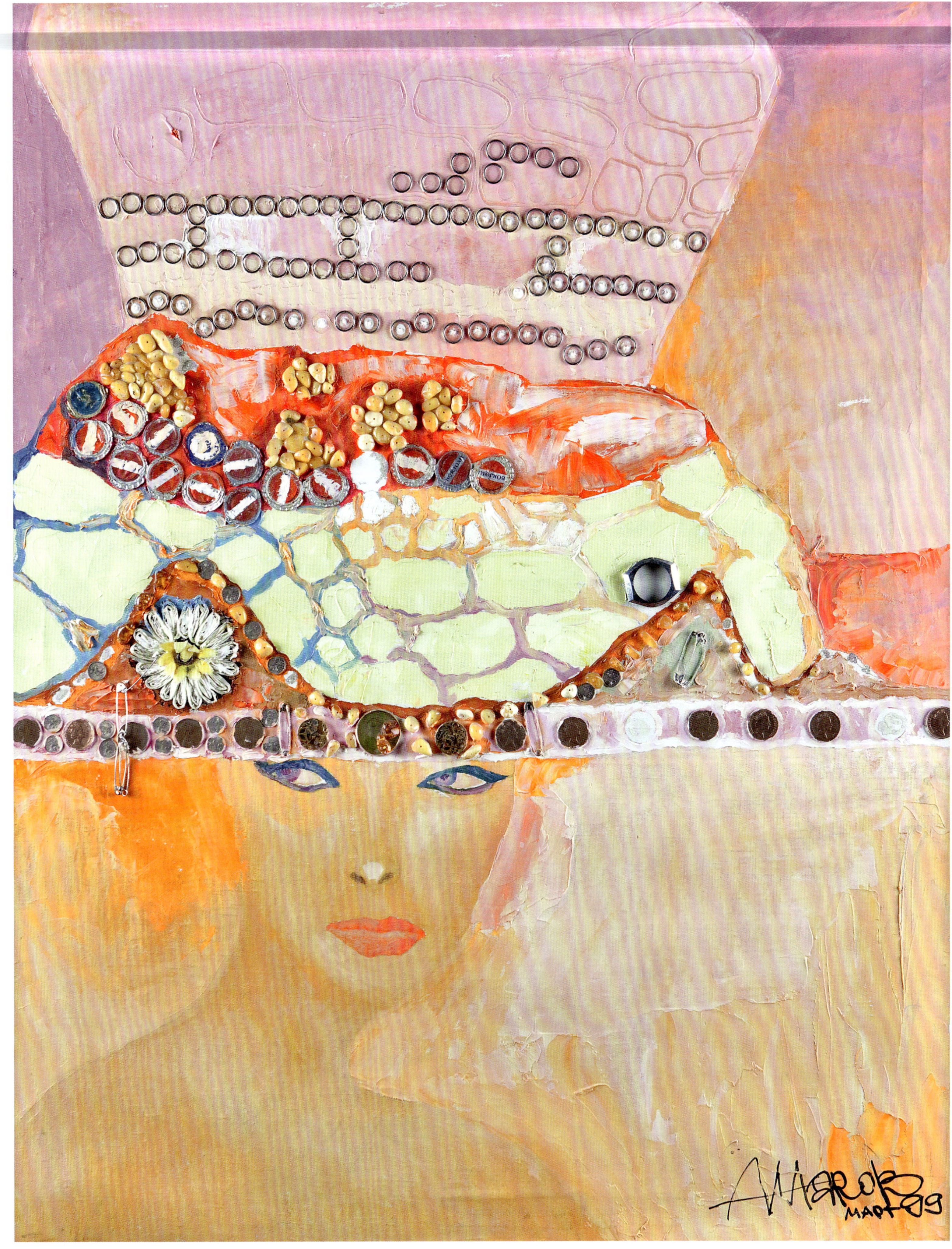

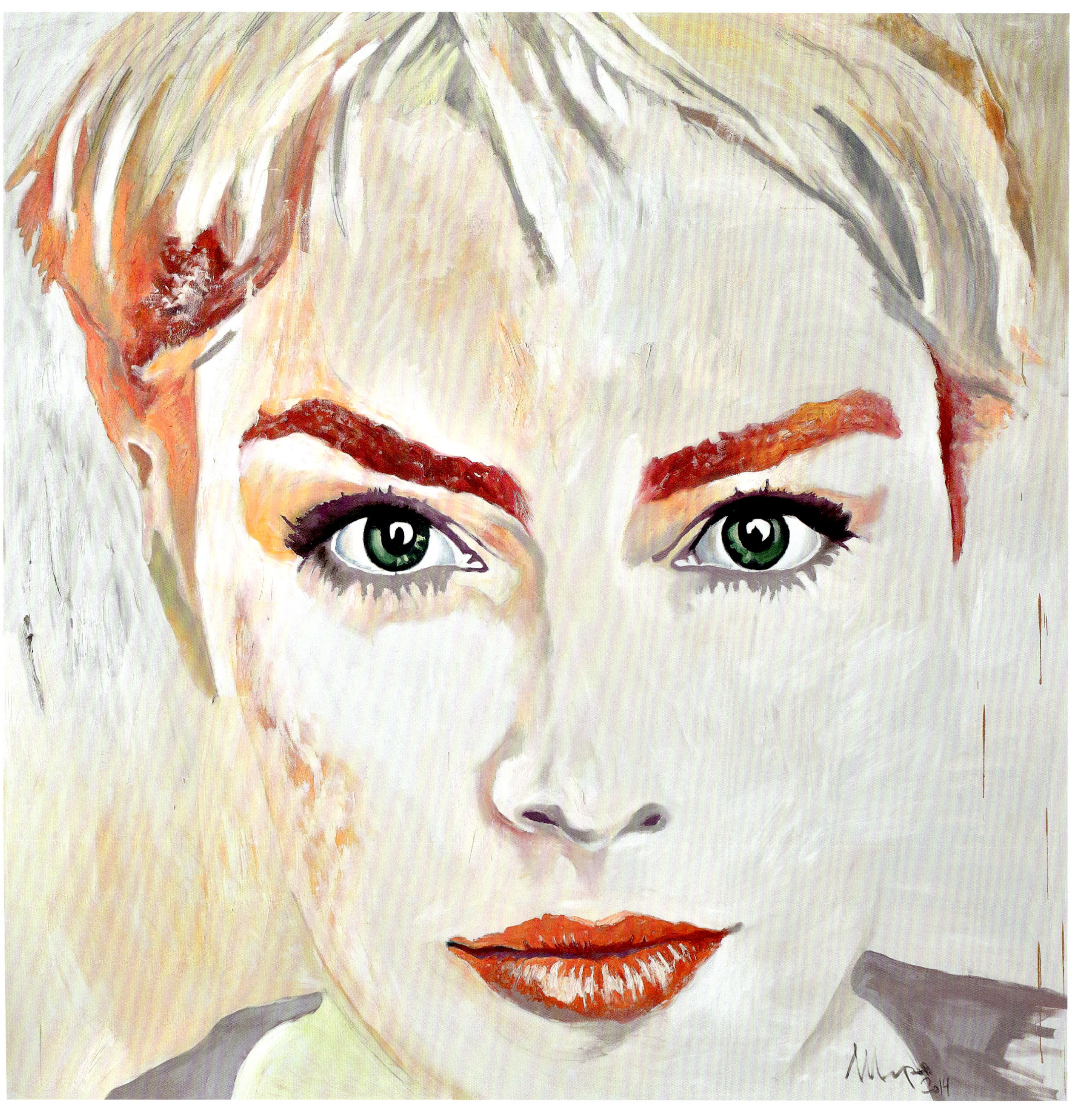

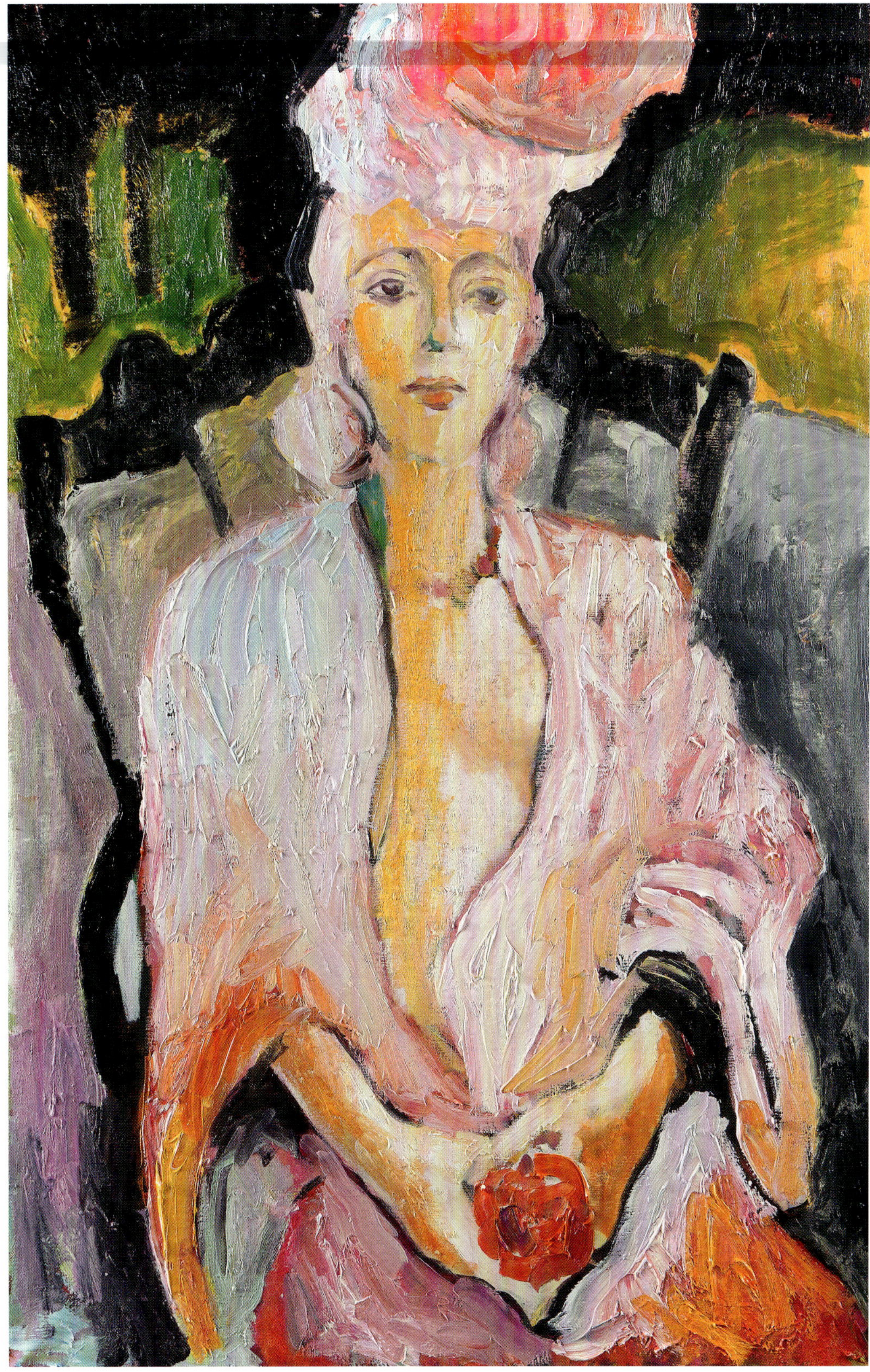

Autoportrait, 2014
oil on canvas, 120 x 100 cm
Property of the artist
Courtesy of the artist and Salamatina
Gallery, New York, Atlanta

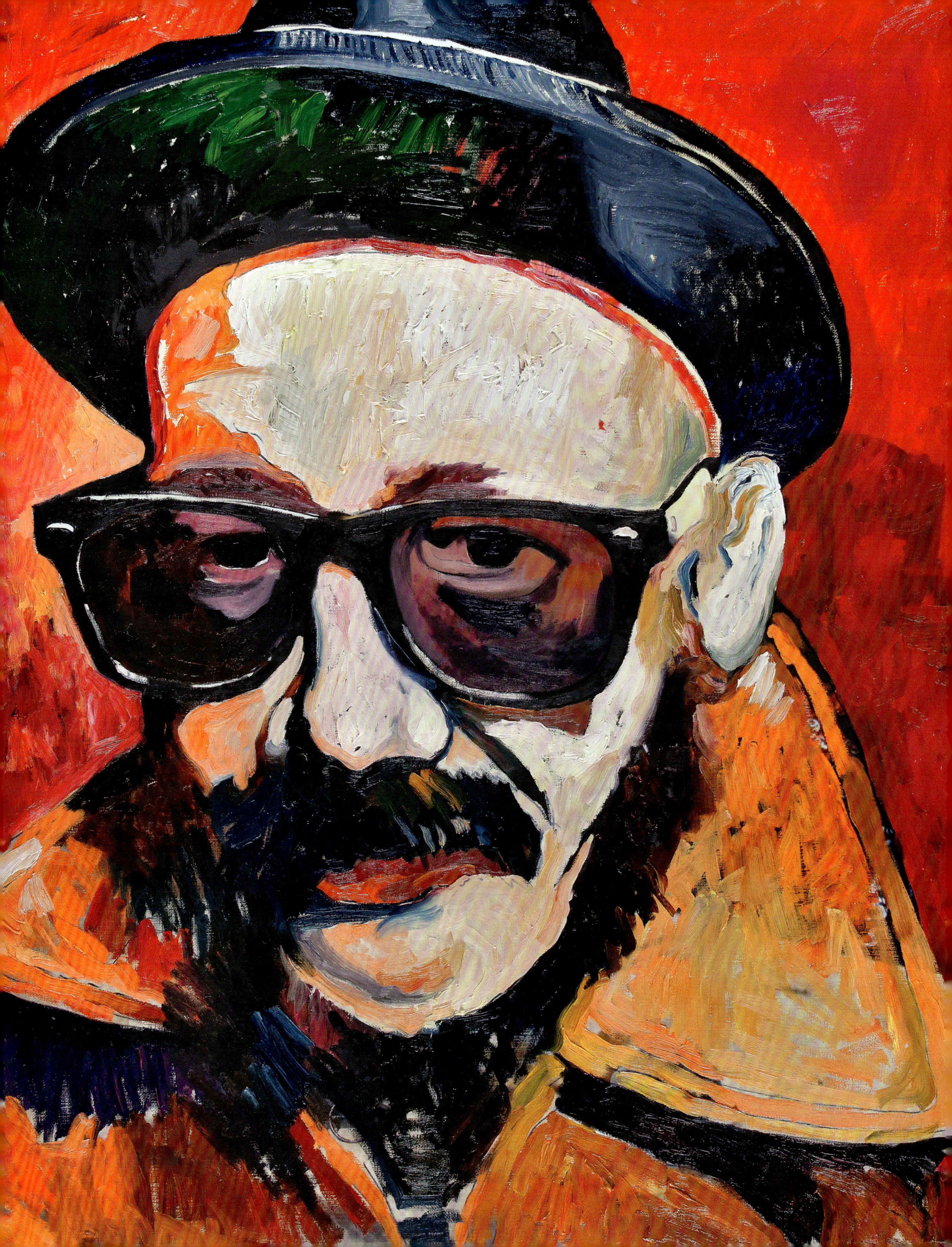

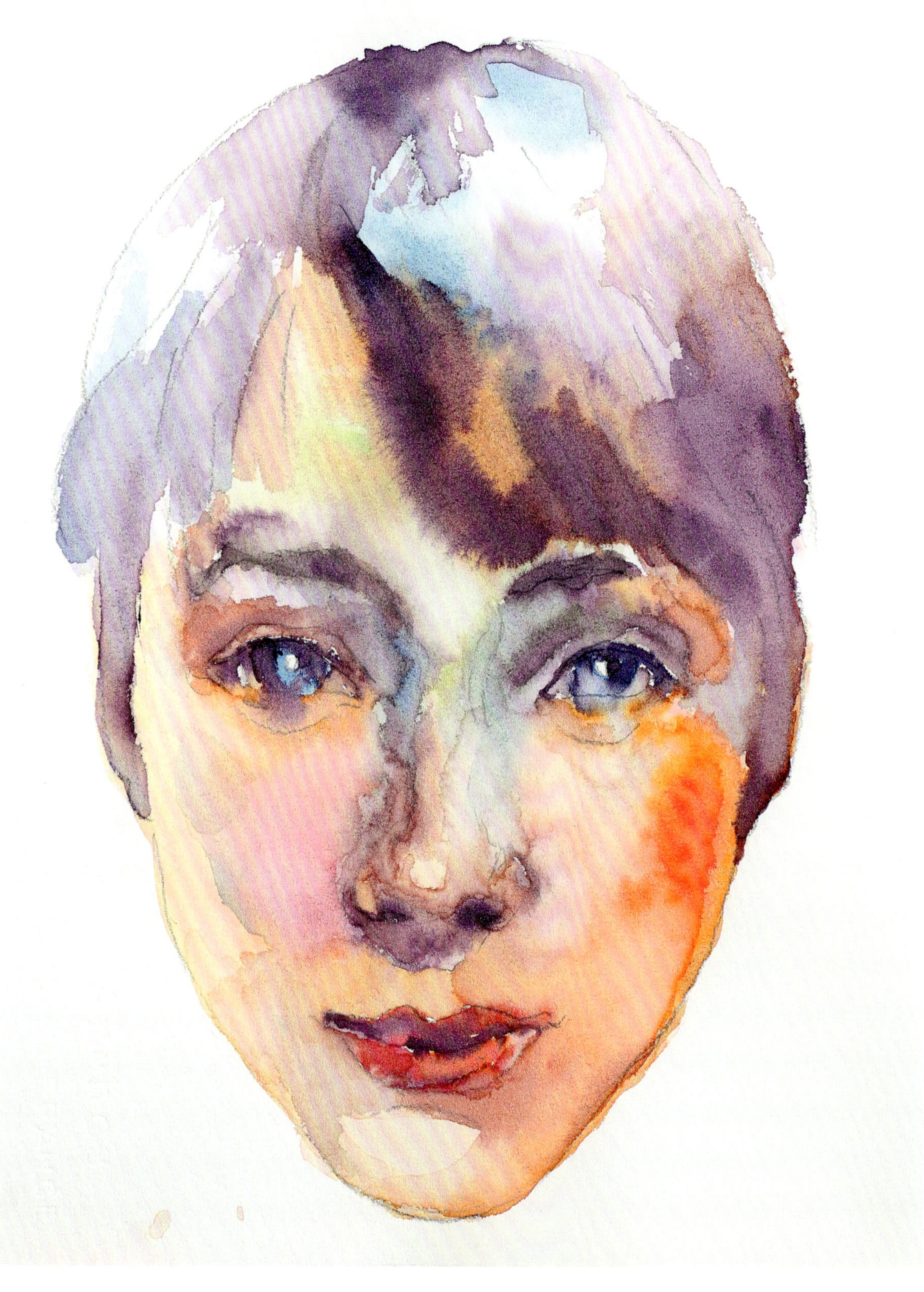

Portrait of Taisiya, 2014
watercolor, 39.5 x 29.5 cm
Property of the artist
Courtesy of the artist and Salamatina
Gallery, New York, Atlanta

Portrait of Varvara, 2014
watercolor, 39.5 x 29.5 cm
Property of the artist
Courtesy of the artist and Salamatina
Gallery, New York, Atlanta

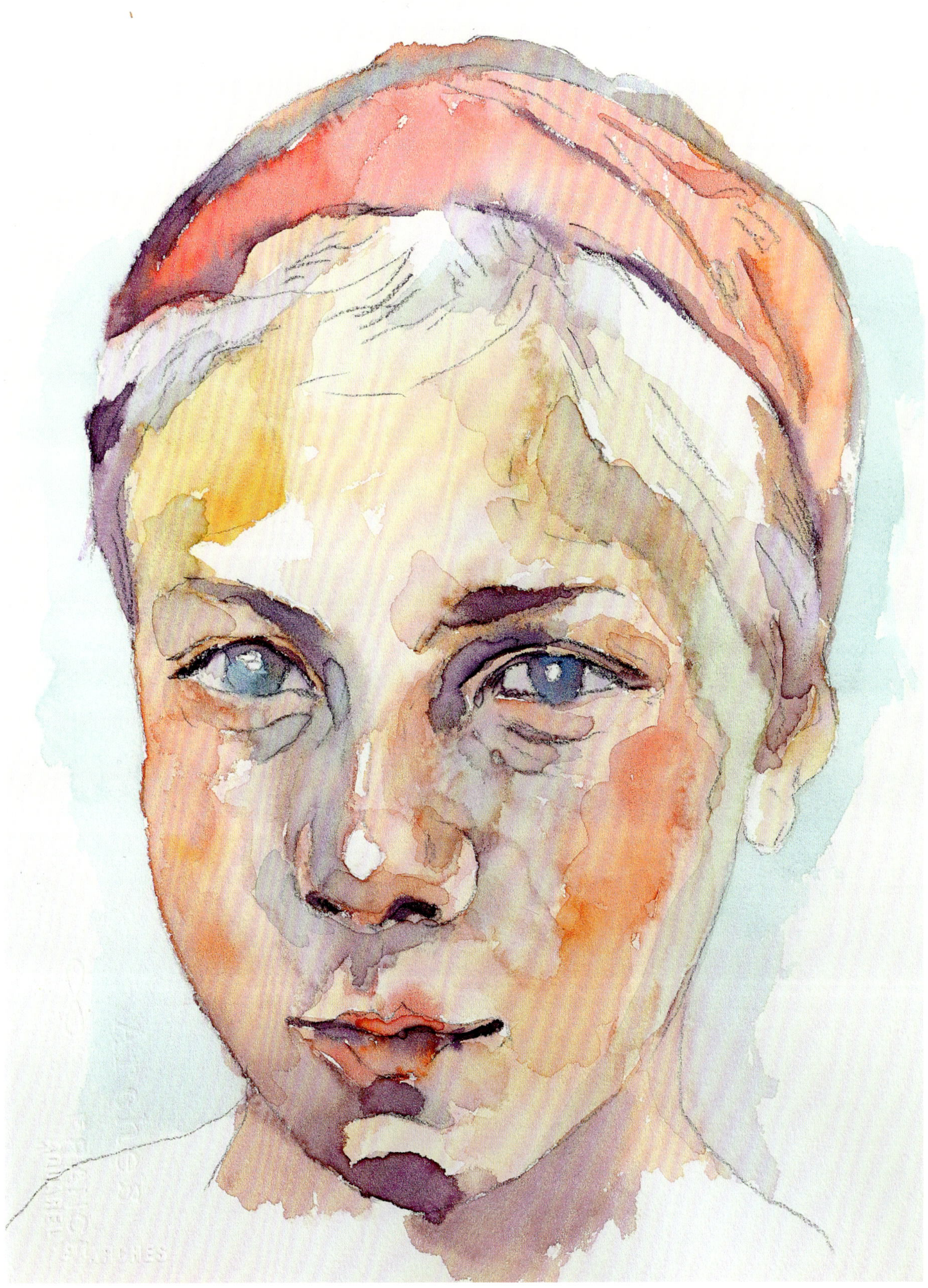

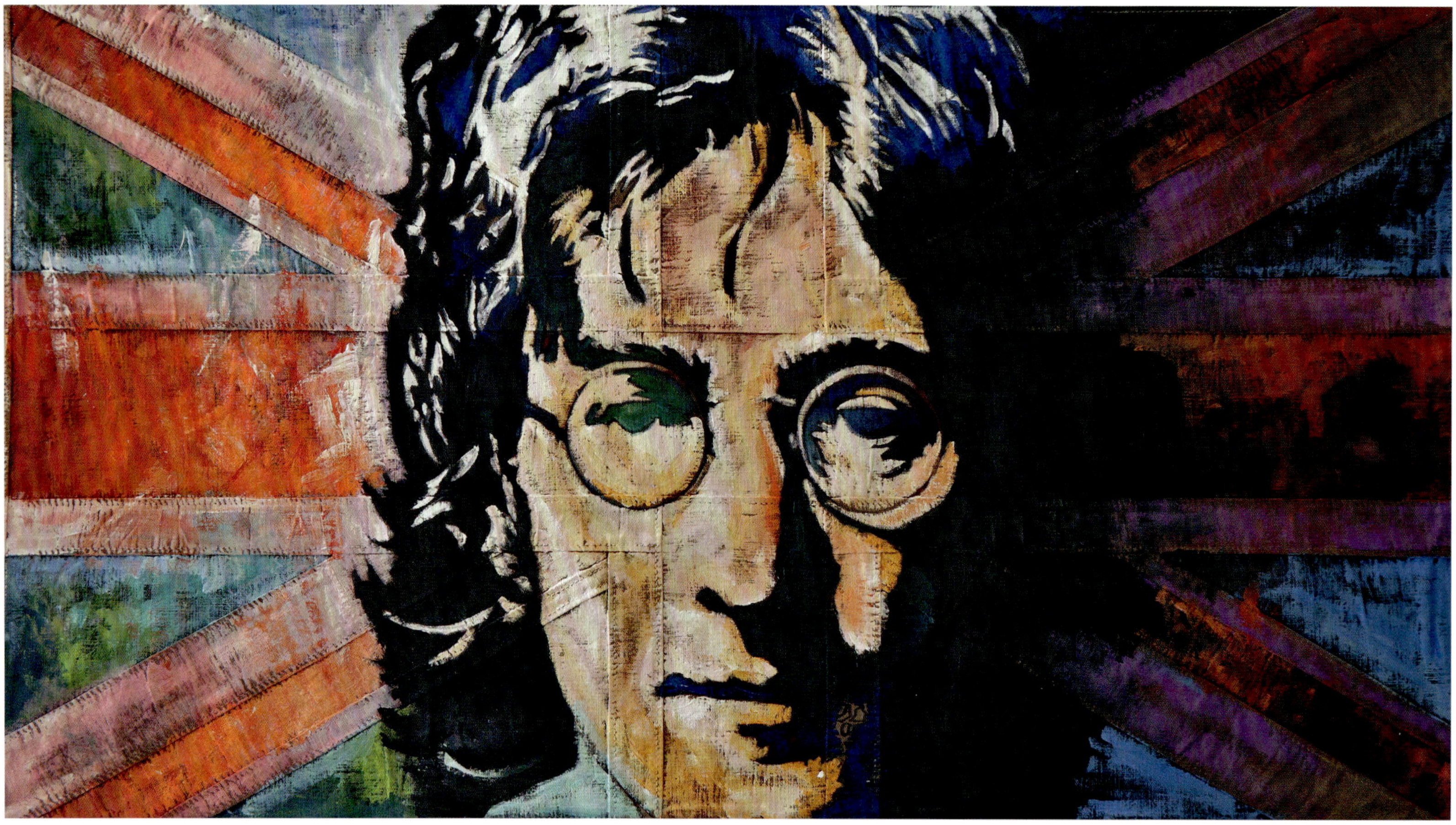

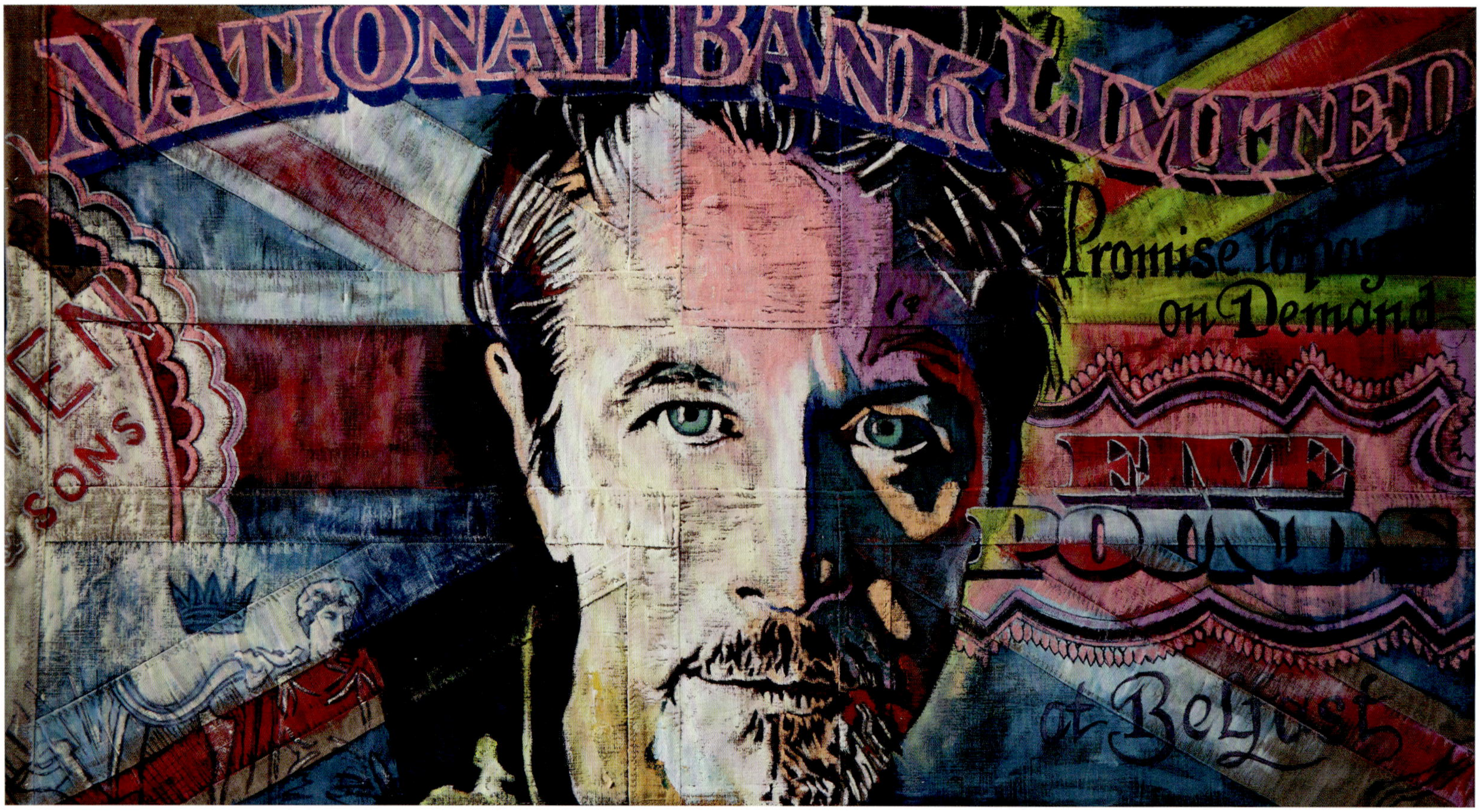

NATIONAL BANK LIMITED
Promise to pay
on Demand
FIVE
POUNDS
at Belfast
SONS

Lennon, 2013
banner/oil, 150 x 90 cm
D. Repinskiy Collection

Harry Oldman, New Money Series, 2013
banner/oil, 150 x 90 cm
V. Klyukin Collection

Sight, 2014
watercolor, 38.5 x 28.5 cm
Property of the artist
Courtesy of the artist and Salamatina
Gallery, New York, Atlanta

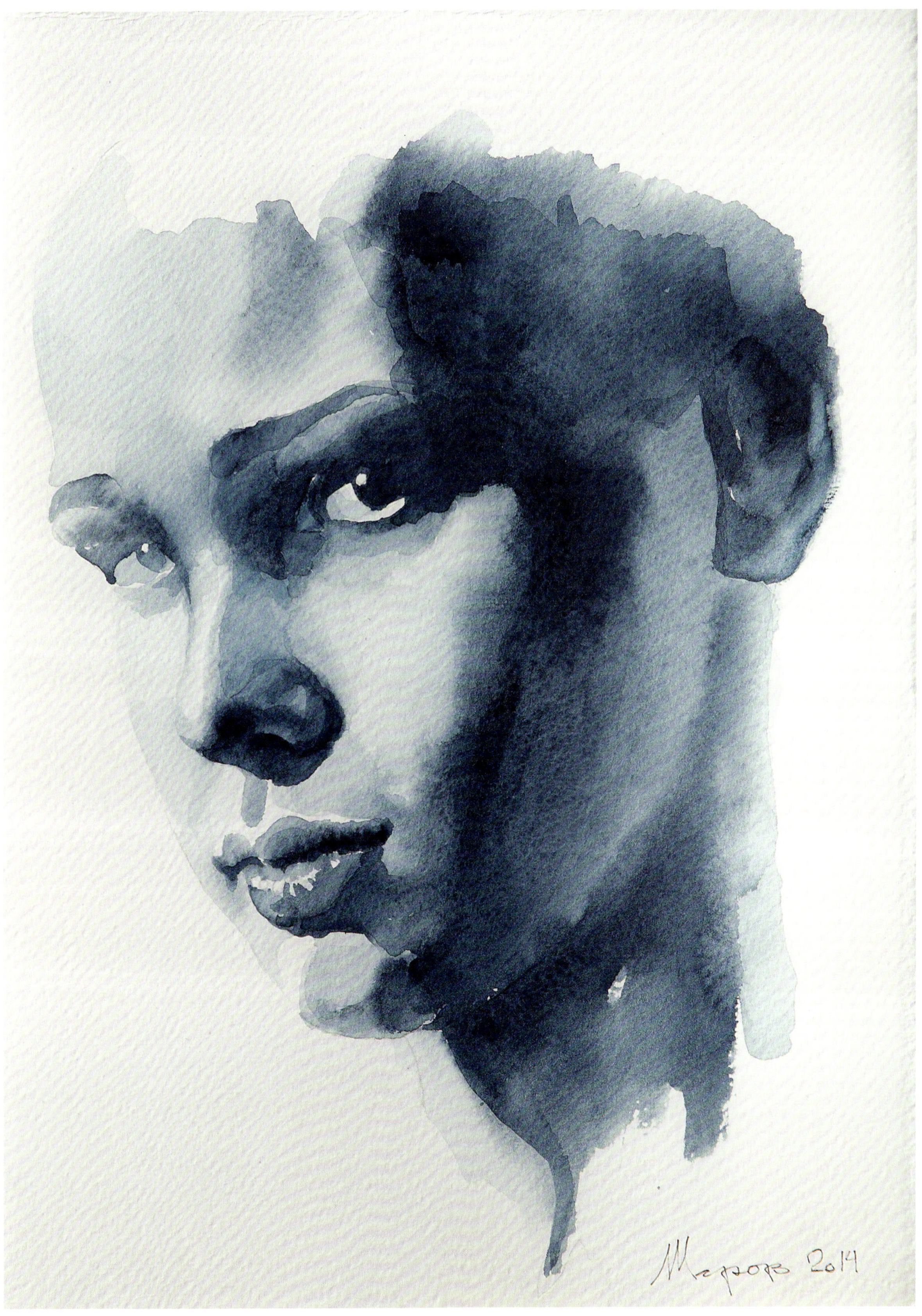

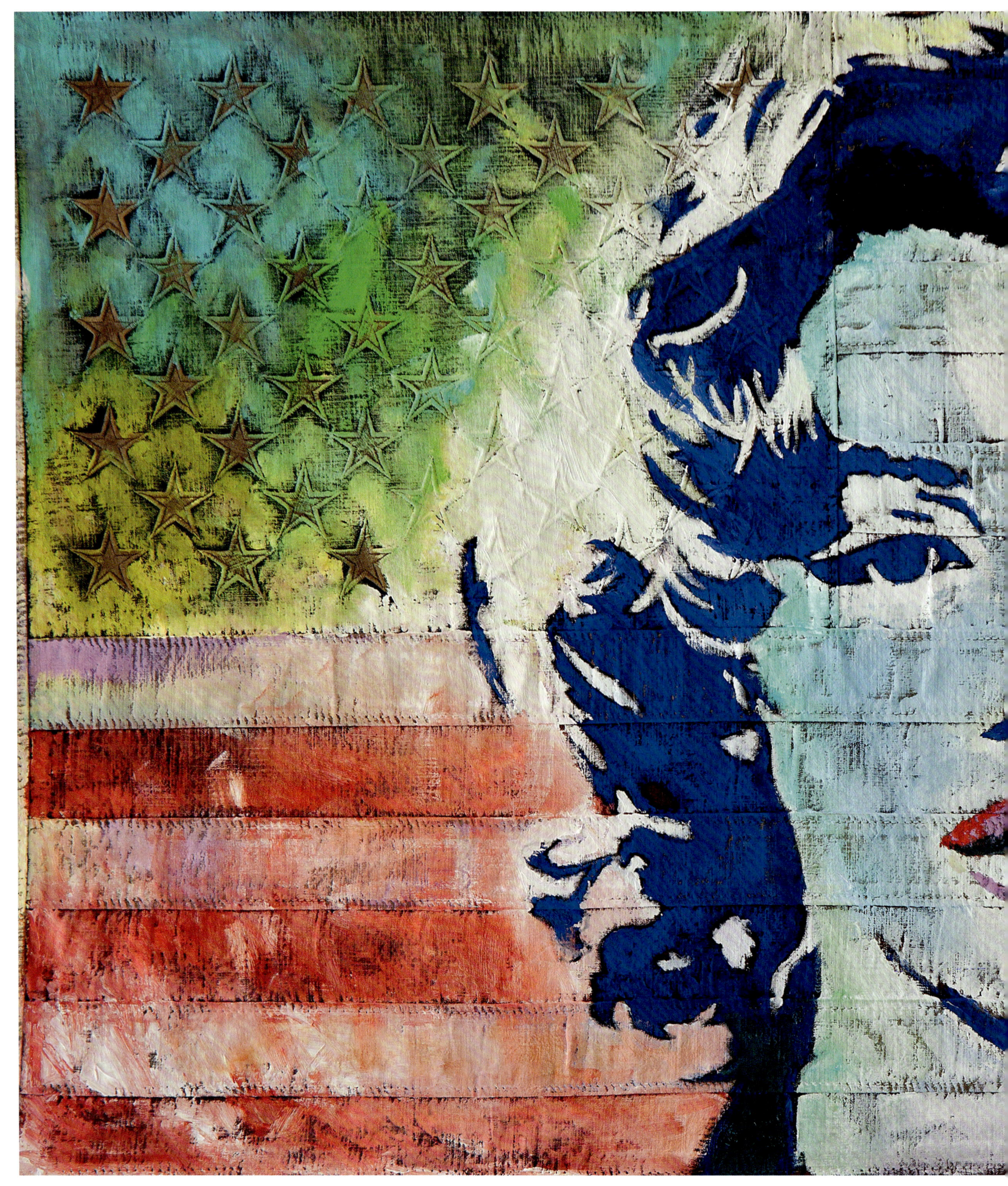

Marilyn, 2013
banner/oil, 150 x 90 cm
V. Klyukin Collection

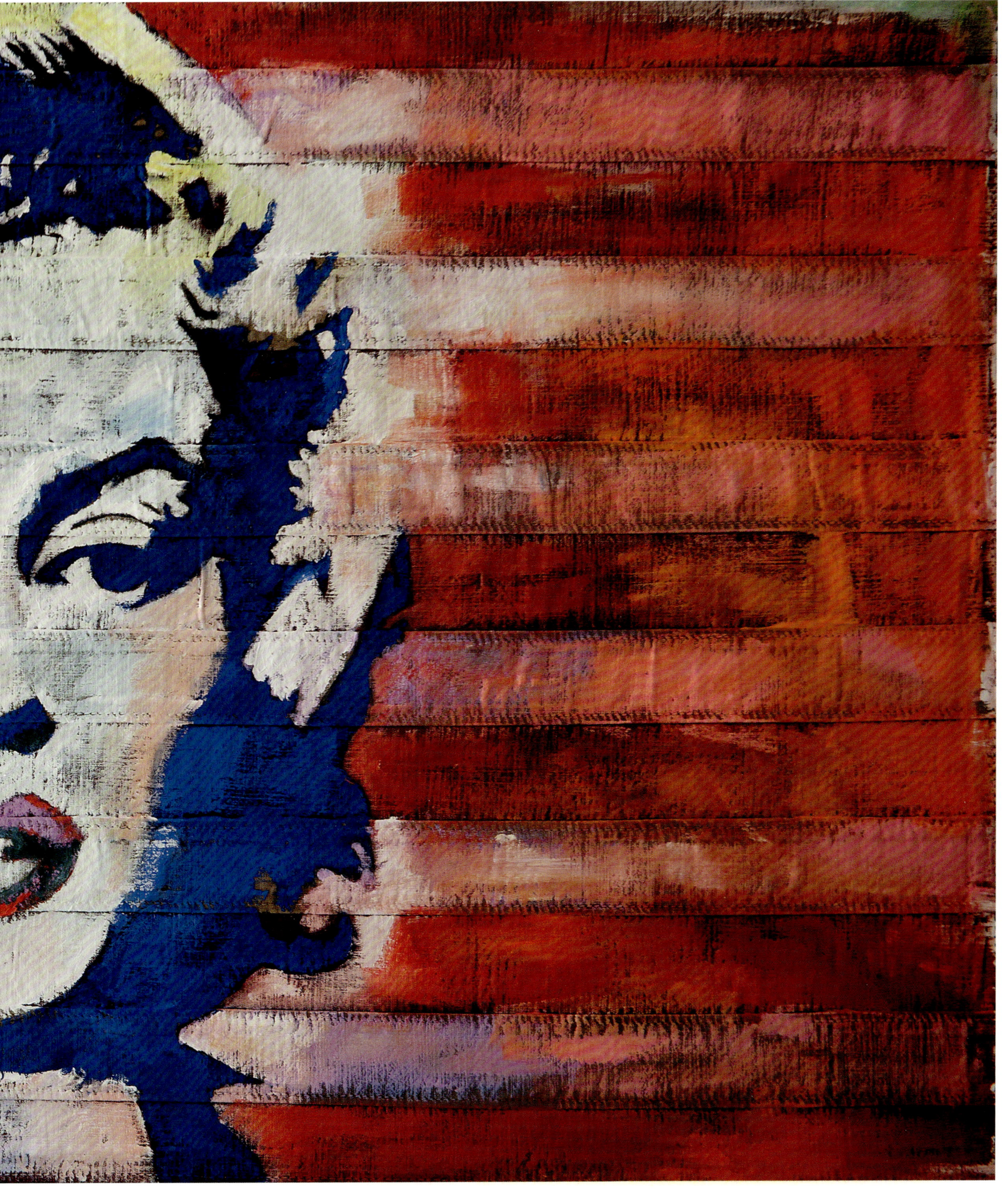

Green Pedicure, 2013
oil on canvas, 160 x 100 cm
Private collection

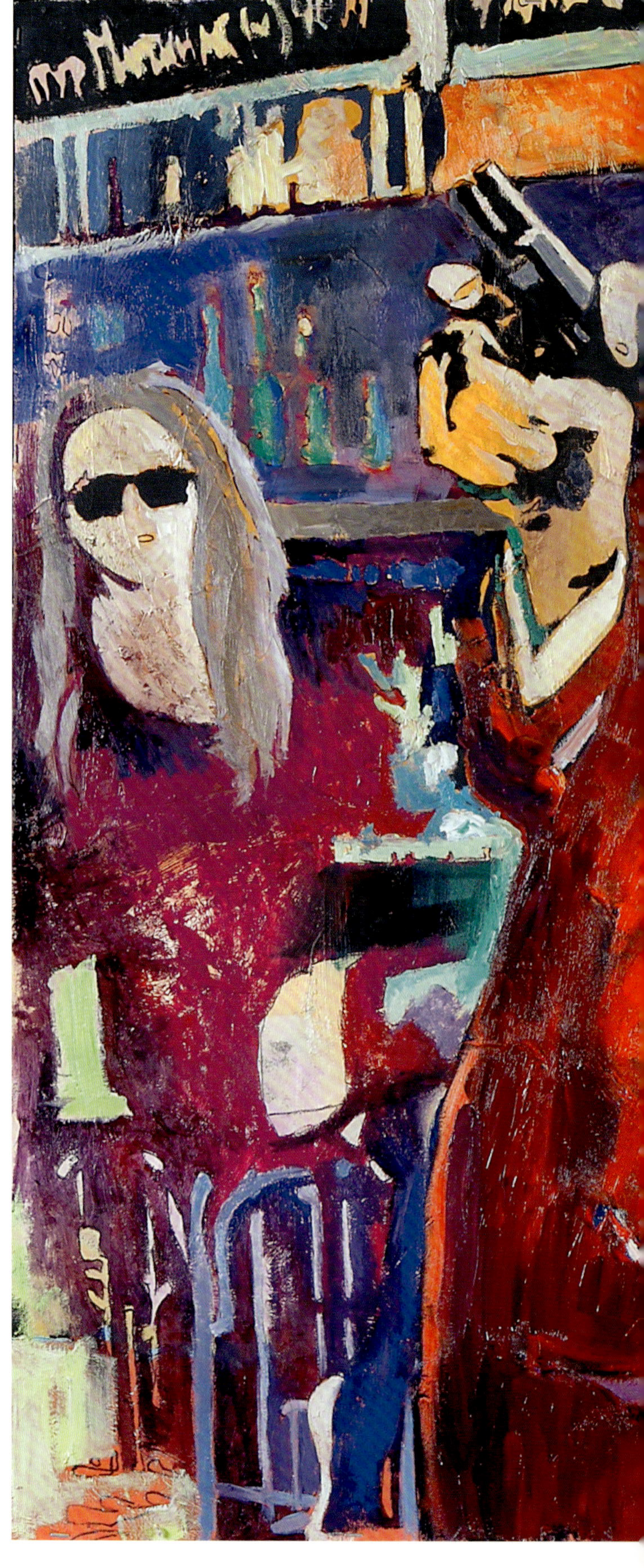

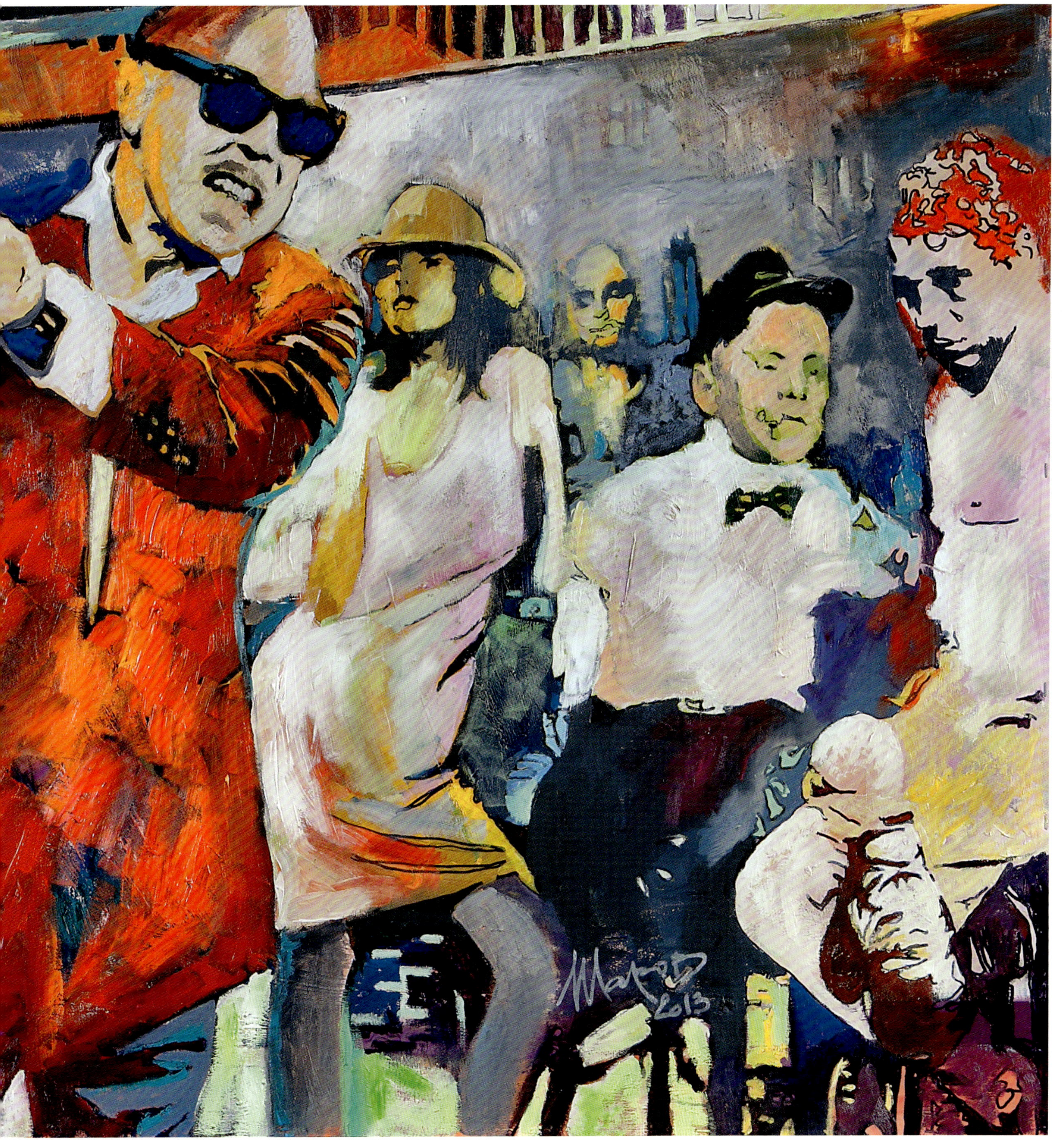

Mark
2013

STILL LIFE

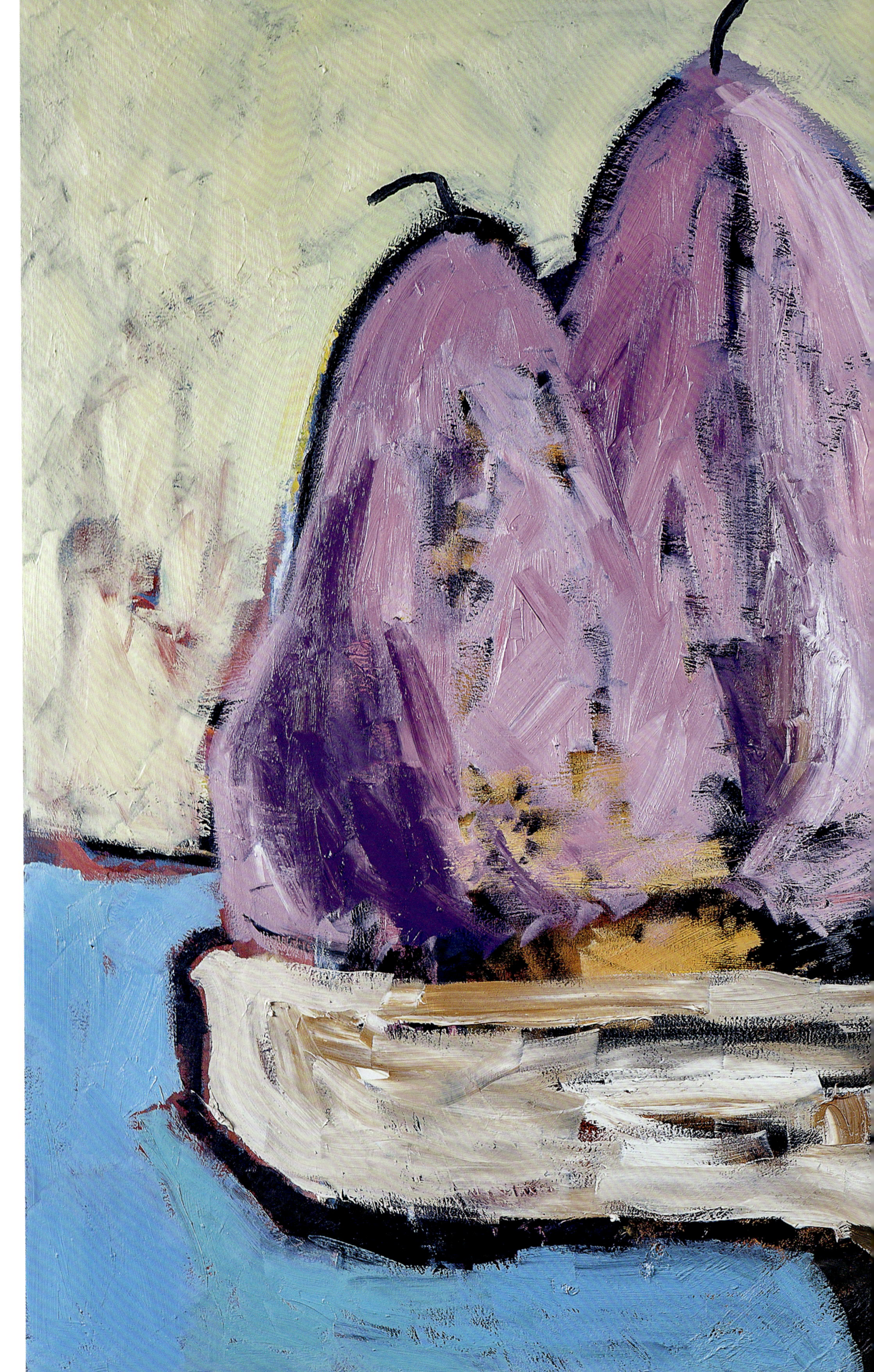

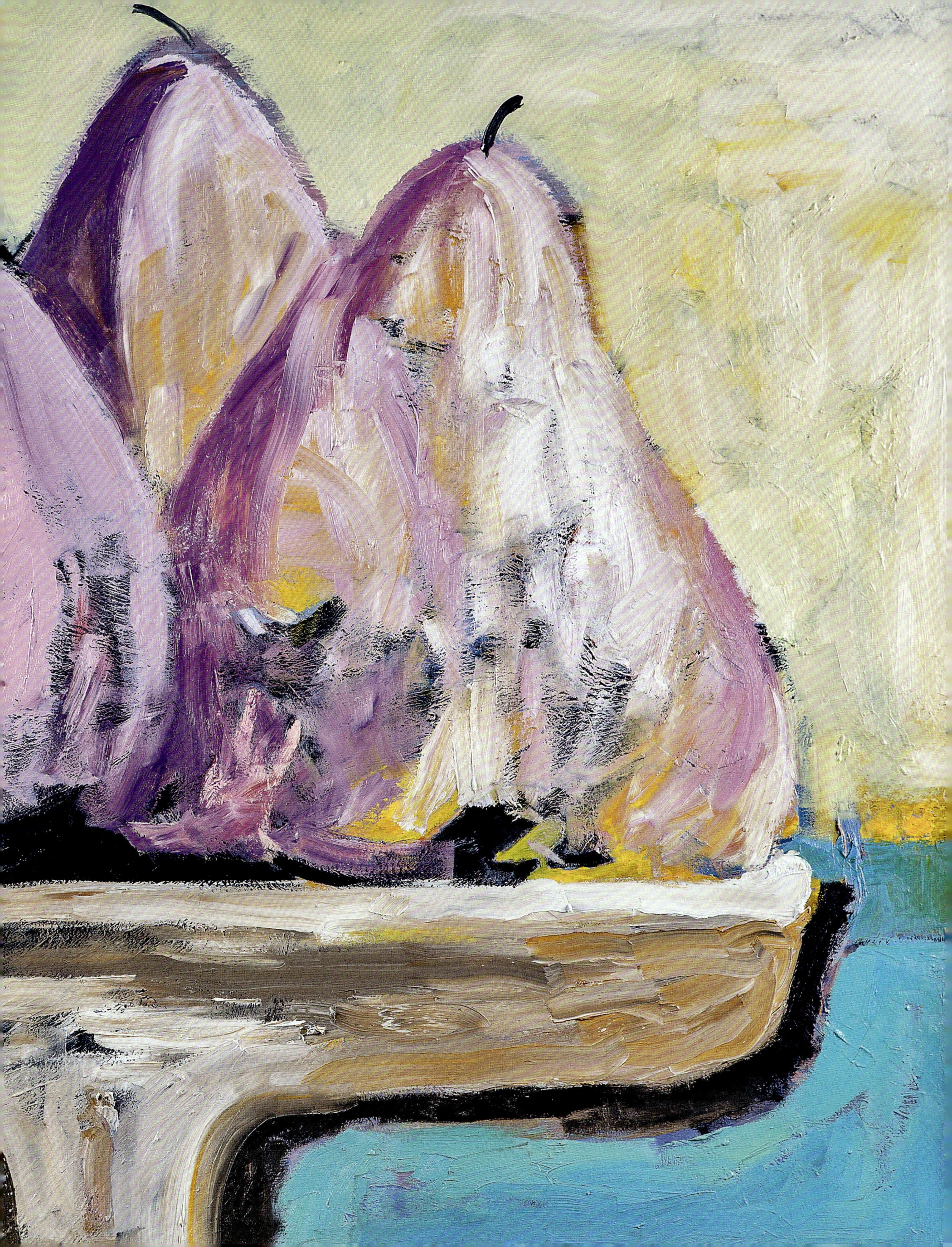

Pages 70–71
Pears No. 5, 2010
oil on canvas, 100 x 150 cm
Moscow Museum of Modern Art
(MMOMA)

Pears No. 3, 2010
oil on canvas, 100 x 120 cm
Moscow Museum of Modern Art
(MMOMA)

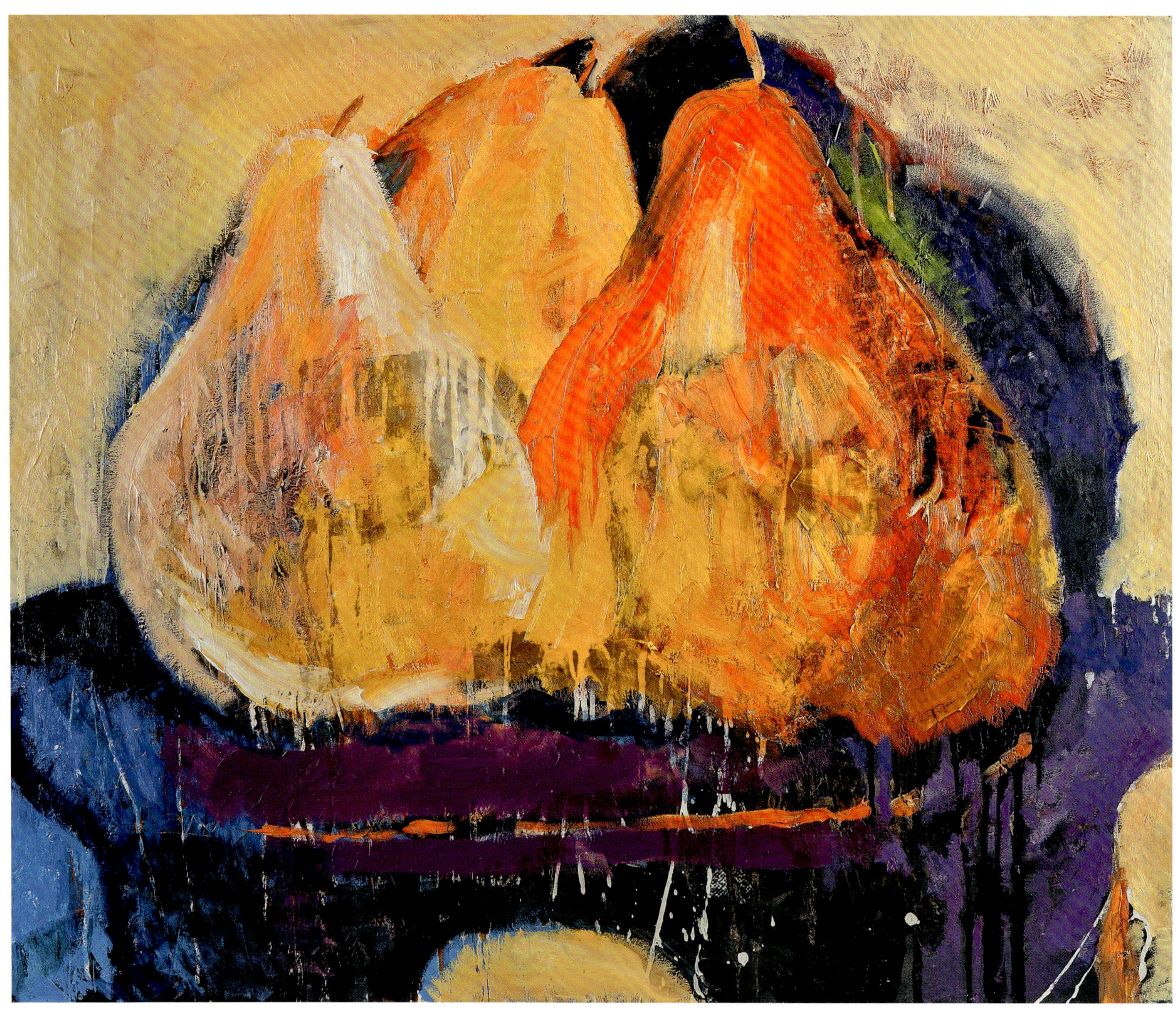

Pears No. 91, 2016
oil on canvas, 100 x 100 cm
Private collection

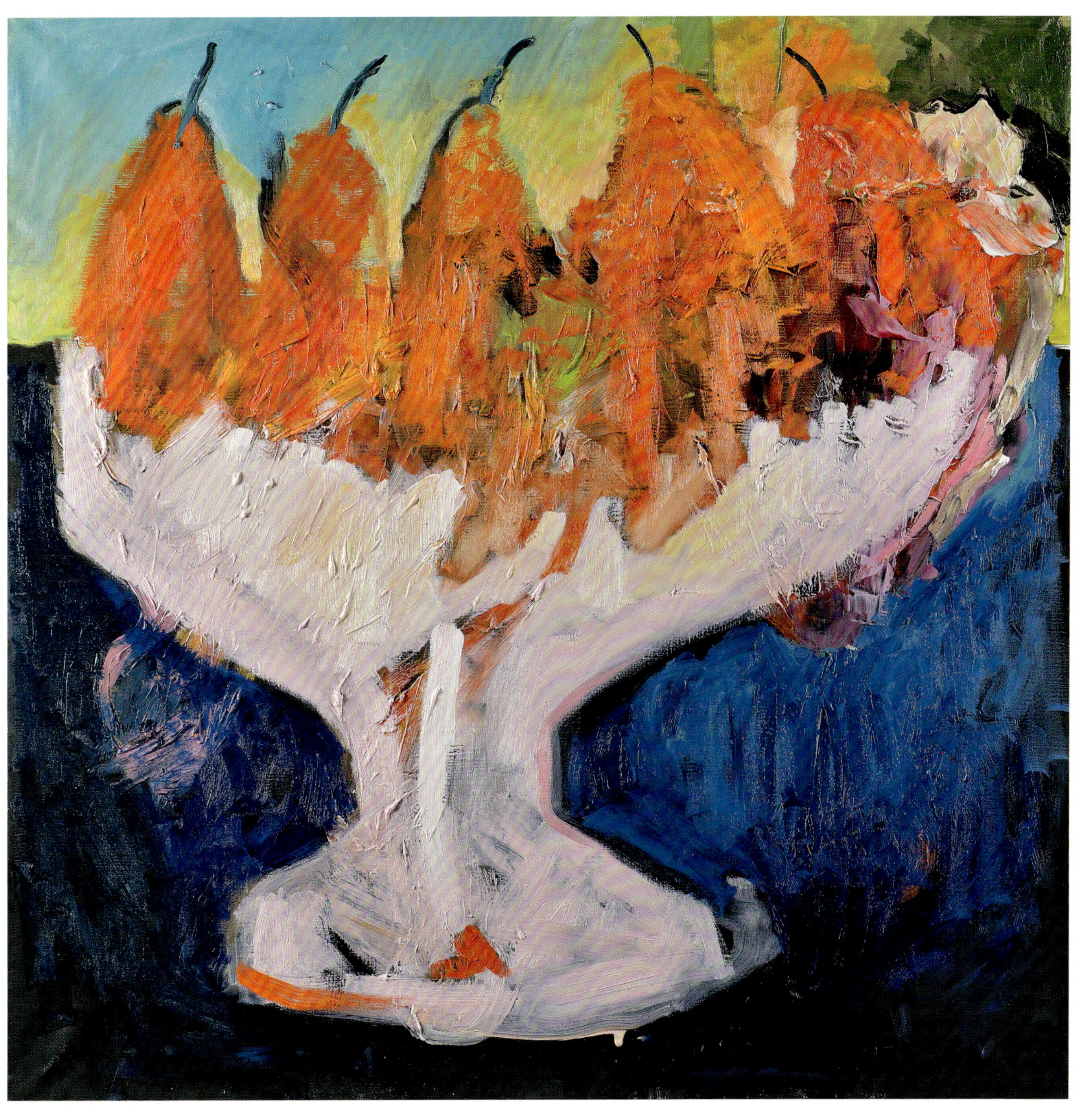

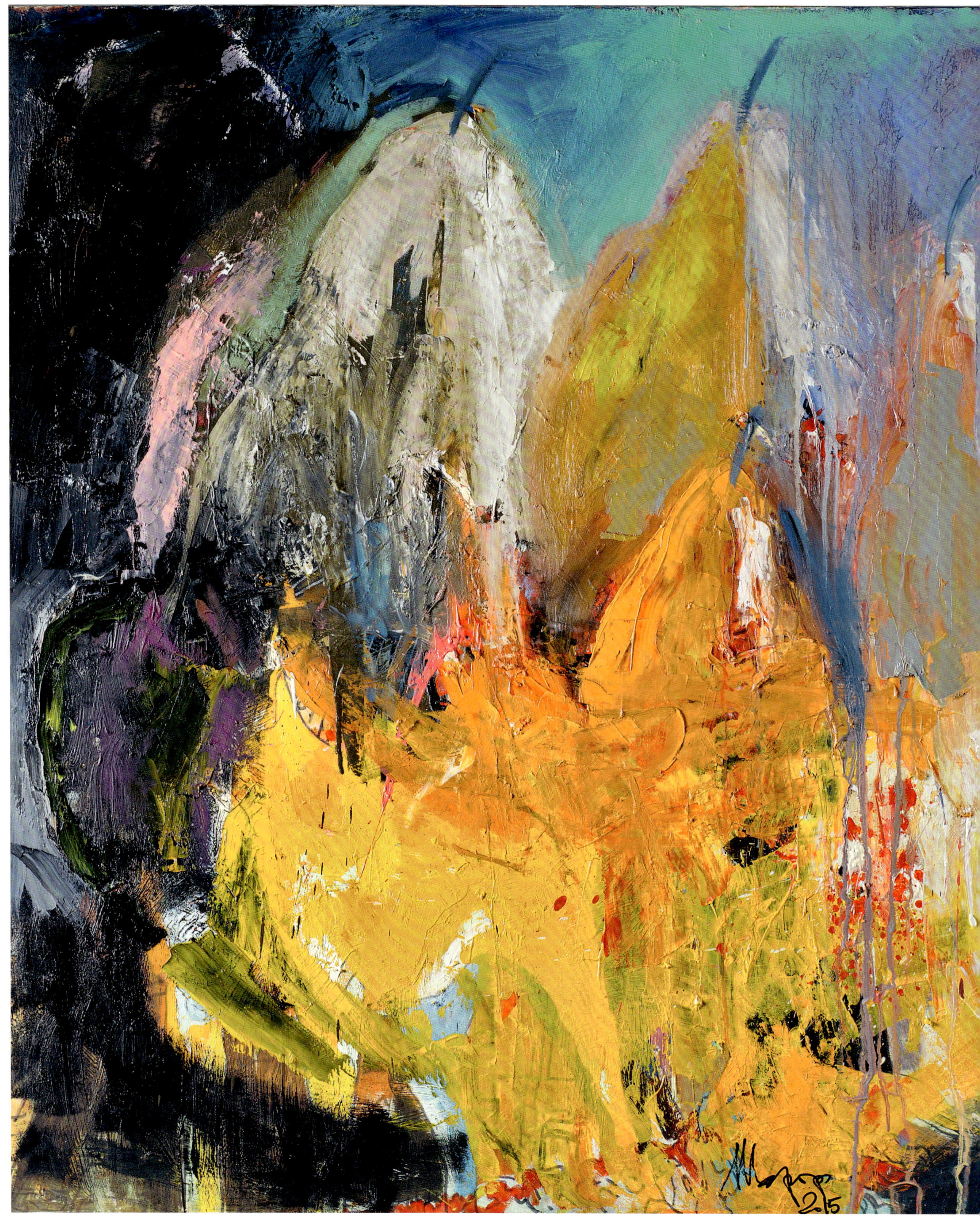

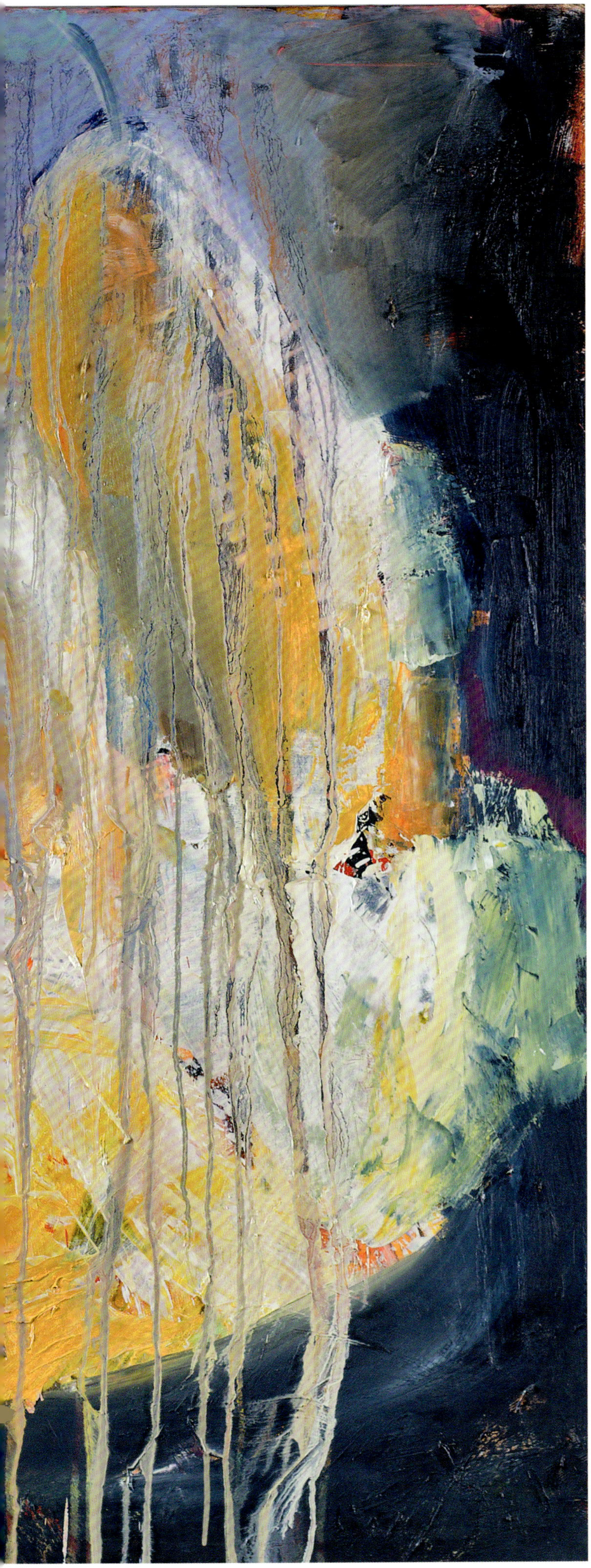

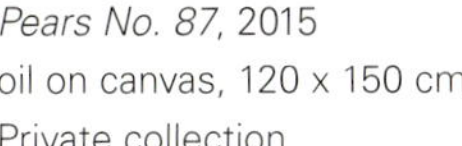

Pears No. 87, 2015
oil on canvas, 120 x 150 cm
Private collection

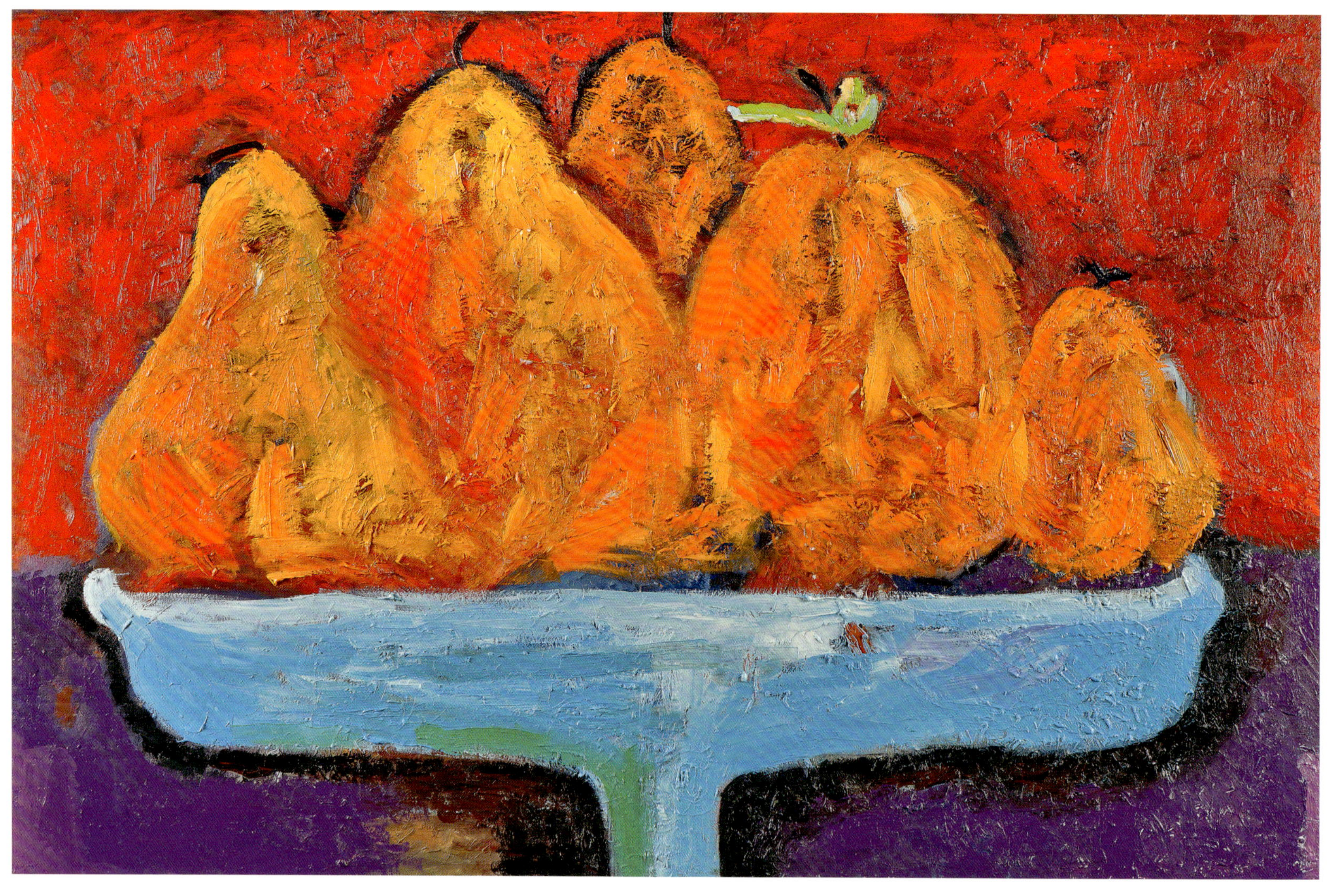

Pears No. 4, 2010
oil on canvas, 90 x 140 cm
Moscow Museum of Modern Art (MMOMA)

Joyful Pears, 2015
oil on canvas, 40 x 60 cm
Property of the artist
Courtesy of the artist and Salamatina
Gallery, New York, Atlanta

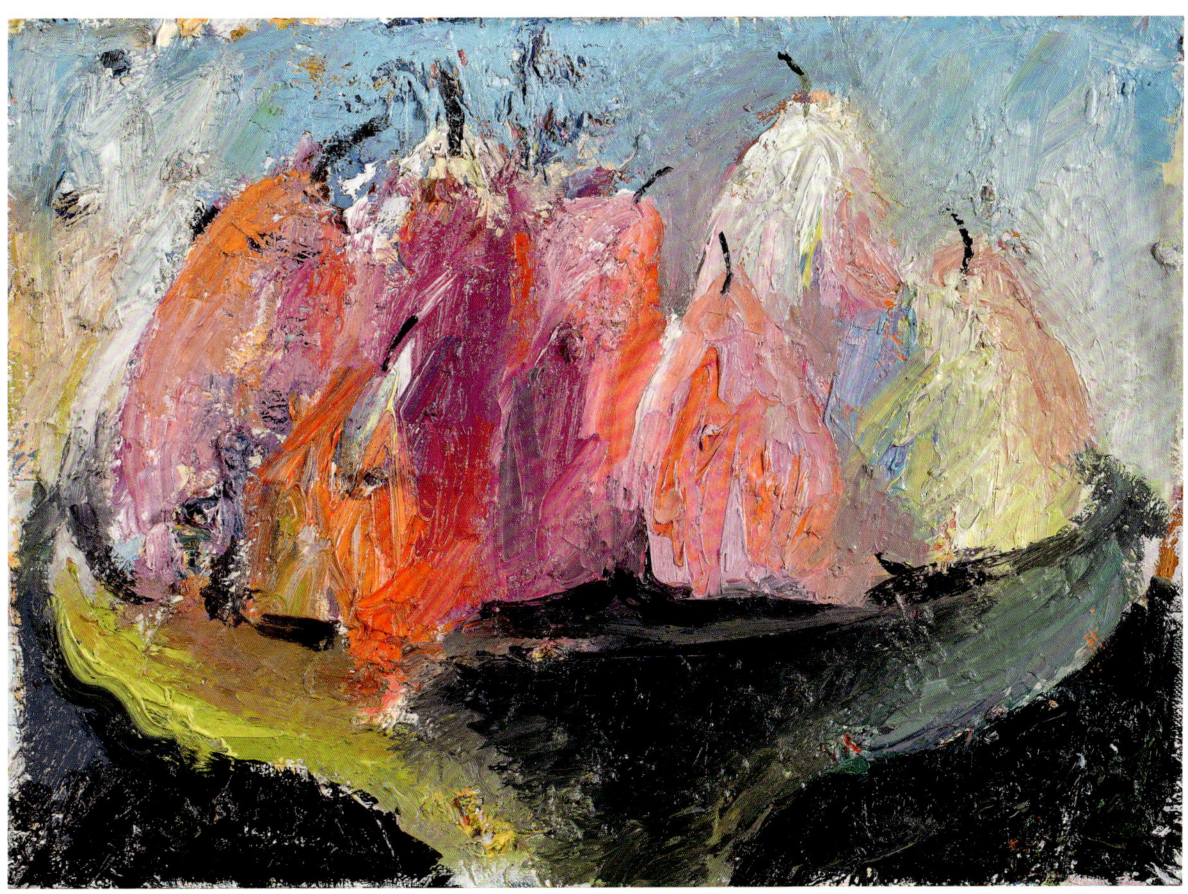

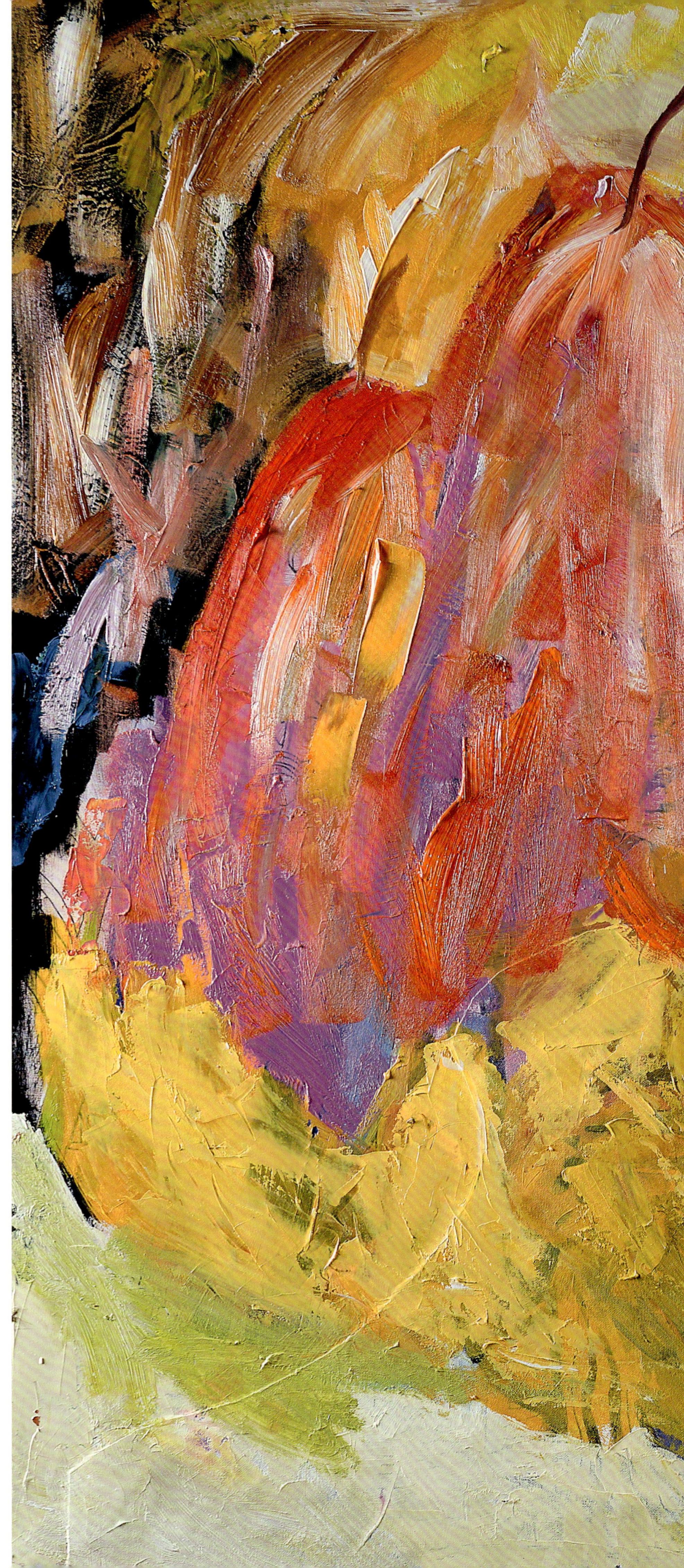

Pears No. 93, 2016
oil on canvas, 120 x 150 cm
Property of the artist
Courtesy of the artist and Salamatina
Gallery, New York, Atlanta

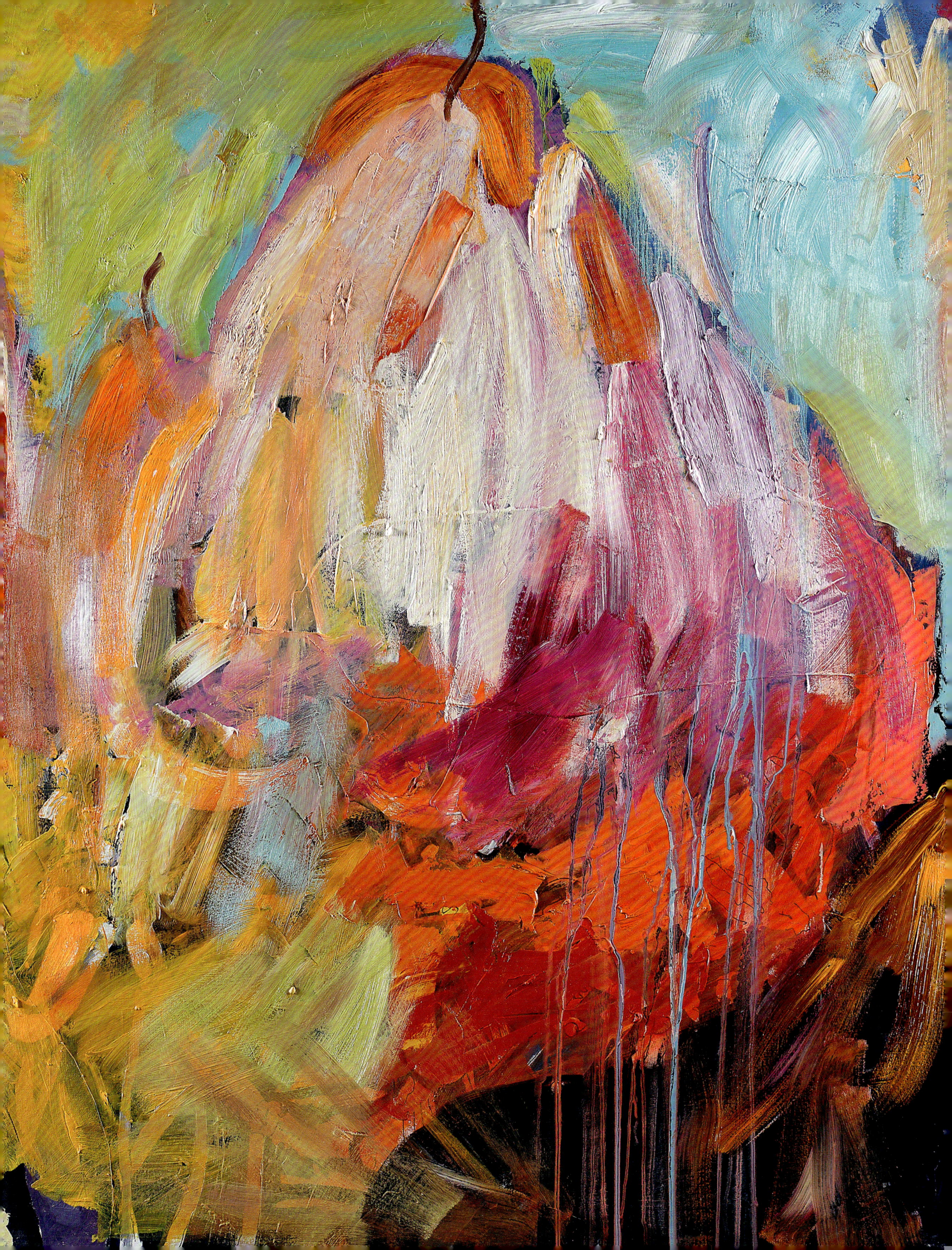

Sunny Pears, 2010
oil on canvas, 100 x 120 cm
I. Ogaryov Collection

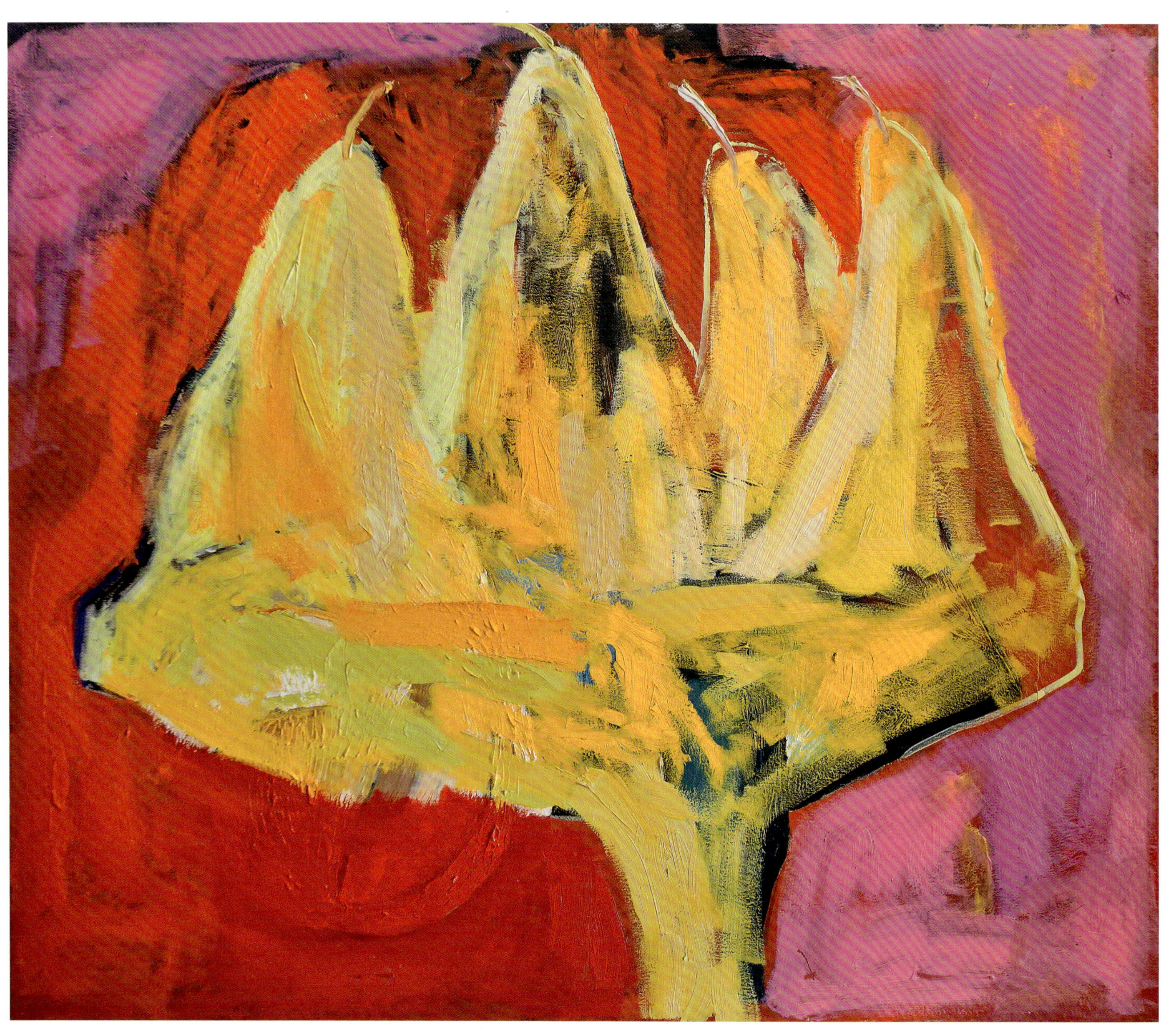

Weeping Pears, 2011
oil on canvas, 60 x 60 cm
A. Groysman Collection

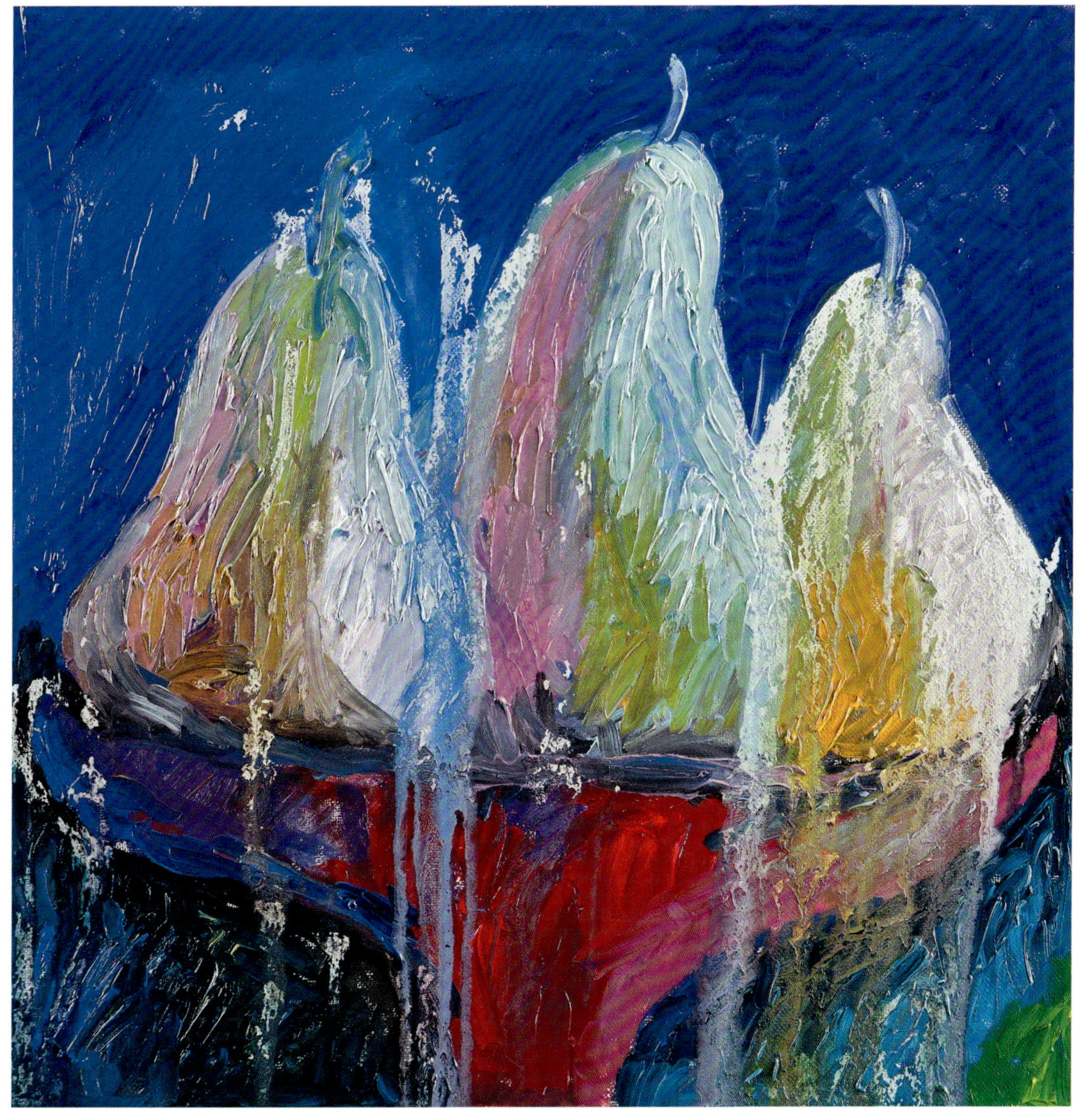

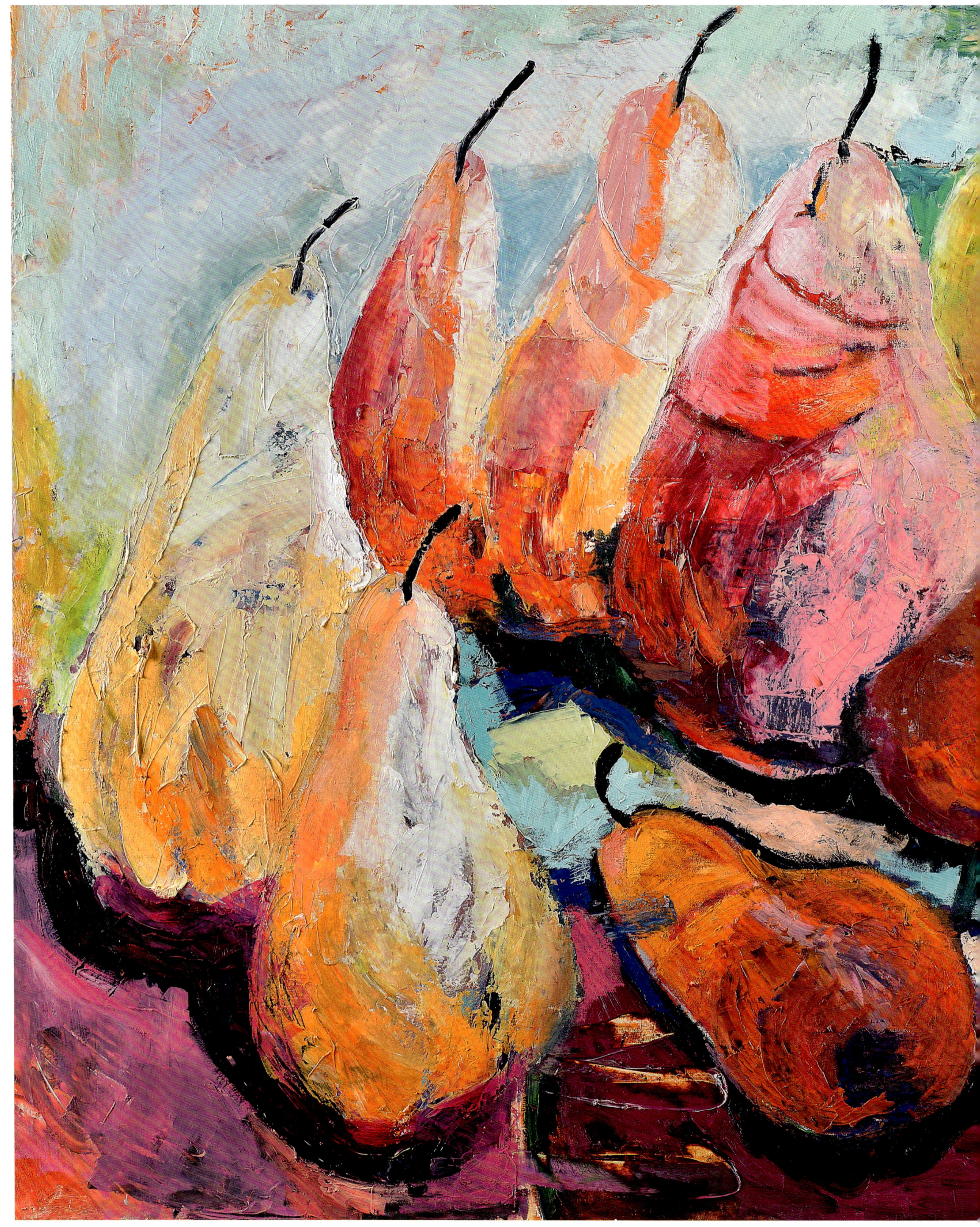

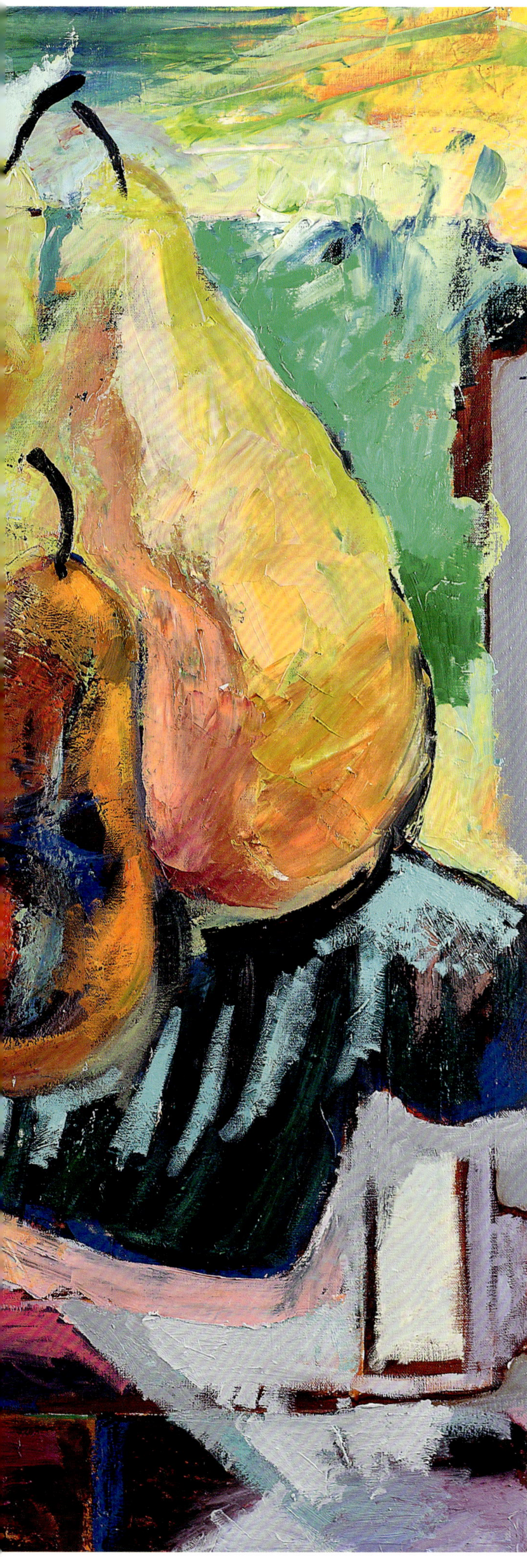

Pears in the Sun, 2016
oil on canvas, 100 x 120 cm
Property of the artist
Courtesy of the artist and Salamatina
Gallery, New York, Atlanta

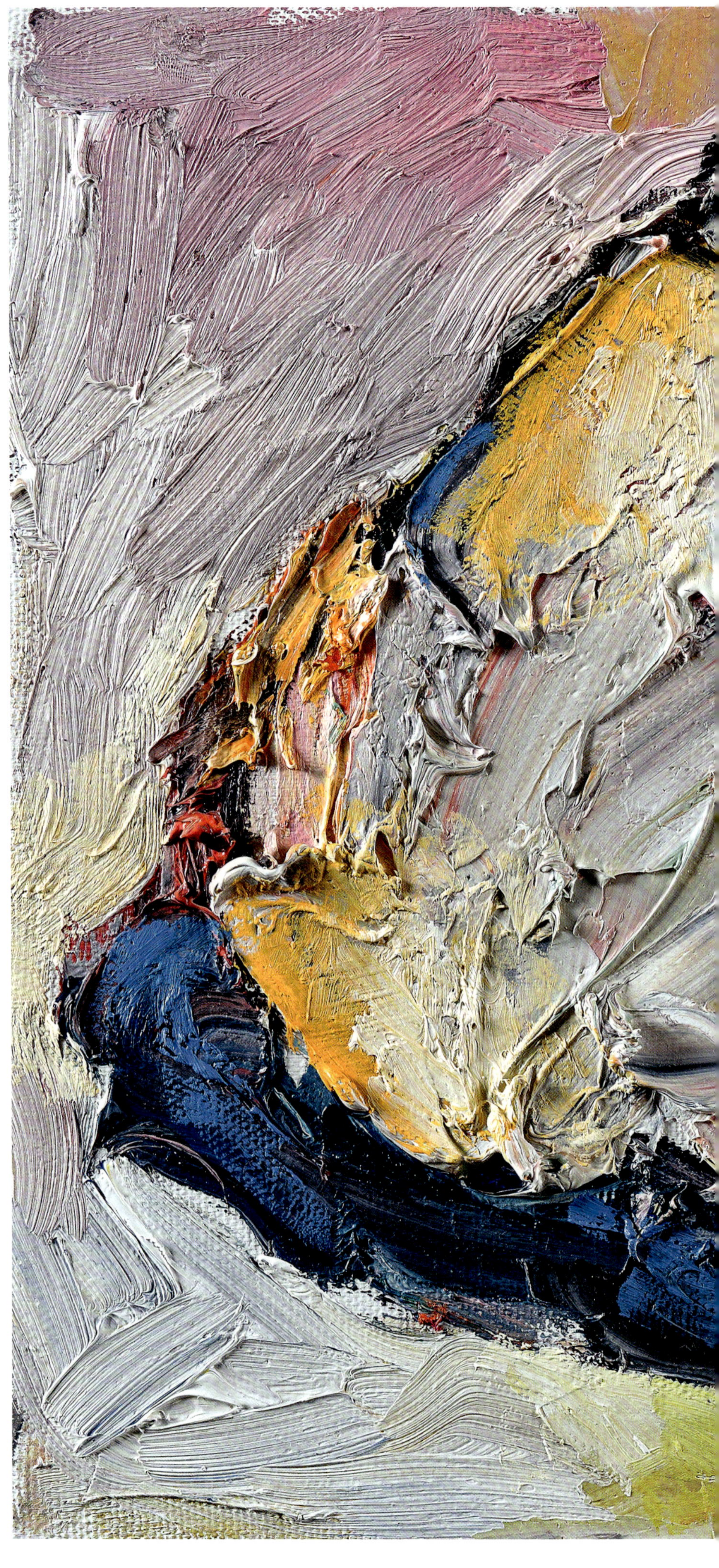

Pears No. 94, 2016
oil on canvas, 40 x 50 cm
Private collection
Courtesy of the artist and Salamatina
Gallery, New York, Atlanta

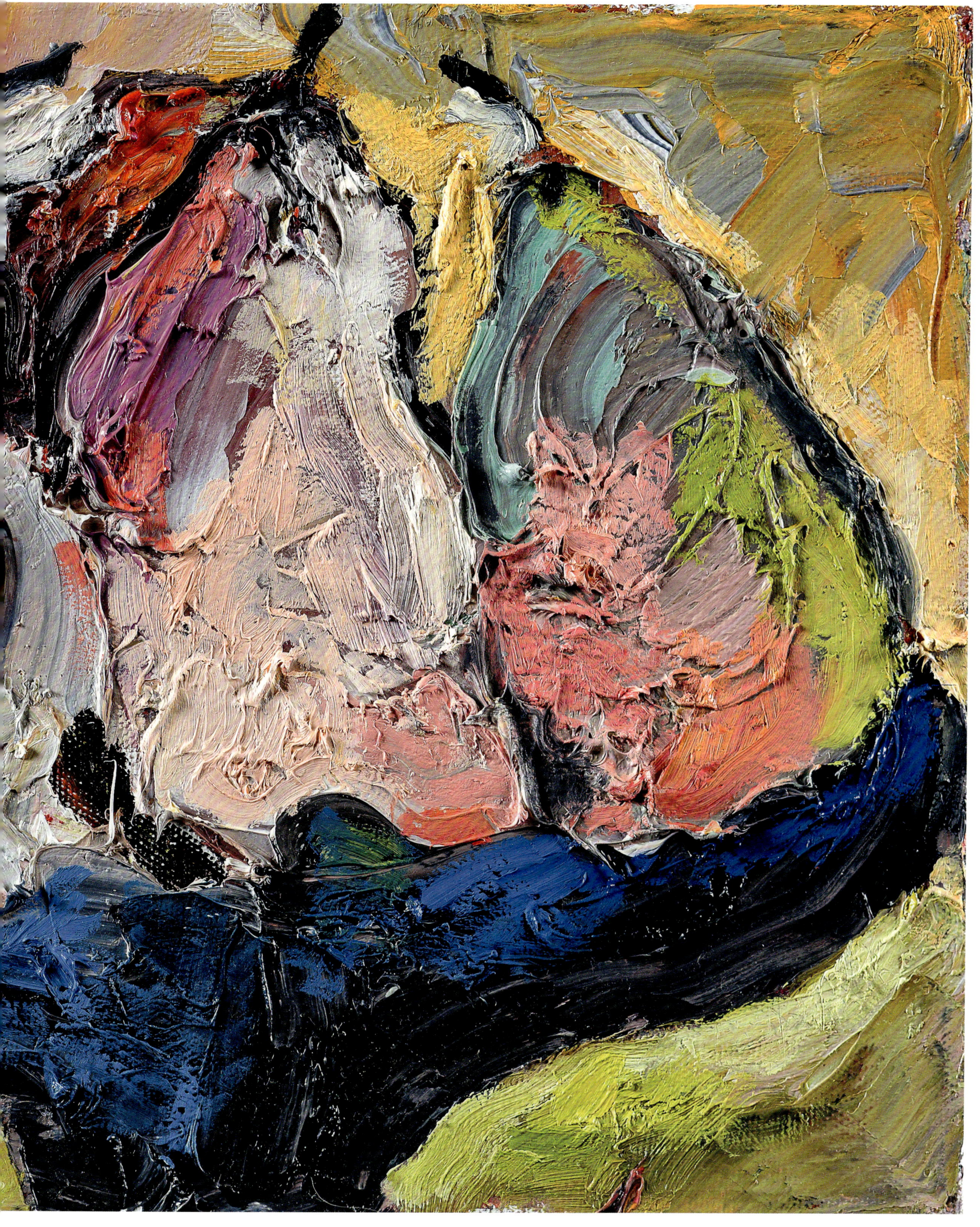

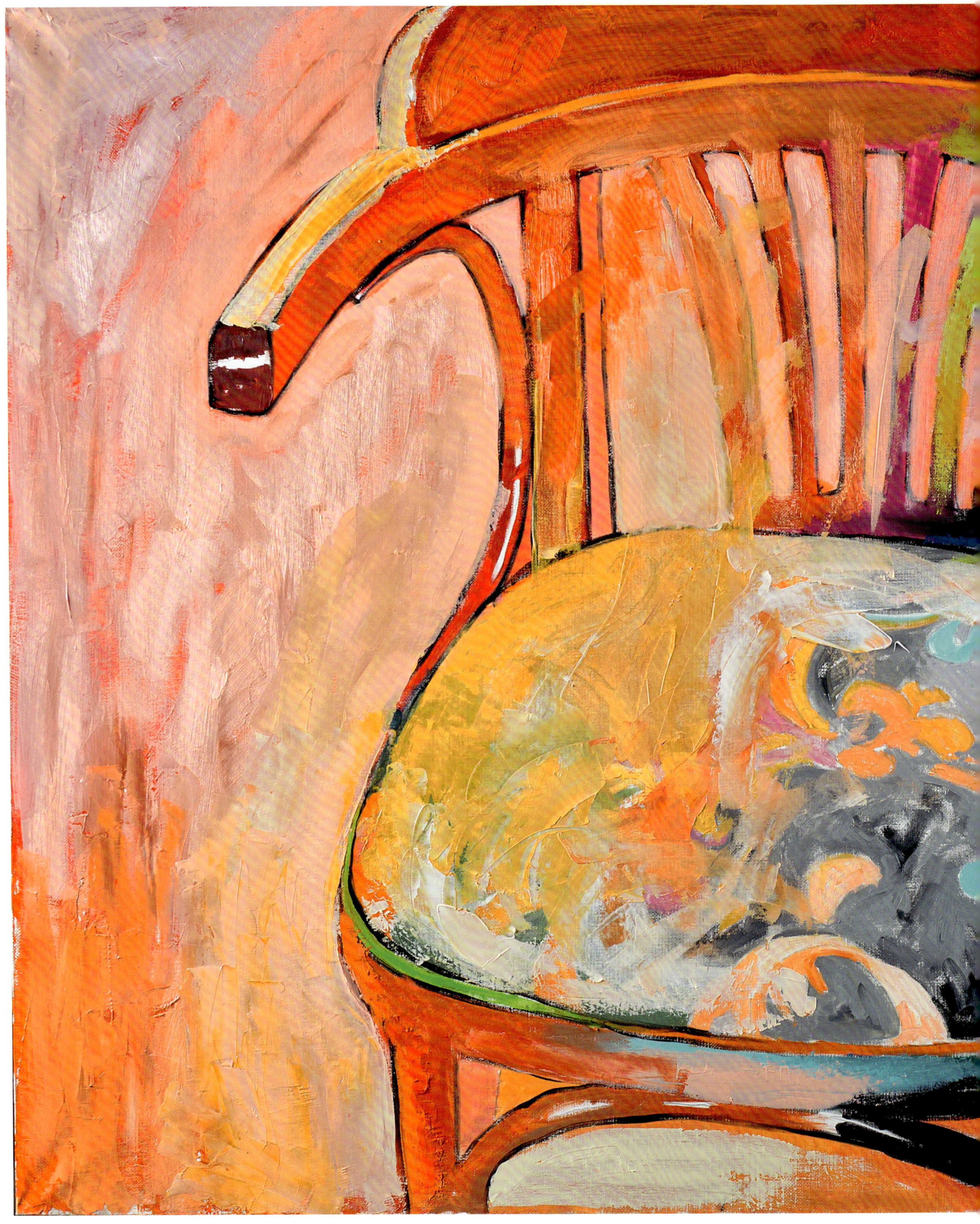

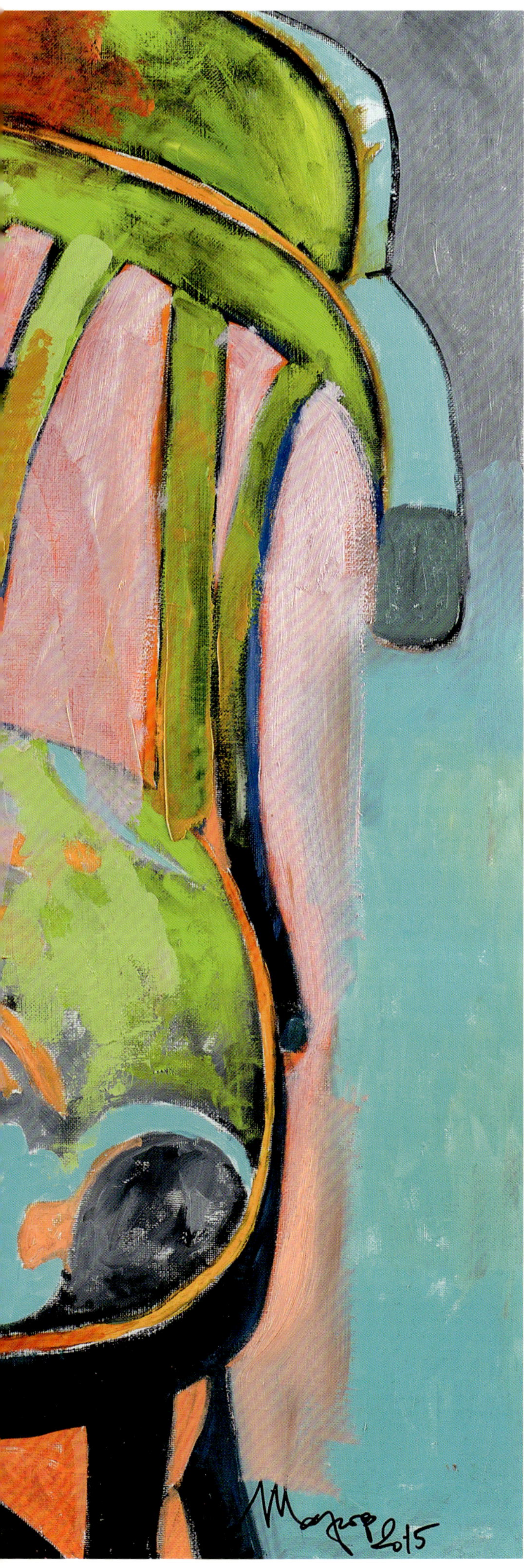

Chair No. 7, 2015
oil on canvas, 100 x 120 cm
Private collection

Page 88
Chair No. 1, 2015
oil on canvas, 120 x 100 cm
V. Klyukin Collection

Page 89
Chair No. 2, 2015
oil on canvas, 120 x 90 cm
V. Klyukin Collection

Page 90
Chair No. 6, 2016
oil on canvas, 110 x 65 cm
Property of the artist
Courtesy of the artist and Salamatina
Gallery, New York, Atlanta

Page 91
Chair No. 7, 2016
oil on canvas, 110 x 60 cm
Property of the artist
Courtesy of the artist and Salamatina
Gallery, New York, Atlanta

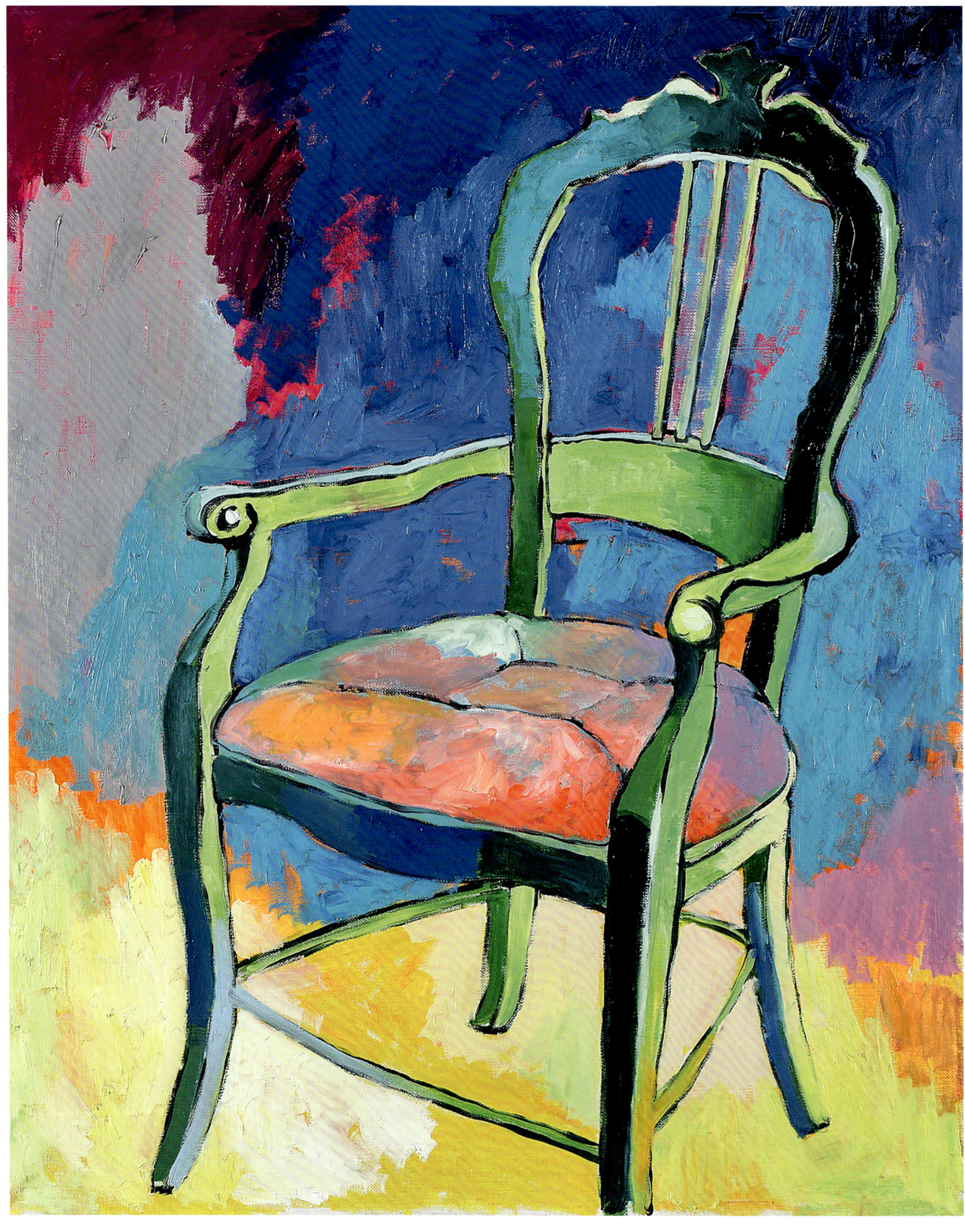

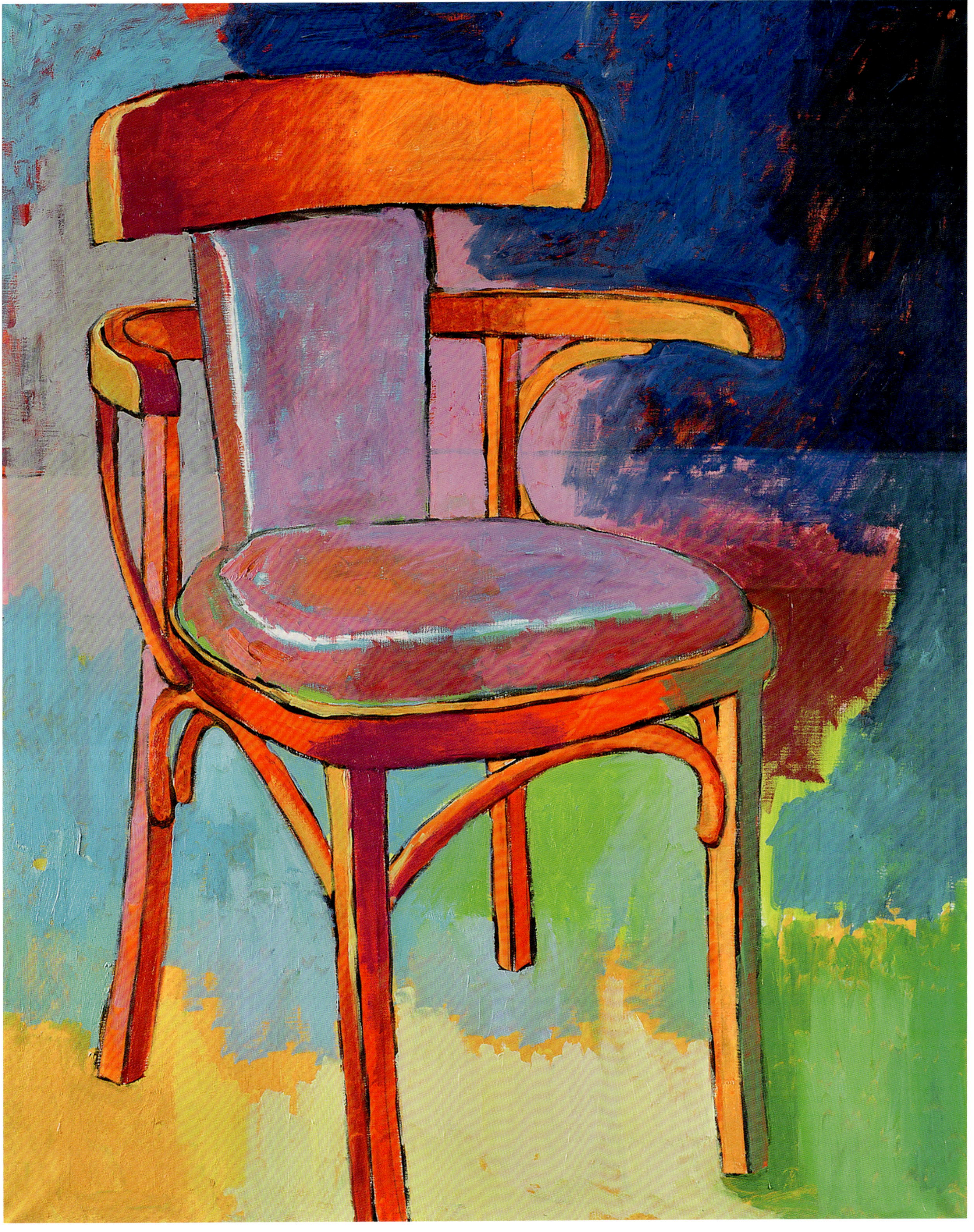

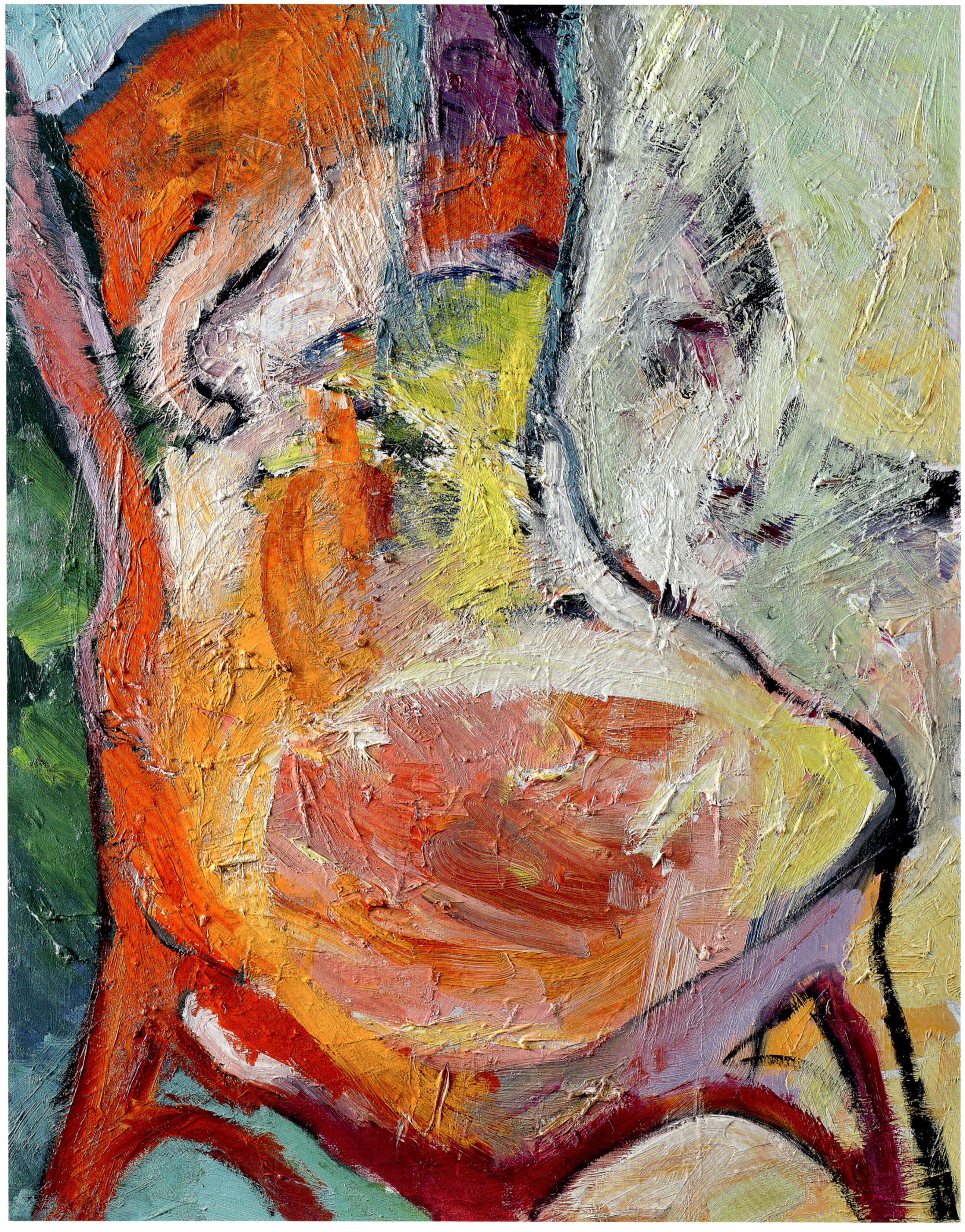

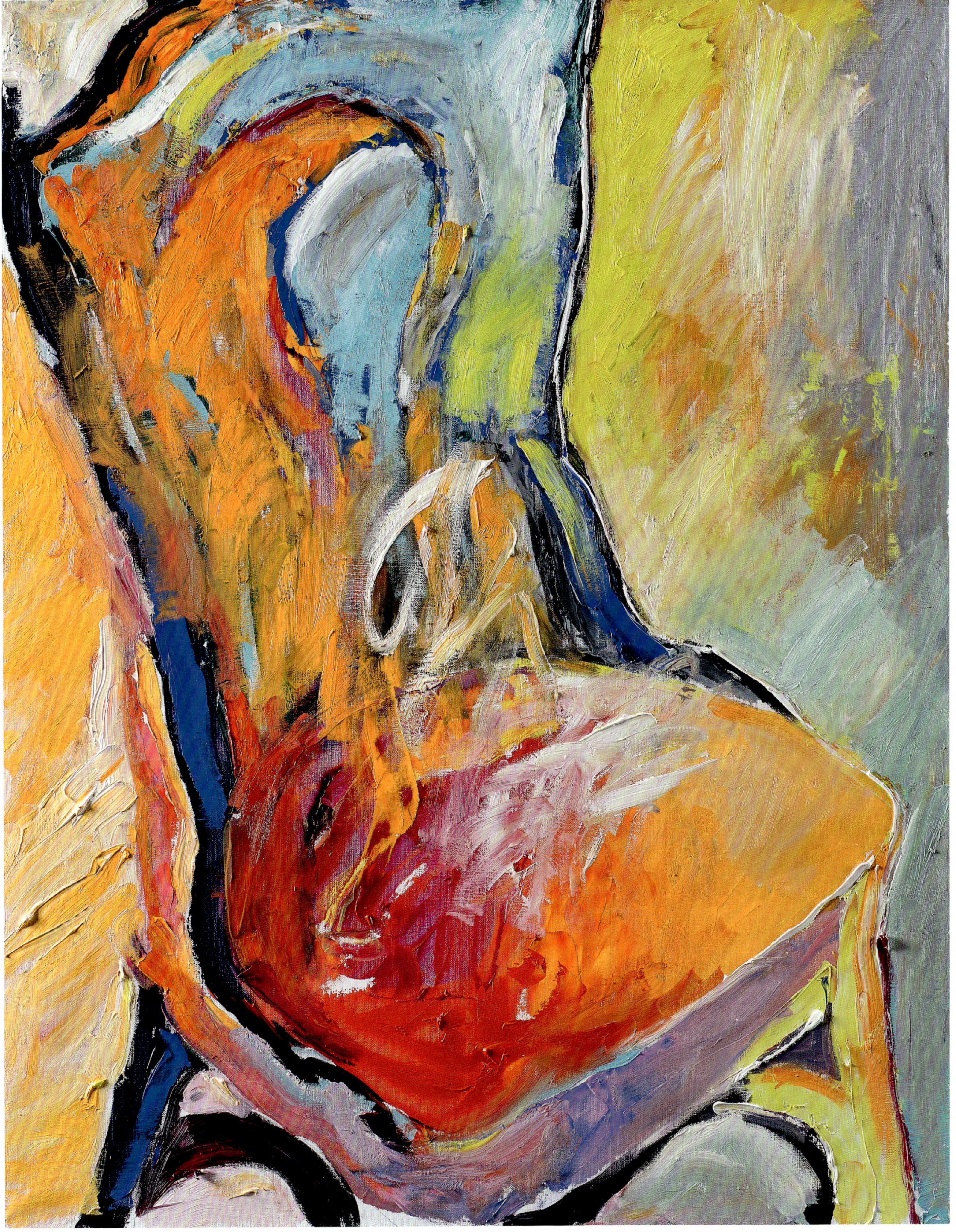

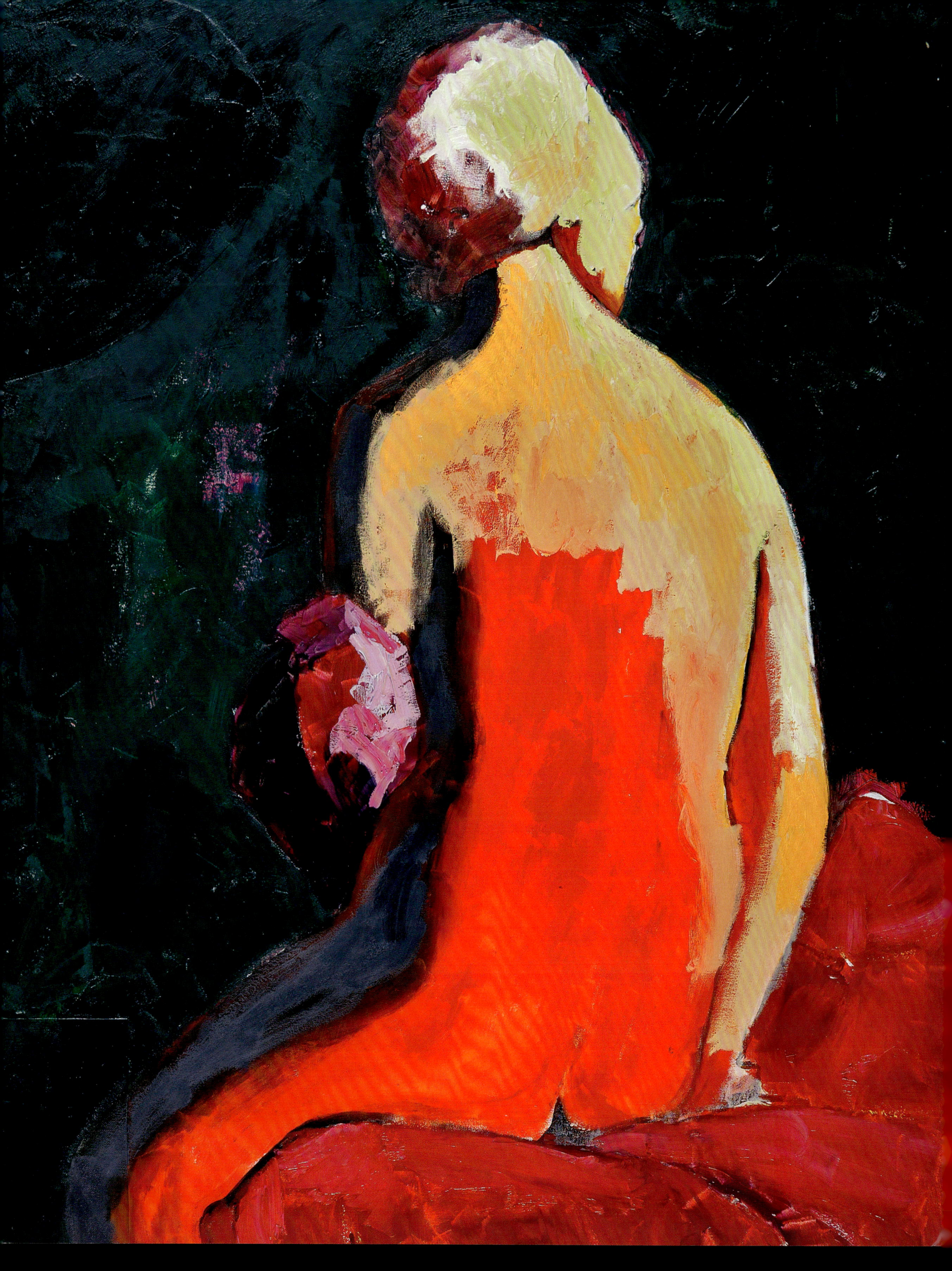

Chromatic Fantasy
The Metamorphoses of Andrei Sharov

Charles A. Riley II

Charles A. Riley II, PhD, is an arts journalist, cultural historian and professor at the City University of New York. He is the author of thirty-one books on art, architecture, business, media and public policy, including *Color Codes* (University Press of New England), *The Jazz Age in France* (Abrams), *Art at Lincoln Center* (Wiley), *Rodin and his Circle* (Chimei), and *Sacred Sister* (in collaboration with Robert Wilson). He is a guest curator at the Chimei Museum, Taiwan, and curator-at-large for the Nassau County Museum of Art and he writes for magazines including *Antiques and Fine Art*, *Art & Auction*, *Art & Antiques* and *Fortune*.

Nude Woman in a Red Chair (detail), 2012
oil on canvas, 150 x 120 cm
V. Klyukin Collection

I. Uncategorized Artist

Chaos shimmers through the veil of order.
Novalis

Even in contemporary art, where cutting edge originality is the coin of the realm, there is room for classical wisdom. The deep truth of the endless, inexorable flux of Ovid's *Metamorphoses* is a timeless favorite of artists from antiquity through the Renaissance and Modernism. Titian, Rubens, Rodin are among the visual translators of these tales of transformation (in Ovid's preface, "animus mutatas dicere formas corpora" or "to speak of bodies changed into new forms"). Like Pygmalion, all artists are by nature agents of metamorphosis. An astonishingly vibrant example of Ovidean polymorphism is the Russian painter (and couturier and theatrical set designer and punk impresario) Andrei Sharov. For the art historian accustomed to framing an oeuvre in terms of period style or ideological affinity, it is refreshing to come across a figure so readily identifiable with a number of movements (he would fit right into many of the circles that were the wheels on which Modernism rolled) who nonetheless shifts shape so persistently that he avoids definite classification. He arrives on the current stage uncategorized, an appealing challenge to look closely at the work.

One way to become an Ovidian artist is to come to a career in art with the diversity of heredity and experience that effortlessly permits change from one field, perspective or medium to another. Sharov's background is tuned to many wavelengths. His father is a physicist and his mother a mathematician. Born in 1966 in Moscow, his path began in the theater as a set designer in 1986 (his bold interpretation of *Anna Karenina* relied on the chiaroscuro of film noir) then progressed to fashion (on the runway, his designs pop dramatically with their Surrealist eyes that stare from metallic gowns or sinister matte Glocks wielded by gloved molls clad in black satin). Critical acclaim for his paintings came early thanks in part to *Bolshepuzui Uhoglaz* (*Big Paunch with Ear and Eye*, 1989, p. 8), a jauntily off-kilter, darkly comic parable in paint channeling Nikolai Gogol via late Philip Guston. The disturbing distension of the anatomy of its bulging eye, clown-like shoes, and the arresting blue of the gloved right hand extended to the viewer is also comparable to such contemporary Mannerists as Caroll Dunham, George Condo and Lisa Yuskavage.

The prescribed career path for Russian artists of the time led through such institutions as the Moscow Technical University, where Sharov headed in 1993, and then the state-controlled Moscow Union of Artists, which he joined in 1996. During a stint in the army he kept his hand in by painting portraits of the officers' wives, an amusing detail that reminds this writer not just of a character out of Bulgakov but of a real-life artist who flits through the biographies of many of the Abstract Expressionists in New York during the fifties and sixties in New York. The suave Igor Pantuhoff was an upwardly mobile protégé of Hans Hofmann and the boyfriend of Lee Krasner among many other insiders whose society portraits and louche exploits made him a fixture of the art scene. Sharov is similarly a public persona not just in Moscow (his massive, two-story studio and garden in the Arbat is a gathering place for collectors, curators, critics and fellow artists, pp. 120–121) but in Monaco (where he maintains a split-level studio and apartment), Amsterdam, Paris and other world capitals. He nomadically rents studio space for as long as he feels the inspiration of the locale, so unlike the nesting instincts of many artists who require the habitual reassurance of the familiar to settle down to work.

Sharov's studio practice is happily, almost innocently devoid of gimmicks, tricks and secrets. He confidently works with rapidity, *alla prima*, eschewing preliminary drawing on the canvas or even on paper, a cavalier fearlessness that probably owes a great deal to his rigorous training not just in fine art but in fashion. He has done the drills that build the skills. Now it is time to let it rip. "I've hated doing sketches since my time in the university," he told curator Oksana Salamatina in a 2014 interview that concludes with a subtly revealing remark about how the lack of resistance at first gives way to a significant uncertainty regarding the way to resolve the coda to the work. "I start my work right away with all my force and energy. I feel the urge to paint and I paint. I work rather fast. In the past I tried to finish a painting without much delay in order to preserve the emotion. It's hard for me to finish the painting later on." We come back to that significant tendency toward delayed resolution in a moment.

II. Flesh for Fantasy

Mine eye hath play'd the painter and hath stell'd
Thy beauty's form in table of my heart…
William Shakespeare, Sonnet XXIV

That brings us to punk. It is difficult to square the Post-Impressionist and Expressionist luxuriousness of Sharov's painterly romanticism with the punk sensibility so evident in his appearance and the aggressive clutter of his Moscow studio, with its drum kit, motorcycle, and graffiti-emblazoned walls with their vast photo-collaged homage to the likes of Sid Vicious and Billy Idol. Punk is generally associated with iconoclasm and defacement, which offers a clue to Sharov's transformations of iconic paintings by Ingres, Schiele and others, and yet it is hard to square it with the eroticism of the paintings.

Punk is also one of the aesthetic movements (rap followed suit) that distanced itself from the very medium with which it is associated. Its proponents insist that punk is *not* music or fashion, despite all that screaming, pink hair, tattoos, black leather and chains. Punk never died in Europe or the United States. It annoyed high society when it was the

shockingly raw theme of the Metropolitan Museum's annual gala and spring exhibition in 2012, and it remains a presence in the gallery neighborhoods of Berlin, New York's Lower East Side, Tokyo, Shanghai and Beijing.

What does punk mean aesthetically? Pushing back against a medium, in this case painting, is one way to keep the dynamism in the relationship to tradition and even one's own past, including academic training. It forces the hand to mar the expectations of formal grace, deflecting beauty's promises and reminding us of its delusional dangers as in Sharov's disturbing revision of Ingres's *Odalisque* in the *Old Courtesan* (2012, pp. 12–13). It is not just that Sharov has taken Ingres's lithe granddaughter of the *Rokeby Venus*, p. 95, and simply aged her. In a similar vein, Shakespeare looks ahead to old age in his sonnets ("O, how shall summer's honey breath hold out/ Against the wreckful siege of battering days"), threatening the muse who spurns him with mortality yet acknowledging her hold. The sonnets and Sharov's paintings are splendidly physical embodiments of cognitive dissonance, honoring eros as they dishonor it. Sharov knows perfectly well how to make a woman look fabulous (as his deft watercolor life studies and his fashion drawings confirm). In the painting he has assaulted her with an insulting fast forward into decrepitude, accompanied by his Billy Idol snarl, the punk threat that sends most of us across the street in alarm to a safe sidewalk from which we stare in trepidation mixed with fascination.

III. One Touch of Venus

Everything that man esteems
Endures a moment or a day.
Love's pleasure drives his love away,
The painter's brush consumes his dreams.
William Butler Yeats, "Two Songs from a Play"

The mask of white and black misshapen mouth of the *Old Courtesan*, pp. 12–13, is a reminder that in addition to his formidable art school and fashion training, Sharov built his repertoire in the theater. The roster of modern and contemporary artists who have made substantive contributions to the stage is formidable, and it is even more intriguing to consider the ways in which theatrical design changed their modus operandi. The most prominent example is Diaghilev's stellar roster of collaborators starting with Picasso, whose décor and curtains for *Parade*, *Le Train Bleu* (p. 96, top), *Le Tricorne* and other works are masterpieces

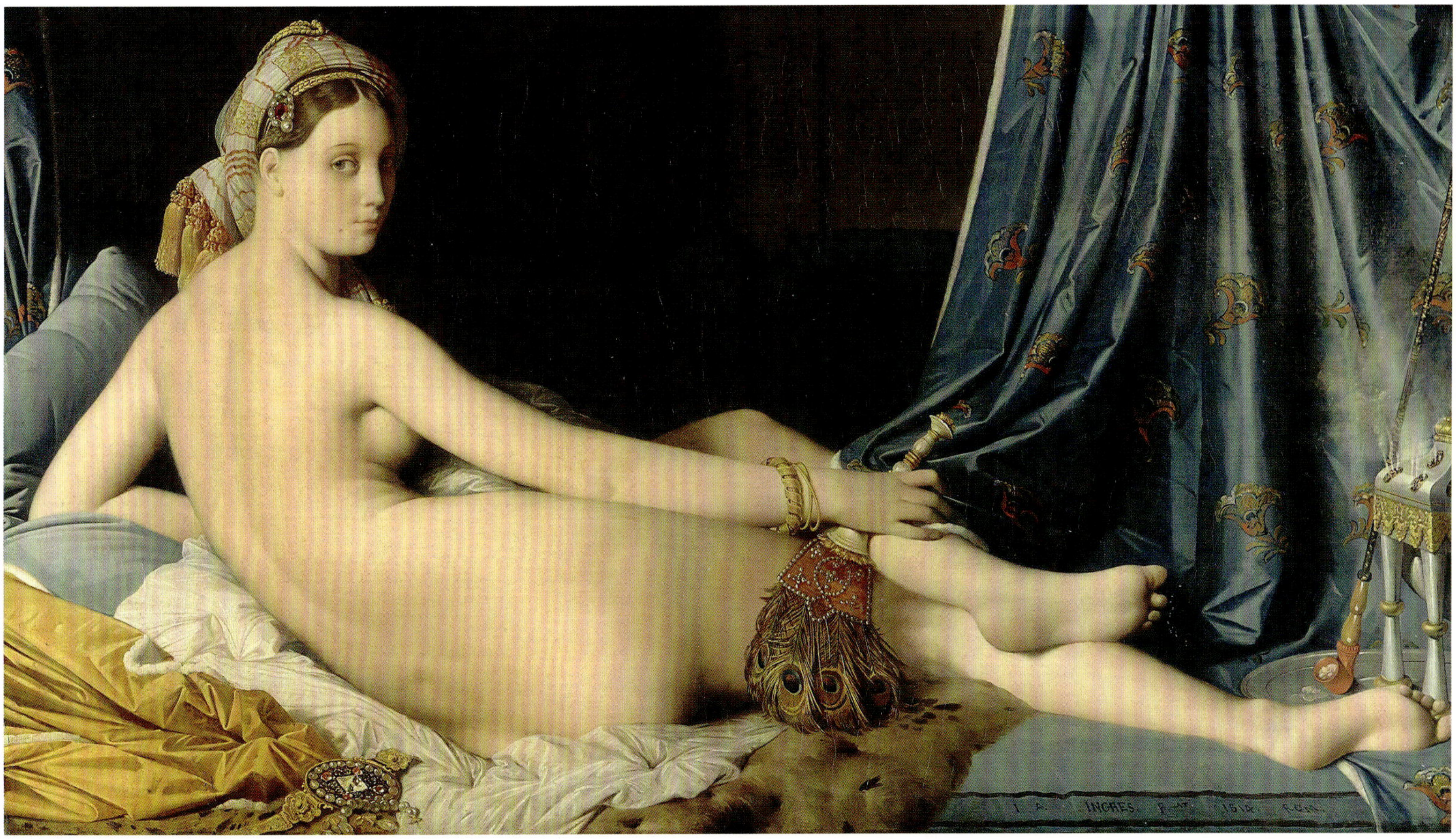

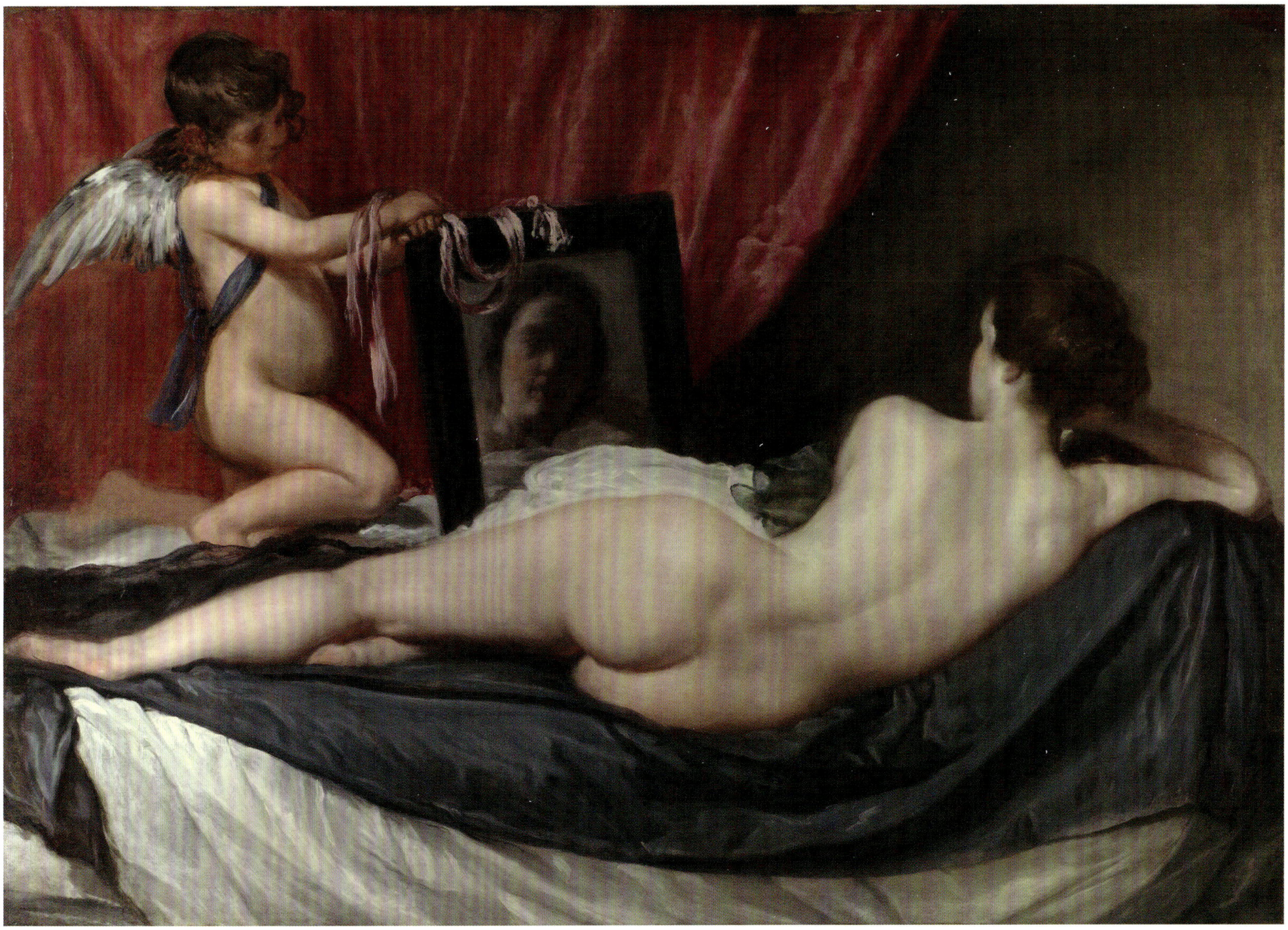

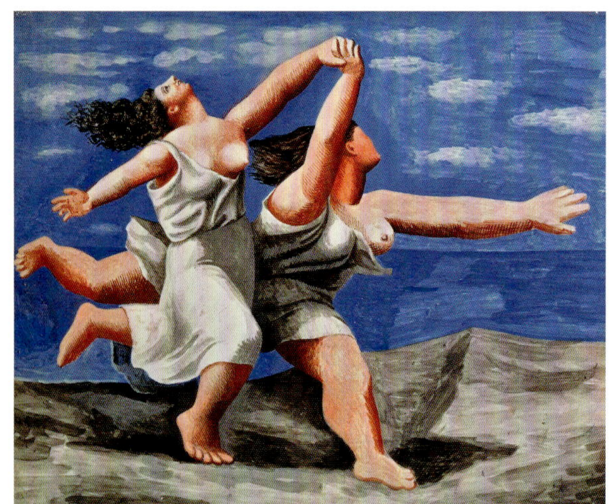

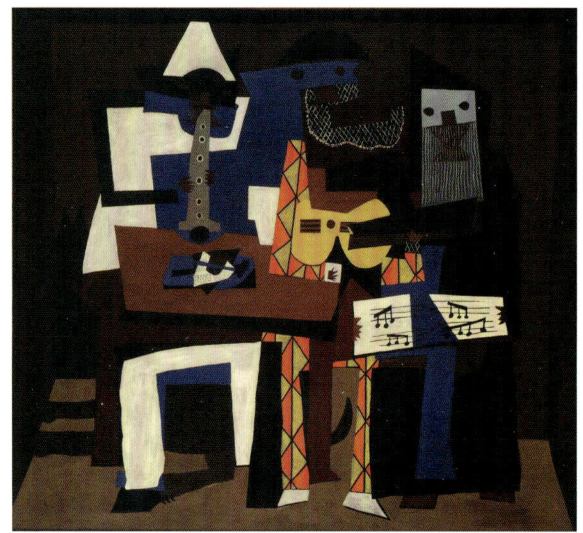

of a particular order. Backstage tales of Picasso's flair for set and costume design (many of them delightfully recounted by Jean Cocteau, blithe spirit of stage and screen) emphasize the showmanship of his virtuosity, whipping up backdrops in minutes before the adoring chorus of ballerinas including the curvy Olga Khokhlova, who in 1919 became Mrs. Picasso Number One. Diaghilev's creative team is legendary, with Stravinsky, Milhaud or Satie at the piano, Picasso, Braque, De Chirico, Laurencin or Matisse with sketchpad in hand, Coco Chanel with a measuring tape around her neck for the costumes and the choreographers Massine, Nijinska (sister of the troubled star of *L'après-midi d'un faune*) and Georgi Melitonovitch Balanchivadze (Balanchine) recently sprung from St. Petersburg via Switzerland while only in his twenties, already devising a neoclassical language that would last so much longer than most modernist styles. As art historian T. J. Clark has recently shown in a convincing book, the specific optical demands of set design had a direct impact upon Picasso's composition in the twenties, evident in the *controlled* recessionary space of a large-scale still life

firmly framed by the proscenium arch of a stage-like room and in the figural groupings of *Three Musicians* (p. 96, bottom) or the titanic running women on the beach he created for the curtain to *Le Train Bleu*.[1] As glamorous as this tale of the Jazz Age can be, it holds a kernel of aesthetic seriousness that serves to guide us to Sharov's own post-theatrical "blocking" (to use the stage term) of figures and his use of pictorial space in the framing of scenes.

The Ballets Russes may have been the most enviable of stage gigs, but many other major artists bear comparison to Sharov, not the least of them Marc Chagall, whose *Magic Flute* (p. 97) for the opening night of the Metropolitan Opera's new Lincoln Center home lingers in the memory of many opera lovers, as well as Balthus, William Kentridge, David Hockney and JR, the eccentric French photographer whose New York City Ballet projects are wildly popular. Each learned the essentials of theater strategies that ensured their formal and chromatic gestures could be read from that last balcony row, and the high-volume graphic fortissimo translated without distortion to their easel paintings. With Picasso, it is evident right there in the bounded areas of high-value blue or red. Sharov, similarly, deploys of bold color in compositions that seize the eye from a distance and reels the viewer in. His work captures the attention in a museum from two galleries away through doors or windows. The picture's edge takes the place of the proscenium, and the directional play of upstage and downstage defy the two dimensionality of the canvas without going as far (metaphorically and literally) as the vanishing point of traditional perspective with its infinite distance from the viewer. Figures and objects read in a certain way from the distance of a last-row balcony seat, and the graphic laws of contrast by which this legibility is achieved inform the technique of the painter, defining the *Reclining Nude* (2012, p. 16) against the dreamy pastoral background that features a Kandinsky-like, brushy haze of blues and greens. The space of a Sharov (like that of a Picasso from the Ballets Russes period) has a paradoxically sincere controlled artificiality that is inherited from the theater, what Clark admiringly called the *truth* of the Picasso paintings, so unloved by those who prefer the Cubist or Blue Period works. The anomaly lies in the overt artificiality of the theater (think of the bias inherent in such words as "stagecraft" or even "staged," and the acid vehemence of the Minimalist manifestos that forbade "theater" in art)

Picasso's stage backdrop for the ballet *Le Train Bleu* (Ballets Russes, 1924)

Pablo Picasso, *Three Musicians*, 1921 New York, Museum of Modern Art

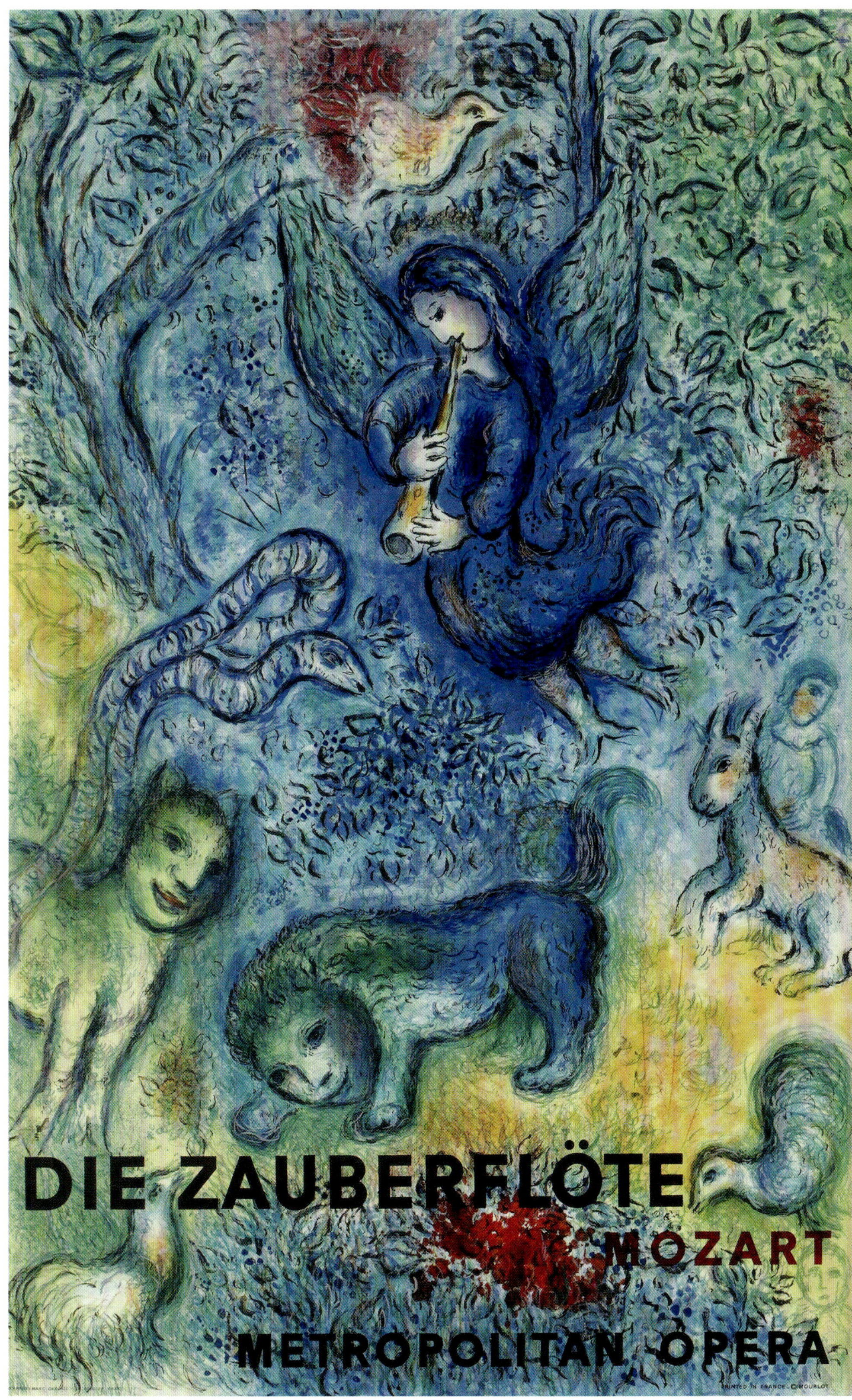

Marc Chagall, *La flûte enchantée*
(The Magic Flute), 1967
color lithograph

by contrast with the candid offering of paint as paint shorn of illusionism.

Not as celebrated as Picasso but certainly as valuable to Diaghilev over the course of decades, Natalia Goncharova is the closest in style to Sharov. Her incandescent sets and costumes for the *Golden Cockerel*, *Firebird* and *Cinderella* share the palette of high-octane reds and flaming golds with which Sharov turns up the heat in his works. Goncharova, Diaghilev, Stravinsky, and even Kandinsky could, as need demanded, play the professional Russian, reciting folk tales via peasant costumes or bulbous church tower iconography and Sharov too has the regional in his repertoire, but thankfully he does not make it either corny or exclusionary. Considering the solar palette of Goncharova and Sharov leads to the always tricky question of color, that most dangerous yet alluring weapon in the painter's arsenal. ("Color deceives continuously," Josef Albers would caution his Yale graduate students on their first day in his epochal course on the subject). Sharov's immediate affinity with the highest values of hue, value and chroma lends a palette that is literally vibrant, the kind of amped up tonality that made the Fauves burn brightly yet briefly. Like the Pont Aven painters, he maintains a studio on the sun-drenched Côte d'Azur not far from Collioure where Matisse, Derain, Vlaminck and Braque unleashed, for a notably brief period of only a couple of years, as though the eye and brain could not tolerate it longer, the rods and cones burnt out by overexcitement. These include a range of high value oranges, reds and pinks in complementary relation with aggressive blues and neon greens.

IV. The Power of the Palette

The starting point is the study of color
and its effects on men.
Wassily Kandinsky

Sharov would have fit right in with the Ballets Russes on so many levels. The other circle he would have instantly been welcomed to had gathered in Munich in the early years of the twentieth century (just before the Ballets Russes had its heyday) when the Blaue Reiter movement was driving color to its limits. Sharov could have spent many an evening sipping Riesling and speaking Russian with principal figures of the movement including Kandinsky, Jawlensky and Werefkin (pupils of Ilya Repin) along with less recognized figures (Mstislav Dobushinsky, Kuzma Petrov-Vodkin, Vladimir and David Burliuk, Vladimir

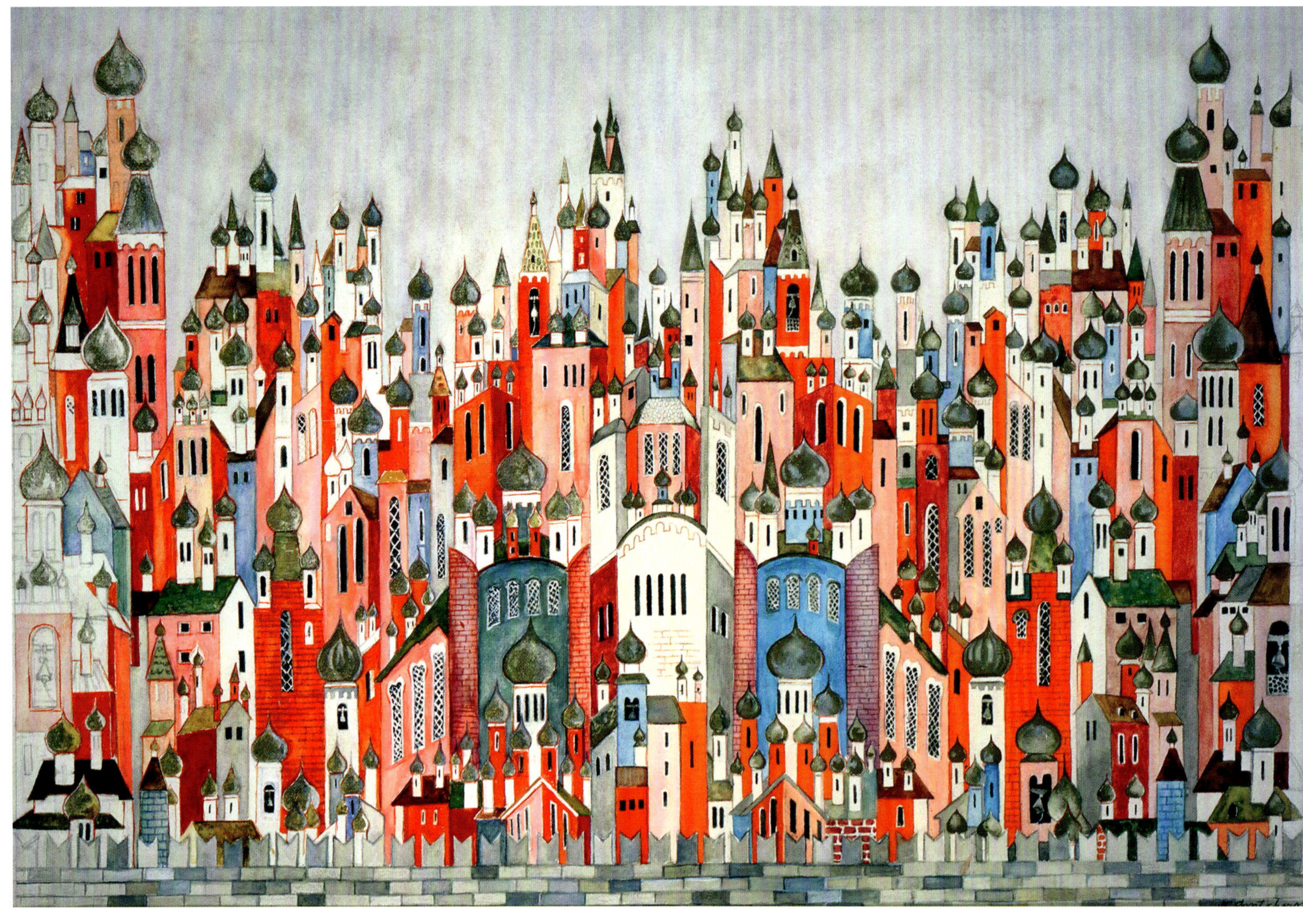

Bechtejev, Alexander von Salzmann, Alexander Mogilevski, Alexander Sacharoff). Kandinsky had actually arrived earlier, in 1896 and his admirers are familiar with the romantic tale of his period in Murnau, a market town near Munich, with Gabriele Münter (his student turned muse, sadly he was married). Their experiments with the local folk art, notably the medium of Hinterglasmalerei (boringly toned painting on glass and mirrors) led not only to the most smoldering palette of his career but to a loosening of the mimetic grip of nature that eventually led Kandinsky, Jawlensky and Klee to full-blown abstraction.

The two historically important exhibitions presented by the group in 1911 and 1912 at the Thannhauser and Goltz galleries included work by Arnold Schönberg, Robert Delaunay (another connection to Sharov, the fashion designs he and his Russian wife created). Franz Marc and Auguste Macke. If you slipped one of Sharov's nudes into the mix, next to a Kandinsky Murnau landscape and Marc's *Red and Blue Horse* (*Rotes und blaues ferd*, 1912, p. 99, top right), his idiom would fit right in with their bold ex-

periment, which influenced the next great Modernist movements such as Cobra (Edvard Munch's group). Comparison with Kandinsky is burdensome but apt, especially as Kandinsky's own stage designs, significantly more advanced even than the Ballets Russes and its "lifestyle Modernism," cast colors in the role of dramatis personae. As a rubric for decoding Sharov, this feeling for color as ethos leads directly to the differentiation of, for example, the tenebrous indigos and burgundies of *Seated Odalisque with Arms Crossed* (2012, p. 99, bottom left), with its bolt of scarlet threatening the background, the similarly immersed *Woman with Blue Hat* (2012) despite the lighter palette from the radiant *Nude in the Sunlight* (2012, p. 17), in which vital greens the color of spring grass and some of the Hofmannesque golds and oranges crowd the cooler blues, the way seasons impinge upon one another at their turning.

The supreme test of color as ethos is the pairing of *Seated Woman in Blue* (2012, p. 103) and *Portrait of a Redhead* (1999, p. 54), with their absent third counterpart the type of Blue Period femmes fatales

Set design for *The Firebird*, Natalia Goncharova, 1926, for Diaghilev's Ballets Russes Moscow, The Tretyakov State Gallery

Wassily Kandinsky, *Murnau View with Railway and Castle*, 1909
Munich, Städtische Galerie im Lenbachhaus

Franz Marc, *Red and Blue Horse*, 1912
Munich, Städtische Galerie im Lenbachhaus

Seated Odalisque with Arms Crossed, 2012
oil on canvas, 120 x 100 cm

Petrov-Vodkin, *Bathing of a Red Horse*, 1912
Moskow, The Tretyakov State Gallery

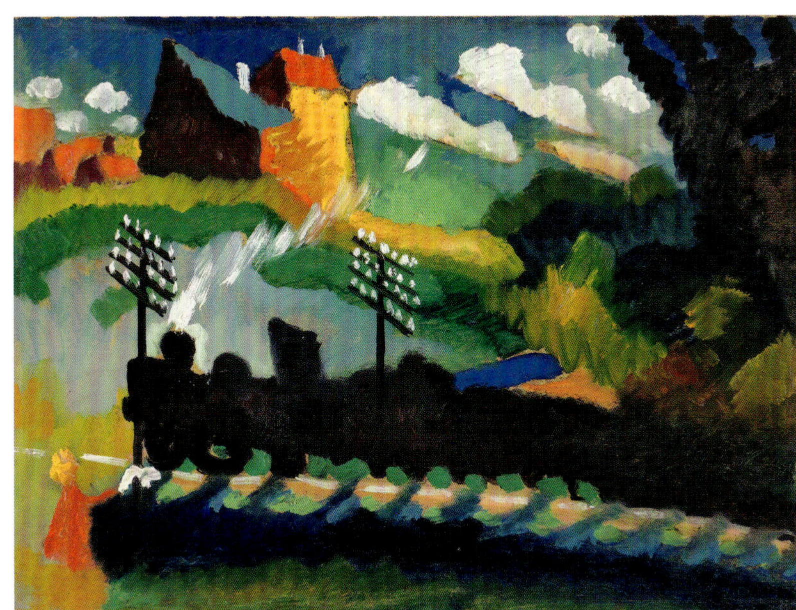

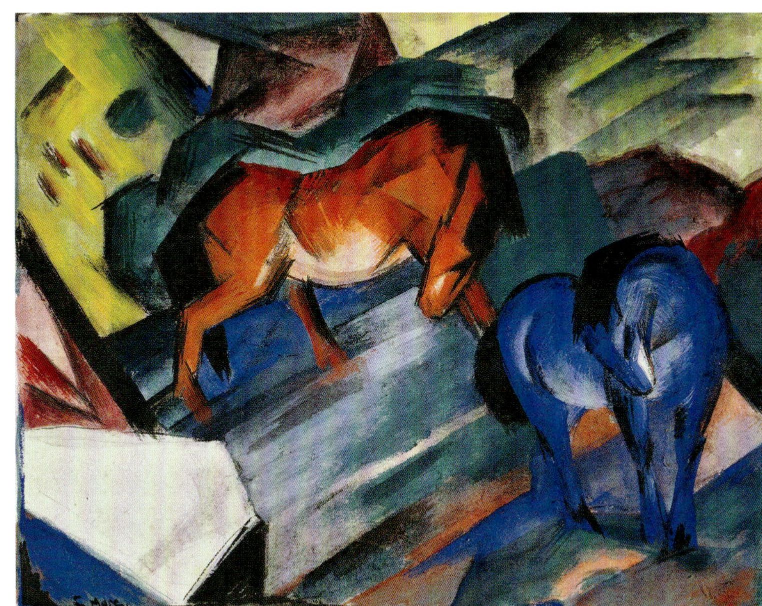

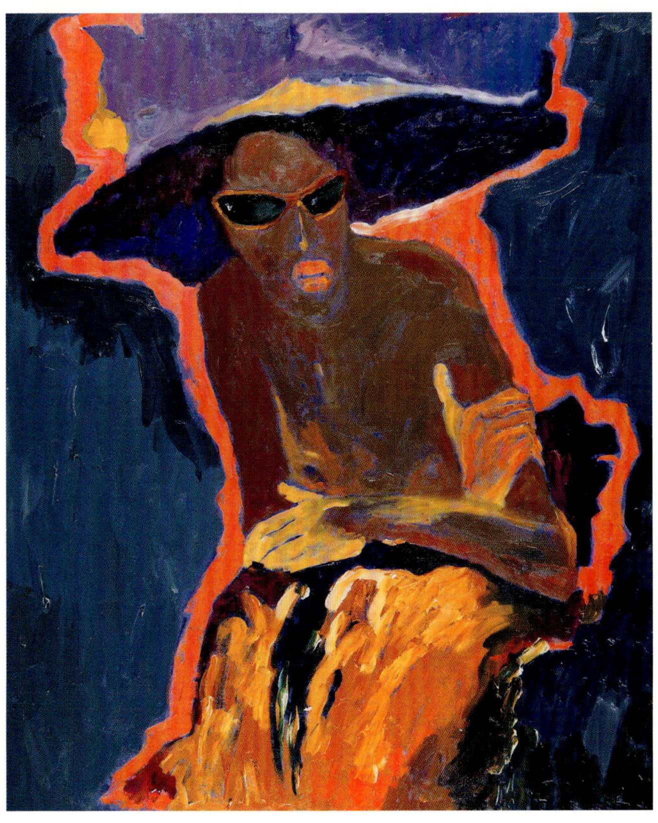

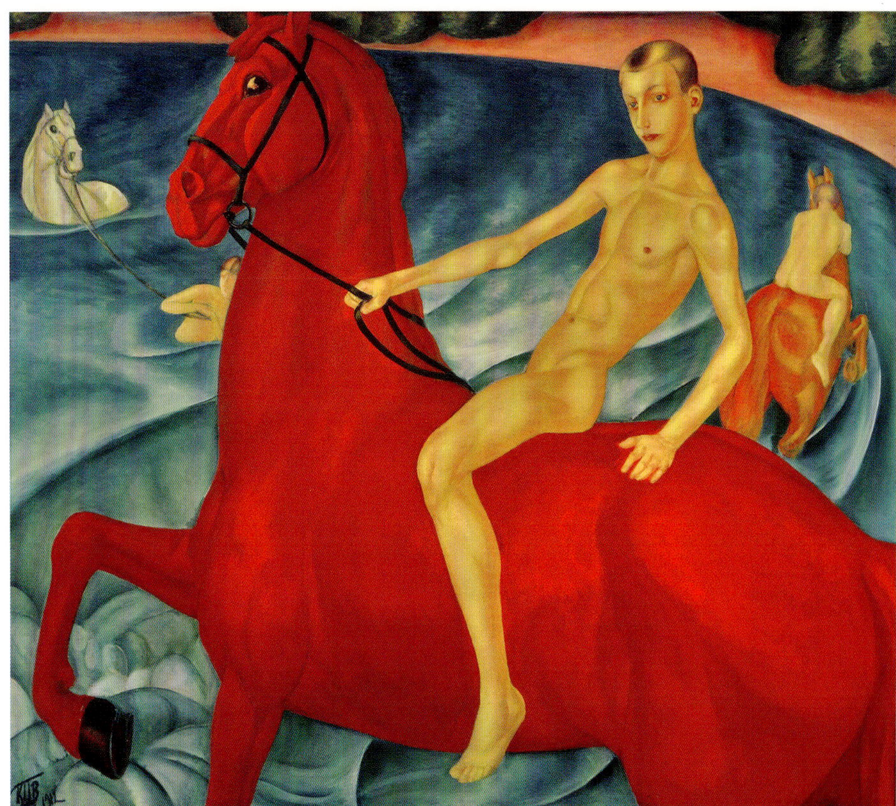

by Picasso, often using his muse Fernande as model (although it is important to note that the work is not an interpretive variation on a specific Picasso, which even this writer quickly and wrongly assumed). The model was a former muse of Sharov's so the style is allusive. The dark, confrontational stare of Blue Period Picasso café scenes is not the only historical allusion in the work—Sharov tucks the legs of Botticelli's dancing graces into the upper right corner inviting further ripples of reference to both Carpeaux and Matisse, for whom the round dance form became a cardinal thematic source. Sharov weaves his own magic on the subject in two very different iterations. The lunar light of *Seated Woman in Blue* intensifies in the pupils and along the highlights of the dancers' legs, even as it drops off into a midnight darkness in the passage over her right shoulder and the red-inflected crown of her hat. Taking on Picasso's blue harmonies is an audacious challenge and Sharov characteristically returns to the broken contour (the brim of the hat offers a quick example—cirrus clouds of blue irregularly thick and thin, and interrupted) the way Liszt turns Wagner's chords into arpeggios, breaking down into consecutive notes (strokes) the massed substance of the urtext. Next we turn to the companion portrait, looking for differences. The proportions as well as palette are altered, and the experience of the character is vastly changed, another Ovidian shift at Sharov's deft hand. The blues recede to an almost Dufy-like haze, while those antiphonal reds, including her unruly auburn hair with a blank white highlight that would never have been admissible in the locked in blue cast of the other painting. A cravat of matching red continues the vertical gesture of the hat (we pause to remember Sharov's professional experience) and the stepwise construction of the crown of the hat, sharpened by the way it is differentiated from their aqua background, is far more focused than the atmospheric hat of the blue portrait. If one is a femme fatale (and certainly Picasso's Fernande as well as the model Germaine, the cause of Casagemas's suicide, were among art history's great femmes fatales) the other is an intense conversational partner, whose range of literary and musical references would certainly include Botticelli, a collector one is pleased to be seated beside a the post-opening dinner in Paris or Chelsea even if her feline eyes are often diverted to her misbehaving husband at the other end of the table. A trick of lighting? On the matrix of a near-identical portrait Sharov builds two distinct personae—this is color not as accent (a sec-

ondary quality, as the philosophers would have it) but as primary matter, the determinant of ethos. Matisse meant something of the kind when he dictated to his students, "Construct by relations of color." The contrast between the works is aesthetic, emotional and epistemological—severing the ties of identity between the pensive ladies. The art historical equivalent was previewed by the unforgettable Picasso/Matisse exhibition of 2003 at the Museum of Modern Art in New York and the Centre Pompidou in Paris, where the blue painting would be the haunted Picasso side and the diurnal brightness of the other the Matisse, profoundly demonstrating the difference that chromaticism and facture can make when the matrix of the theme and variations of nearly uniform.

The steady appeal of Sharov across these metamorphoses is tribute to his Ovidean versatility. From one subject, several fully realized paintings are capable of emanating. As the distinguished critic Lilly Wei notes in an essay on the artist that is essential reading for students of his work, "Sharov likes to play with narrative intention and to find unexpected associations."[2] While the blue seated figure recedes into a spectral unreality, the red lady advances like a *salonnier* on the offensive, bearing down on her fatuous yet adoring interlocutor for the pleasure of a Proustian kill. We know from Schiele's title *Scornful Woman* that the glare of the woman in the hat is accompanied by a similar hauteur, but immersed in shadow and surrounded in such a hazardous red she gains, by one of Wei's "associations," the vulnerability lent by mortality. Refer back to the original and you will find that Schiele surrounded her in a vigorously brushed band of white which Sharov has diabolically translated into molten red, igniting a whole new range of narrative associations. Where the starting text is supplied by classical icons, such as the Odalisque of Ingres, Sharov's retelling can even seem cruel—his Odalisque is shockingly past her prime, encased in layers of suffocating pigment like the mask of lethal white lead cosmetics Elizabeth I wore on her deathbed. An excess of color reverses the Gauguin-esque erotics of the palette as in Munch, Goya and some Klimt, ruining the conventional beauty of the young original with a ruthlessness that may tap the punk fundament of Sharov's personality.

The seamless transitions that Wei identifies are not just narrative in nature. They have their visual dimension as well, most clearly seen in the play of figure and ground within series. The arabesques descending from the shapely legs of the Botticelli danc-

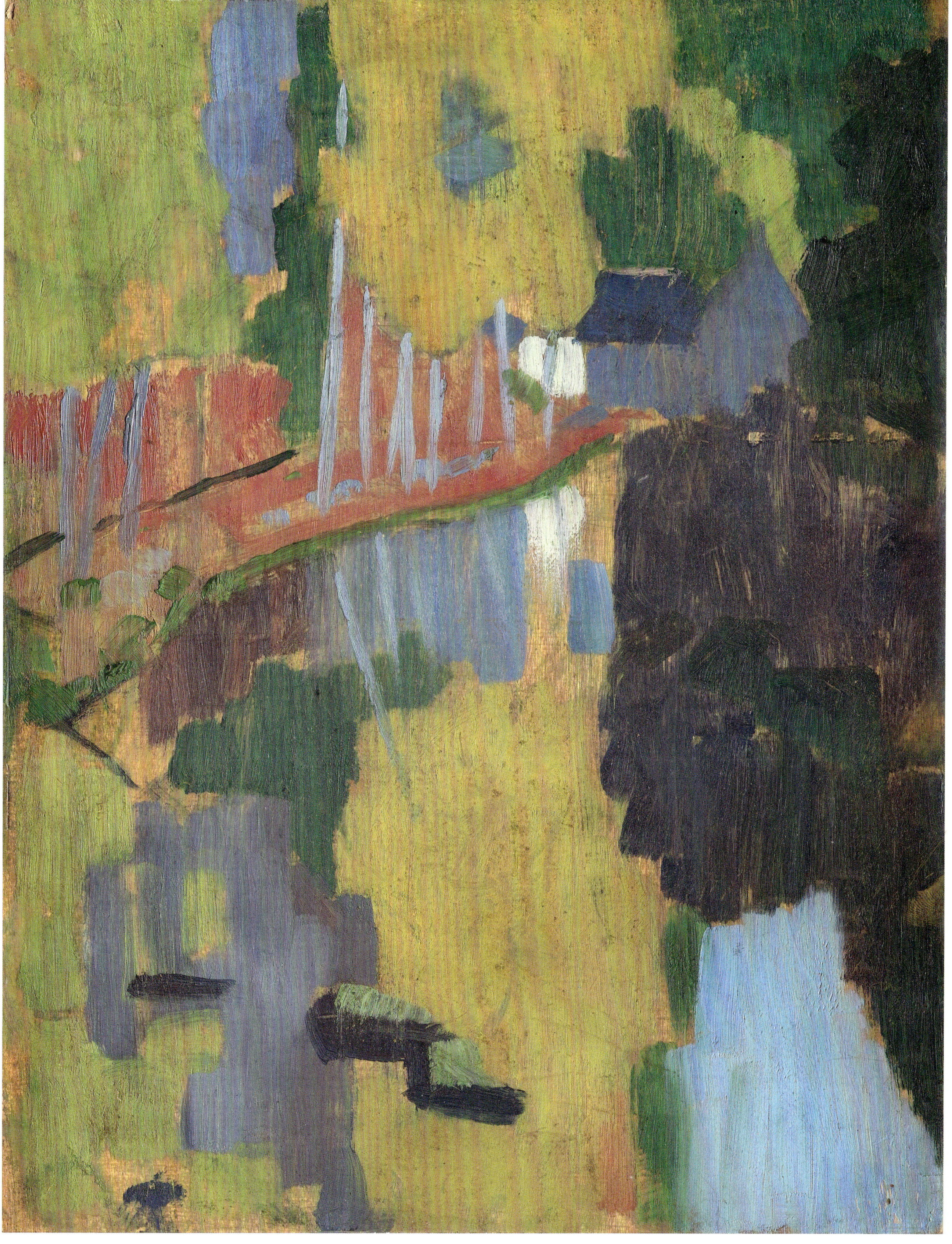

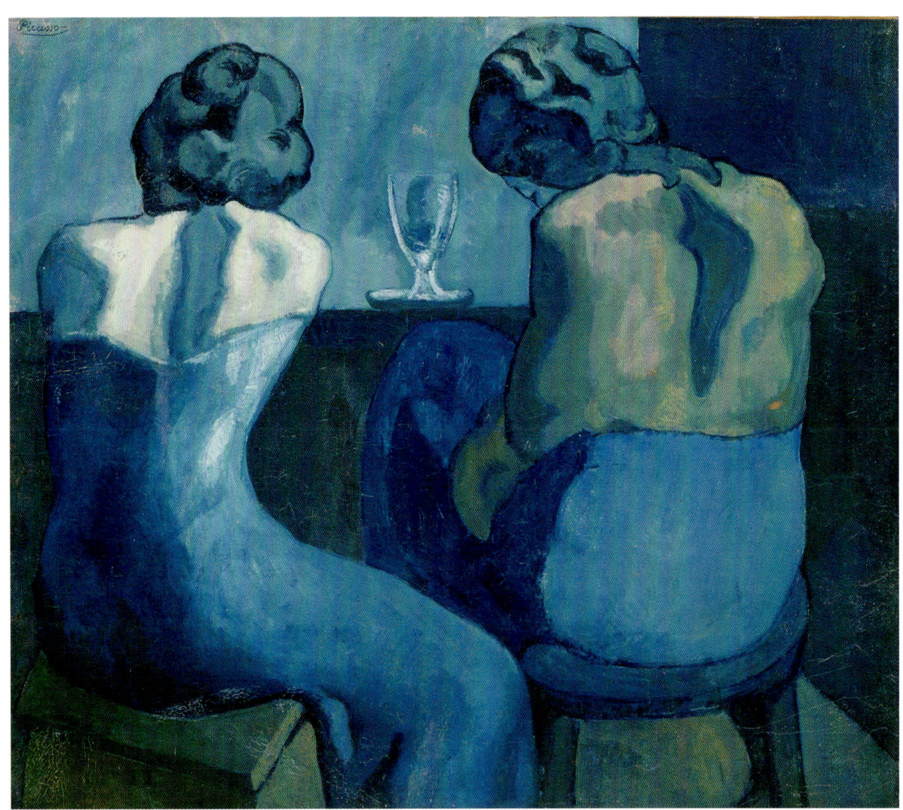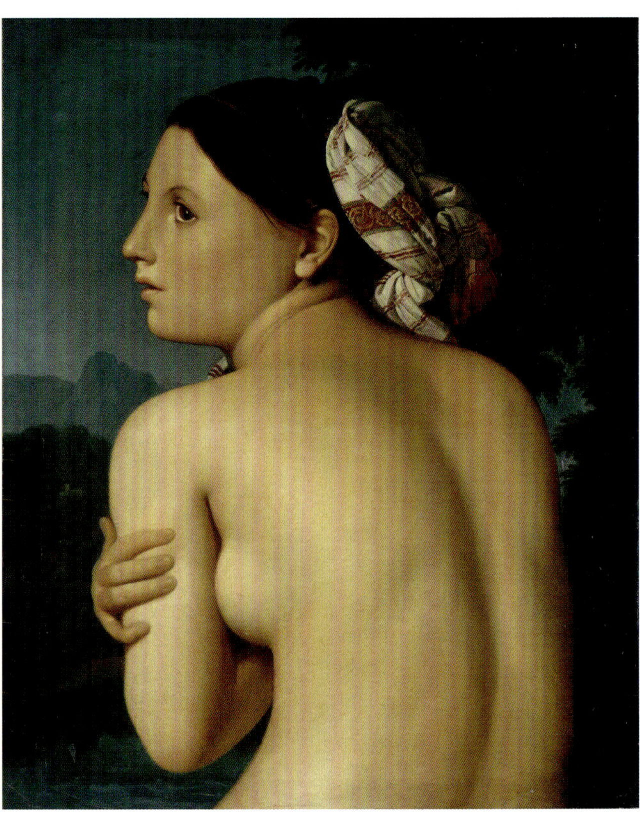

ers, descend from the top of *Seated Woman in Blue* (p. 103) through the echoing curves of her hair with the inverted image of the fingers propping her chin which correspond in scale as well to the legs and even a few of the billowing brush strokes from which her mantle is constructed—curve answering curve in a flowing manner that invokes the creamy currents of color in a Renoir portrait. The aura of radiant red and orange, even the shadowy purple in *Nude Woman in a Red Chair* (p. 92), or the pulsing contours of *Nude with Towel* (2012, p. 18), resonate from implied figures. The sensuality of *Nude with Apple* (p. 114), in which Rubens meets Modigliani and Matisse (the space of the Red Studio) is similar to the dissolved radiography of *Nude in the Sunlight* (2012, p. 17), which echoes the magnificent miniature *Le Talisman* (p. 101), by Sérusier, the mighty amulet of the Pont Aven school (a love letter to Gauguin). Sharov the arch-colorist is also like a Medieval illuminator of manuscripts, surrounding the central black and white text (an historical image by Ingres, Botticelli, Schiele) with his own lively commentary in vivid hues, all the incident and emotion rushing to the borders of the rectilinear form, drawing the eye and heart from the doxology at the center (art history as starting point, them upon which the variations are lavished).

Confronting these aggressive colors flooding an adoptive imagery, many would leap to a comparison with Andy Warhol, whose deployment of color over figure always hollowed out the image to a stencil's emptiness, further devaluing emotionally by sheer quantitative excess. I propose a significant divergence from Pop and its irony, in the hope that it prompts you to examine Sharov's palette all the more attentively. As *Color Chart*, an important thematic exhibition at the Museum of Modern Art in New York demonstrated in 2008, the "industrial" colors of Warhol (along with Donald Judd, Gerhard Richter and other important figures in the show) broke from the expressionist tradition in color theory (including the Fauves, the Austrians, Die Brücke and Cobra) by stridently inviting the products of the paint factory as well as car and office furniture manufacturers into the gallery. Where Warhol's palette adhered to the facetious orthodoxy of commercial graphics, Sharov remains an old school mixer of paint, the sort of palette that Derain or Vlaminck or Matisse could have picked up still wet and put to use immediately in the studio. Consider the divided reds and oranges, cut with white, that lava-like sea in *Reclining Nude, Head Resting on Right Arm* (2012, p. 16), its horizon shimmering with heat through the veil of lime green. The blue caressing her breasts and thighs is straight out of the Fauve repertoire, while Bonnard would have smiled to see the lambent gold and pink of that Mediterranean sky as it lit her eyes and mouth and wound its luminescent way along the edges of her figure, blue meeting red, a human (not mechanical) interaction of primaries that is anything but the chemical objectivity of the indifferent Warhol, who was cool

Pablo Picasso, *Two Women seated at a Bar*, 1902
Hiroshima, Hiroshima Museum of Art

Jean-Auguste-Dominique Ingres, *The Half-Length Bather*, 1807
Bayonne, Musée Bonnat

where Sharov is hot. Even when Sharov comes closest to Warhol in form and function, as in the portrait of the pop singer Madonna all tarted up with flickering brush strokes, he remains on the Expressionist side of the border with Pop.

More than the fixed rationality of line, the tremulous exuberance of color lends itself to Ovidian nature of art past, present and future. Sharov does not just speak this language of change, he sings it, sometimes as mellifluously and harmonically as the Postimpressionists and sometimes with the harsh dissonance and growling rhythms of his punk heroes. Much as Ovid endures (even in exile he could defiantly predict "wherever Roman power extends… I shall live") in this Darwinian world of genetic mutation and this post-Einsteinian universe of sub-atomic super-string flux, so too Sharov's rhapsodies will echo, their notes so passionately struck as never to be stilled. One of the reasons for this marvelous anomaly (the permanent legacy of art dedicated to impermanence) in the case of both Ovid and Sharov is their darkly comic streak, sometimes mocking and sometimes lusty, which finds even in intimations of mortality the pleasures of a free spirit. They do not take themselves or the portentous themes of the time as seriously as they do the imperative to paint or write well, to accomplish what Pygmalion did with ivory (bringing it to life) and to revel in art as its own reward.

New York, October 2014

[1] For example, Clark notes, "Objects and bodies are only given weight and identity in painting by being enclosed—by existing in relation to a finitude they call their own. Being is being in." T. J. Clark, *Picasso and Truth* (Princeton: Princeton University Press, 2013), p. 104.
[2] Lilly Wei, "At Home in the World," in *Andrei Sharov* (New York and Monaco: Salamatina Gallery, 2014), p. 15.

Seated Woman in Blue, 2012
oil on canvas, 120 x 120 cm
Private collection

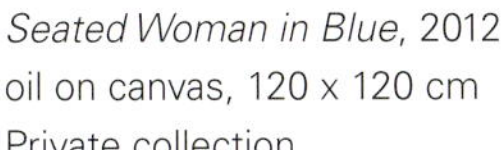

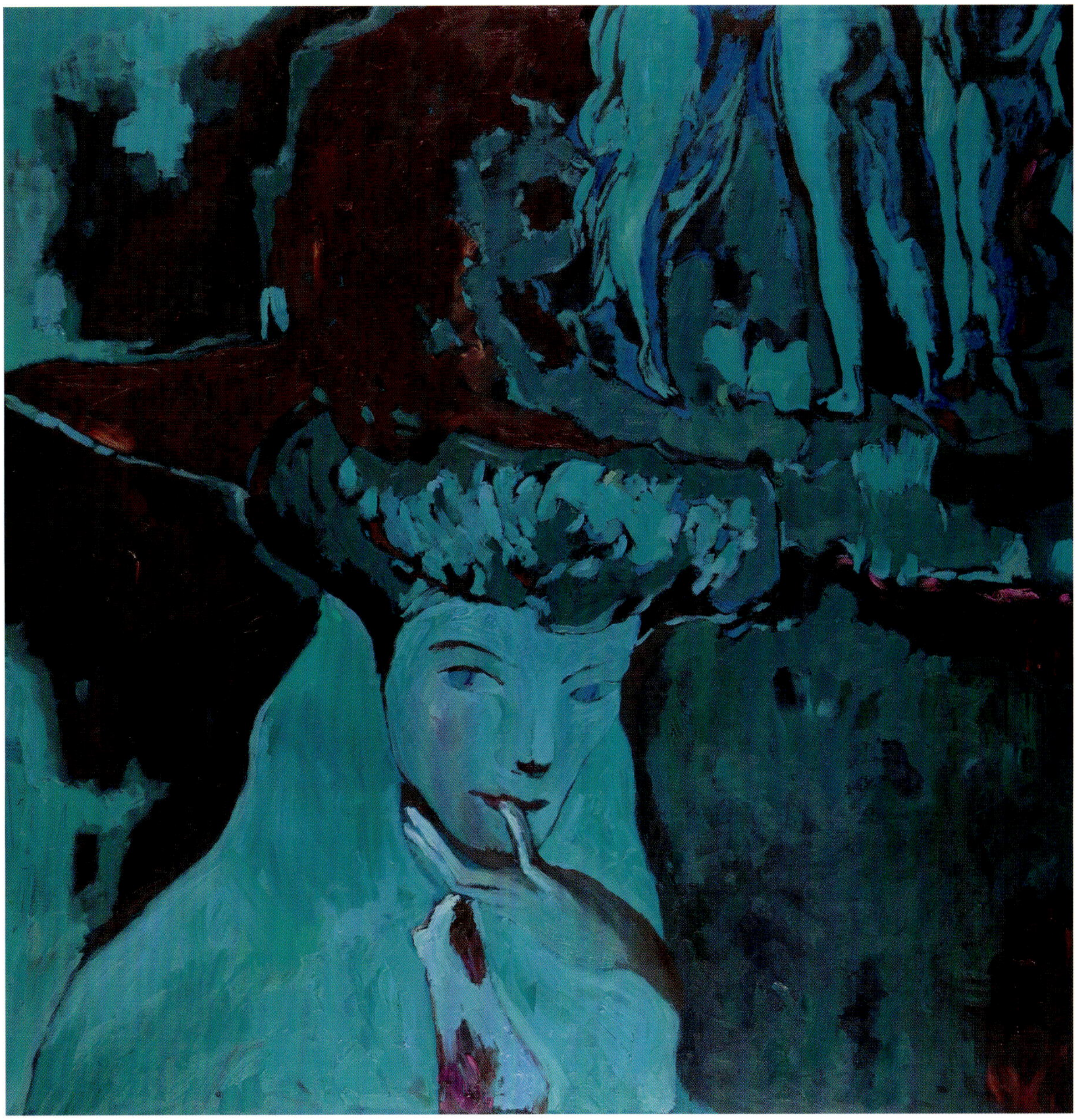

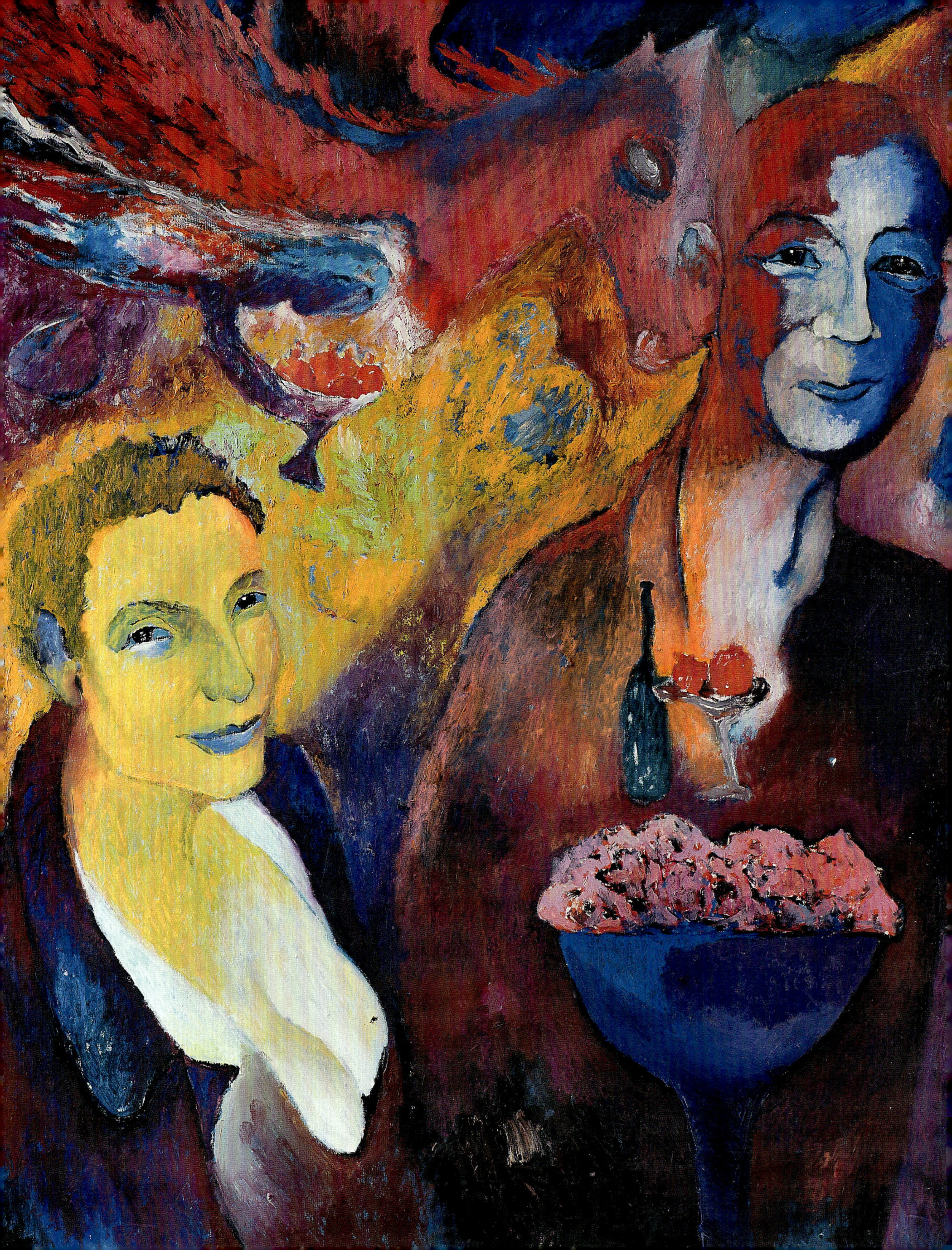

Andrei Sharov
A Russian Firehorse

Simon Hewitt

A rtist. Theater Designer. Fashion Designer. Sharov has mastered at least three "trades" with style, panache and an amiable equanimity that earns him friends wherever he goes.

Nothing in his family background destined him for such a life.

He was born in Moscow in 1966 into an environment more attuned to science than art. His mother Lydia was a mathematics teacher. His father Yuri was a government physicist who liked hiking and playing the guitar—a member of what Andrei calls "the Lyricist-Physicist Generation."

As a schoolboy, Andrei was "more attracted by the humanities and literature" than science—above all by history, geography and writing. He wanted to become a novelist.

But some artistic seeds had been subconsciously sown. His mother liked to flick through a book of paintings with her young son; Vasiliev, Korovin and Vrubel caught his eye. His father was "actually not a bad artist himself." Andrei used to help him copy out illustrations.

His parents would be proud, if surprised, supporters of their son's unexpected artistic career.

It began in mid-adolescence. Andrei Sharov had "never tried painting" when, at the age of 15, he suddenly begged to attend art classes. His parents arranged lessons with Sergei Shlykov—an accomplished, if largely forgotten, draughtsman in the Garif Basyrov mould—who didn't come cheap and wasn't close. His studio was in Bibirevo, on Moscow's leafy northern fringe, a 40-minute trek from the Sharov apartment near VDNKh.

Maybe Andrei's parents thought art lessons would keep their son out of trouble. He was "an active participant" in the gang warfare between kids from VDNKh and their local rivals from the Botanical Gardens, who fought over the coins they fished out of the Peoples' Friendship fountain at VDNKh. "Tourists threw them in for luck," remembers Sharov. "The bottom of the fountain was covered with coins every day. Serious money!"

He took lessons at Shlykov's studio for three years, day-in, day-out ("Shlykov used to say an artist doesn't have weekends!"), sometimes even staying overnight.

Shlykov gave drawing lessons, and sent Sharov to Sergei Silitsky to learn to paint: first geometric forms (cones and cubes), then faces.

However, when the 18-year-old Sharov applied to enter Moscow's premier art academy, the Stroganov Institute, he was turned down. His brief, atypical artistic training cannot have helped. He enrolled at the city's Technological University instead, studying Fashion. Despite having "good young teachers," his nine-year university career would prove chaotic—coinciding with Perestroika, national service and the break-up of the Soviet Union. He never graduated.

His dreams of working as an artist were rekindled by Gorbachov's reforms. When Sharov returned to civilian life from the army in 1987, he "discovered another country"—one, notably, where post-war foreign art could be seen. Jasper Johns, with his flag paintings, and Andy Warhol, with his stylized portraits, would become lasting influences.

Sharov began to frequent Artists' Alley (Аллее Художников) outside Izmailovo Flea-Market in search of clients—accompanied by fellow-artists Gosha Os-

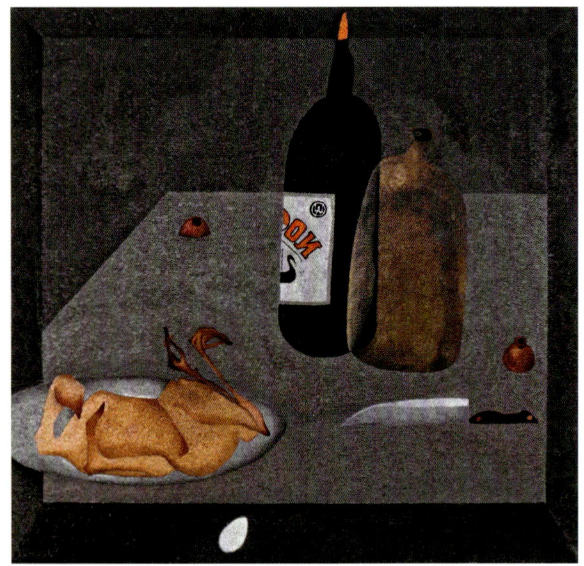

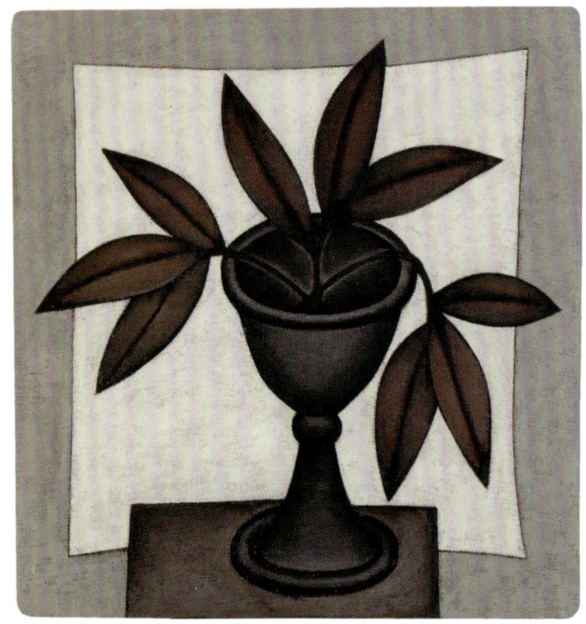

tretsov, Sergei Pakhomov and Andrei Kryukov—and managed to sell his first picture in 1988. He didn't know how much to charge, so accepted 100 rubles without haggling. It was the first time he had seen a 100-ruble note: perhaps why banknotes (usually dollar bills) would later become a leitmotif of his work.

The buyer said he'd come back later to collect the picture, but didn't. Showing characteristic doggedness, and honesty, Sharov returned to Izmailovo every day for a month before he finally saw his client again and handed over the painting, disingenuously entitled *Vase with Fruit* (its main subject was a statuesque nude). Sharov regretted that he never took a photo of it—at least, not until 2012, when he was contacted by a neighbor of the buyer, who had just died; the picture had been found among his discarded belongings.

Buoyed by this initial success, Sharov painted busily in the late eighties and early nineties. His

works were shown at Moscow's Art Manège fair; in Kiev, London and Cologne; and at the Paris gallery of Marie-Thérèse Cochin.

These early paintings were "varied: abstract and realism united." There is a Chinese-style pattern to one painting, visible in a 1989 photograph of Sharov in John Lennon sunglasses and sockless sandals, sitting cross-legged on the floor. The painting is signed with an elegant, Oriental-style monogram which the artist soon discarded. Another work features a seated woman in a blue dress, against a disjointed background that is part domestic interior, part pure abstraction. Seated women in flattened perspective (and often hats) would become a recurring theme in Sharov's work.

So would humor. His 1989 *Bolshepuzui Uhoglaz* (*Big Paunch with Ear and Eye*, p. 8) has a Gogolian sense of the absurd. A 1993 pencil drawing shows a long-necked woman with a head like an ostrich.

A variety of artistic influences are apparent in these early works. Petrov-Vodkin's red horse, albeit without a rider, puts in the first of several appearances spanning Sharov's career. The blank face, and particularly lurid tone of green, in *A Woman In Green* (1993) echo Samokhvalov's famous *Tram Conductress*. Semi-abstract still lifes have thick angular brushwork like Nicolas de Staël's. A grey-ground *Still Life with a Chicken* (p. 106, top) spoofs Krasnopevtsev. Frequent recourse to blue and rose-pink brings to mind early Picasso.

The most powerful painting from this period is a portrait of *Mary Stuart Before the Execution* (p. 107), intended for an illustrated history that was never published. The tragic queen's emaciated face, her right ear and two bony, Schiele-like hands emerge from a sea of abstract-patterned scarlet, interrupted only by a splodgy white ruff.

While hesitant and exploratory, these youthful works glisten with original talent. But painting could hardly offer Sharov a sustainable income straight from university, and his first job was at the innovative Roman Viktyuk Theater in Moscow. It was the start of an illustrious theater career: he has since worked as a set- and costume-designer for over 40 plays—earning the prestigious Chaika [Seagull] Award for his costumes for Maupassant's *Bel-Ami* at the Mossoviet Theatre in 1997.

The nineties also saw Sharov build on his university course to establish a reputation as a fashion designer, starting with his *Vesenny Prisyv* collection

Still Life with a Chicken, 1989
oil on canvas, 100 x 100 cm
Property of the artist
Courtesy of the artist and Salamatina Gallery, New York, Atlanta

Dmitriy Mikhaylovich Krasnopevtsev
Still Life with Flower, 1964
Private collection

Mary Stuart Before the Execution, 1993
paper, oil, feather, pencil, 40 x 30 cm
Property of the artist
Courtesy of the artist and Salamatina Gallery, New York, Atlanta

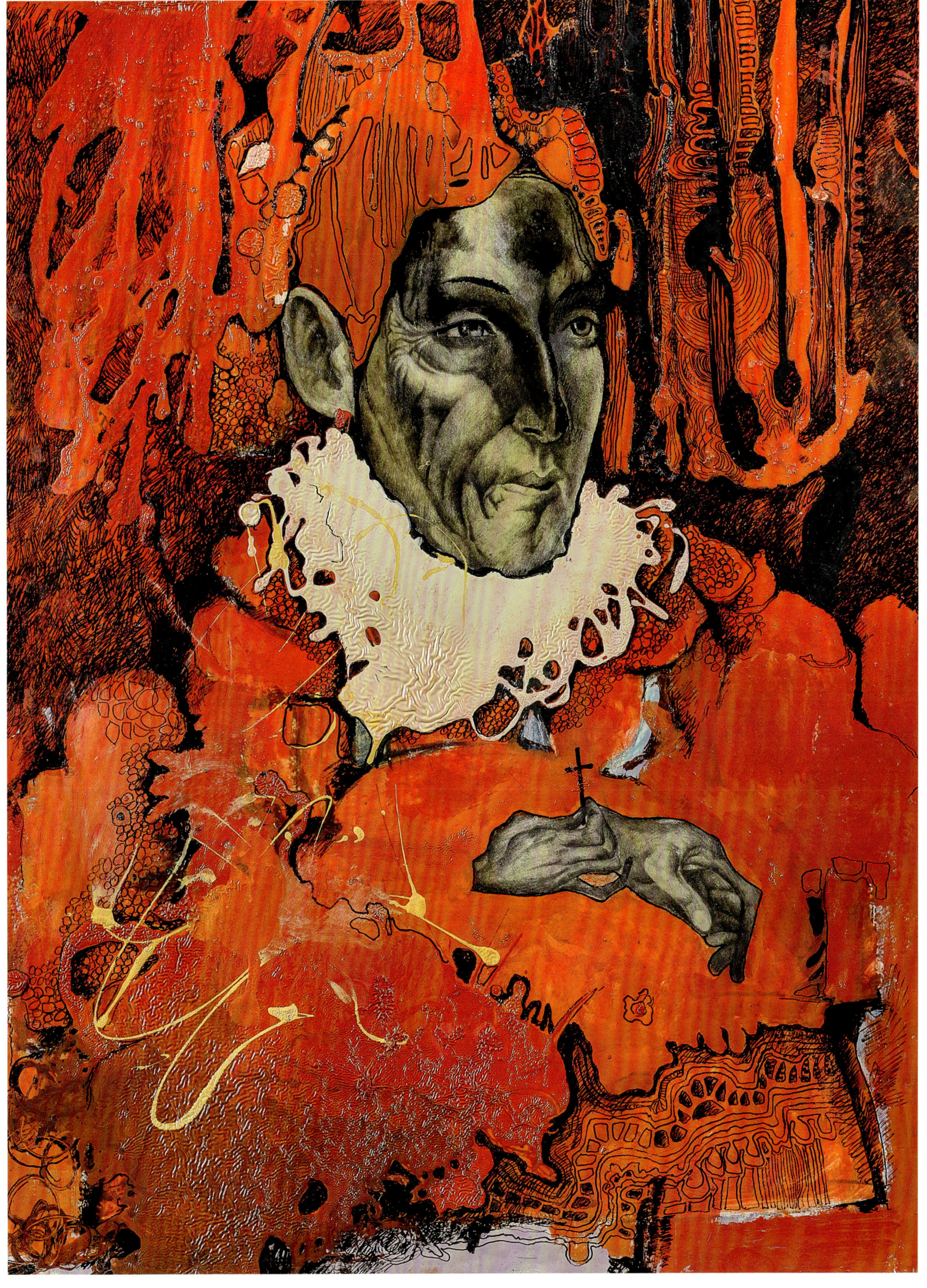

from 1992 and leading ultimately to the creation of his own fashion line, *Bureau 365*.

This commitment to theater and fashion shifted Sharov's focus away from painting for most of the decade, although in 1996 he was admitted to the Moscow Union of Artists and moved into a new studio: one of the most historic in Moscow, superbly located on a quiet, old street (Bolshoi Afanasyevsky Pereulok) on the edge of the Arbat.

This studio is a handsome, pedimented nineteenth-century building in a leafy courtyard, set well back from the street behind a German Language School. It has two large windows and a third, smaller one above its metal doors, which have been neatly spray-gunned with four cryptic red and black initials: not by Sharov, he reports, but by "some hooligan." The term seems a little vehement, given Sharov's empathy for Street Art.

The doors are leather-padded on the inside but, apart from a mattress in one corner, the studio offers cold comfort. The brickwork is painted white, the walls lined with pipes; one window is shuttered, the others partly blocked. Even during the day, electric light is needed. Wires trail. Bulbs dangle.

The studio is bizarrely cluttered with sculpture. Mayakovsky is present in duplicate: in one corner standing, in the other via a large bust topped by an irreverent beret. A cluster of heads hobnob upstairs around a wooden platform, like rats in a trap. The sculptures were in the studio before Sharov arrived: a previous occupier was the famous sculptor Nikolay Andreyev, whose presence is signalled by not one but two Cultural Heritage plaques on the wall outside. One shows him in bearded profile above a laurel branch. Both recall that this illustrious sculptor "lived and worked in this building 1900–1932." Another Communist icon, "Iron Felix" Dzerzhinsky, gazes down from the studio wall in an unusual dot portrait: a birthday present from friends, artist unknown. An arched recess harbors an army of black-and-white photographs of living people—with, in the center, Sharov's own portrait framed by red-and-silver tinsel. He is smoking a cigarette and, aping the Andreyev plaque outside, wearing a crown of laurels.

High up the back wall is a vinyl portrait of a reclining girl in stiletto heels, which Sharov says he is restoring for a friend. In one corner is a large Audrey Hepburn in a purple hat, sunglasses dangling from her mouth. An even larger portrait of a fetching young lady hangs above the mattress like a family icon. She emerges from the same strident yellow ground employed for a portrait of a youthful Bob Dylan, shown behind a plant and lonesome red chair that nods to Van Gogh. Alongside lurks a pastiche of Repin's *Cossacks Writing to the Sultan*, with the cossacks transformed into Punks—part of a Punk nostalgia project Sharov is co-authoring with Triumf Gallery supremo Dima Hankin.

Sharov's studio is disorientating. If you forget the art and the misleading sculpture, it could be a night club. There is a small stage in one corner; tables; a roll-down cinema screen; a stooled bar unit; candlesticks made from bottles of Cointreau; spotlights on the wall; a piano; spotlights on stands; and a drum-kit emblazoned with German imperial crosses and the word FUCK. An amplifier is smothered in a Union Jack made from red tape, with the motto DIE YOUNG and a central skull-and-crossbones.

There's something of the pirate about Sharov—and a macabre sense of humor (one of his flag portraits shows the skull of Queen Elizabeth II). A bust of an elderly gentleman has been painted silver, with black lips, purple beard and purple eyebrows. It is positioned beneath a psychedelic stenciled Punk frieze with a sign saying OPASNAYA ZONA (danger zone).

"Russian Punk was my youth," smiles Sharov.

A large clock on the wall by the studio door refuses to tick. Time stands still for this Eternal Punk, whose sets and costumes helped Mike Packer's *Anarchy* attract full houses to Moscow's Sovremennik Theatre in 2012–13. Even though this play (originally entitled *tHe dYsFUnCKshOnalZ!*) is about British Punk, it was dear to Sharov "because it held echoes of my youth."

The play's publicity blurb, however, talked about "mid-life crisis and what happens when Punks get old and sell out."

In seventies Britain—where I grew up—Punk stood for rebelliousness, cacophony and ugliness. Punk Reality in eighties Russia, Sharov explains, was slightly different.

OK, in St Petersburg Punk was "brutal and marginal." But, in Moscow, Punk was "for kids from respectable, intellectual families—for the élite!"

Sharov's preferred subjects come from the world of Showbiz: actors like Bruce Willis, Anthony Hopkins, Jack Nicholson and Monica Belluci, or musicians like Jim Morrison, John Lennon, Sting and Madonna. The usual suspects. There is a sprinkling of predictable political icons (Che Guevara, Abraham Lincoln) but, except for Mayakovsky (and some irreverent penguins with CCCP across their chests),

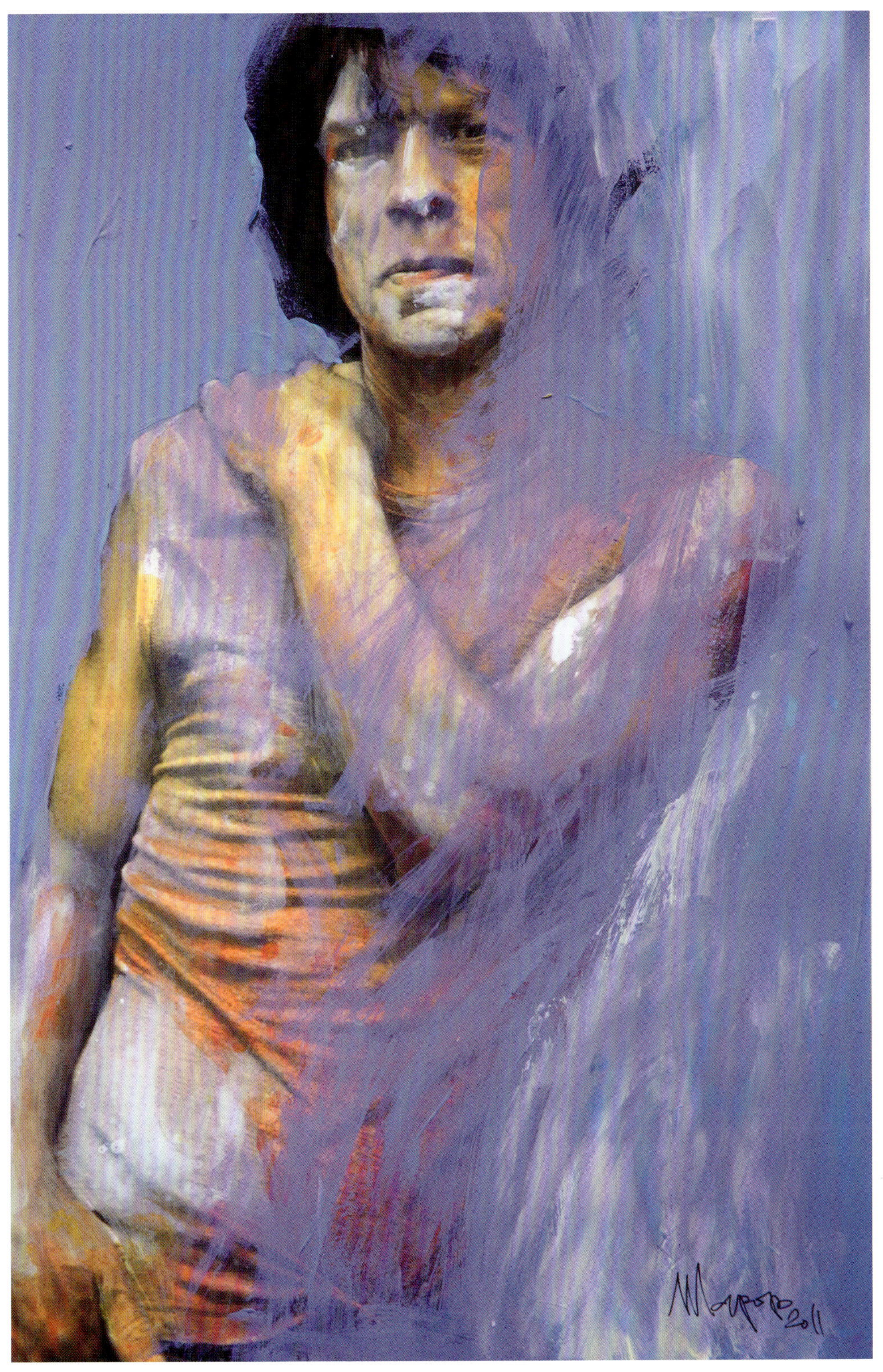

Jagger, 2011
acrylic on canvas, 150 x 100
Private collection

inforced by chunky steel frames (selected by Sharov himself), boy do these works have wallpower!

Two subjects recur. Sharov has painted Jean-Michel Basquiat at least seven times, in various poses and styles. "Basquiat gives me such a thrill!" he explains. "He was a very colorful character! A punk at heart!"

Sharov's definition of a punk is revealing: "Punks live brightly, but not for long." Where does that leave Sharov? He has morphed from a mousy, smooth-haired, Soviet pretty- boy into a macho, tattooed, balding bruiser, constantly accompanied by a jaunty cigarette, held half-smoked in his left hand. He wears T-shirt and jeans but loves dressing up—not just as a finger-jabbing Punk, but as personas ranging from a demure Renaissance burgher in velvet cap to a long-bearded, Kulik-like figure posing in front of his own painting of an orange-faced Albrecht Dürer wearing a *Campbell's Soup* T-shirt (ho-ho).

Sharov remains a man of the stage. Some of his best portraits—with their abrupt contrast of black shadow and milky-white skin—are indebted to theater spotlights.

His other favorite subject is the ultimate anti-Basquiat figure: Audrey Hepburn. Hollywood movie-star, fashion icon and Swiss-based humanitarian worker: the artful Sharov could not have selected a more glamorous, wholesome, cosmopolitan mascot.

He usually shows her in her iconic, wide-brimmed hat from *Breakfast at Tiffany's*. Large hats litter Sharov's paintings. One, reworked in a stormy blue palette indebted to Vrubel, is based on Gustav Klimt's *Schwarze Federhut*. Another quotes Modigliani—with a hat made up of Cadillacs.

Zany, Surrealist humor is never far from Sharov's brush. Some of his young ladies compensate for their lack of clothes with fantasy head-dresses made up of flamingos or swans (another nod to Vrubel). Whole flocks of them.

The Fashion World influence on Sharov's art often induces kitsch, especially when he parades his erudite knowledge of the classics in fantasy contexts. He lands the *Venus de Milo with Siamese Cats* (p. 110), Botticelli's *Three Graces with a Grazing Zebra* and *Michelangelo's* David *with Dogs on Times Square* (p. 110).

Sharov also verges on kitsch when he bases paintings on photographs: his *Ali* (Joe Frazier v. Cassius Clay, p. 111) is a good example. The approach is reminiscent of Picabia's late recourse to images from girlie magazines.

Sharov largely eschews Russian subjects. His musical pantheon is determinedly Anglophile—with no room for Vysotsky (or even a cigarette-shrouded Gainsbourg).

Many Sharov portraits take the form of Banksy-like stenciled images (Sharov even portrays Banksy's spurious alter ego, *Mr Brainwave*) on a cotton background of flags or bank-notes. Such works can seem trite and formulaic, scarcely more worthy of critical attention than, say, the creations of Italy's Gerardo Colombo or St Petersburg's Egor Bogachev. But, re-

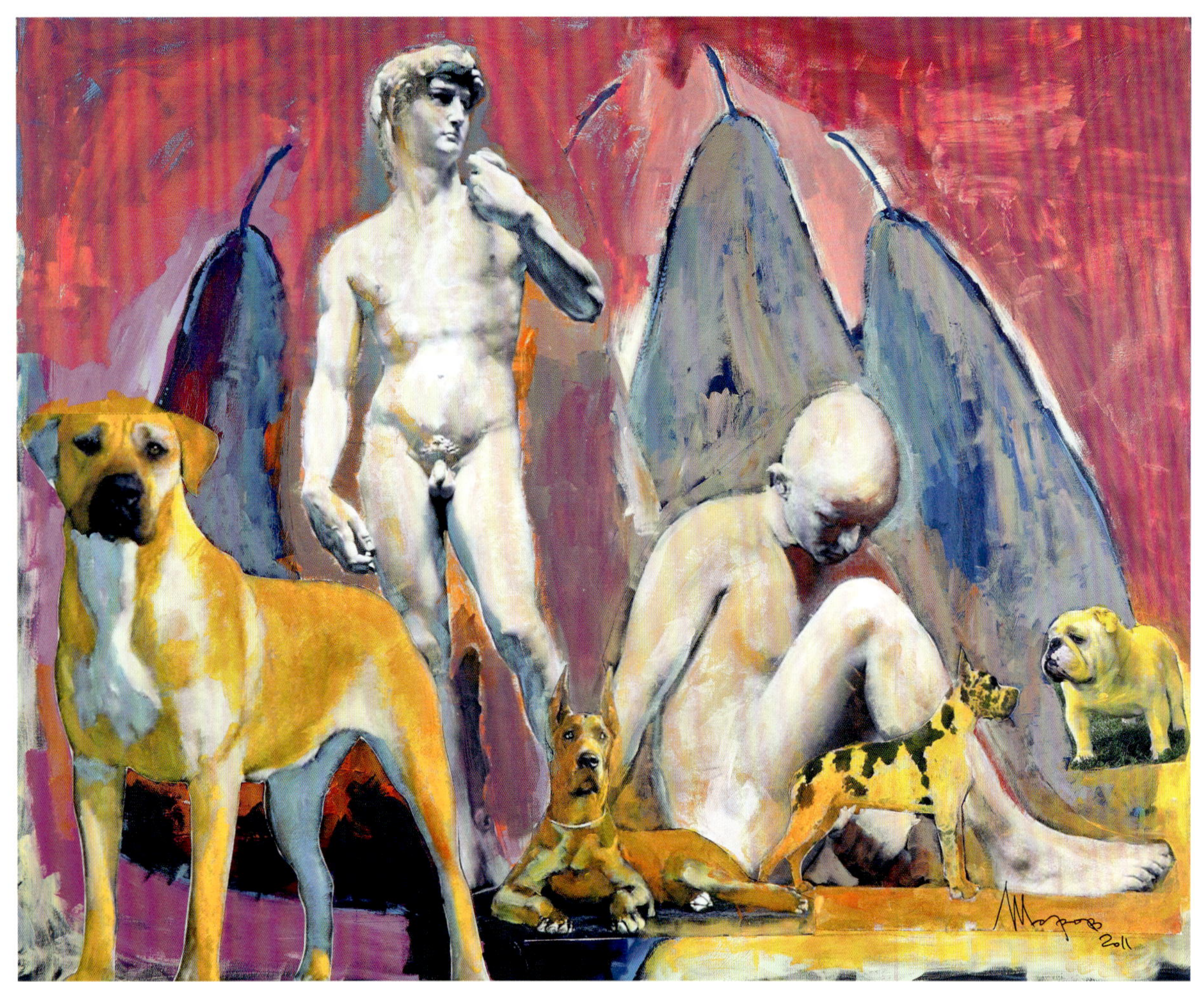

Michelangelo's David *with Dogs
on* Times Square, 2011
oil on canvas, 120 x 150 cm
V. Klyukin Collection

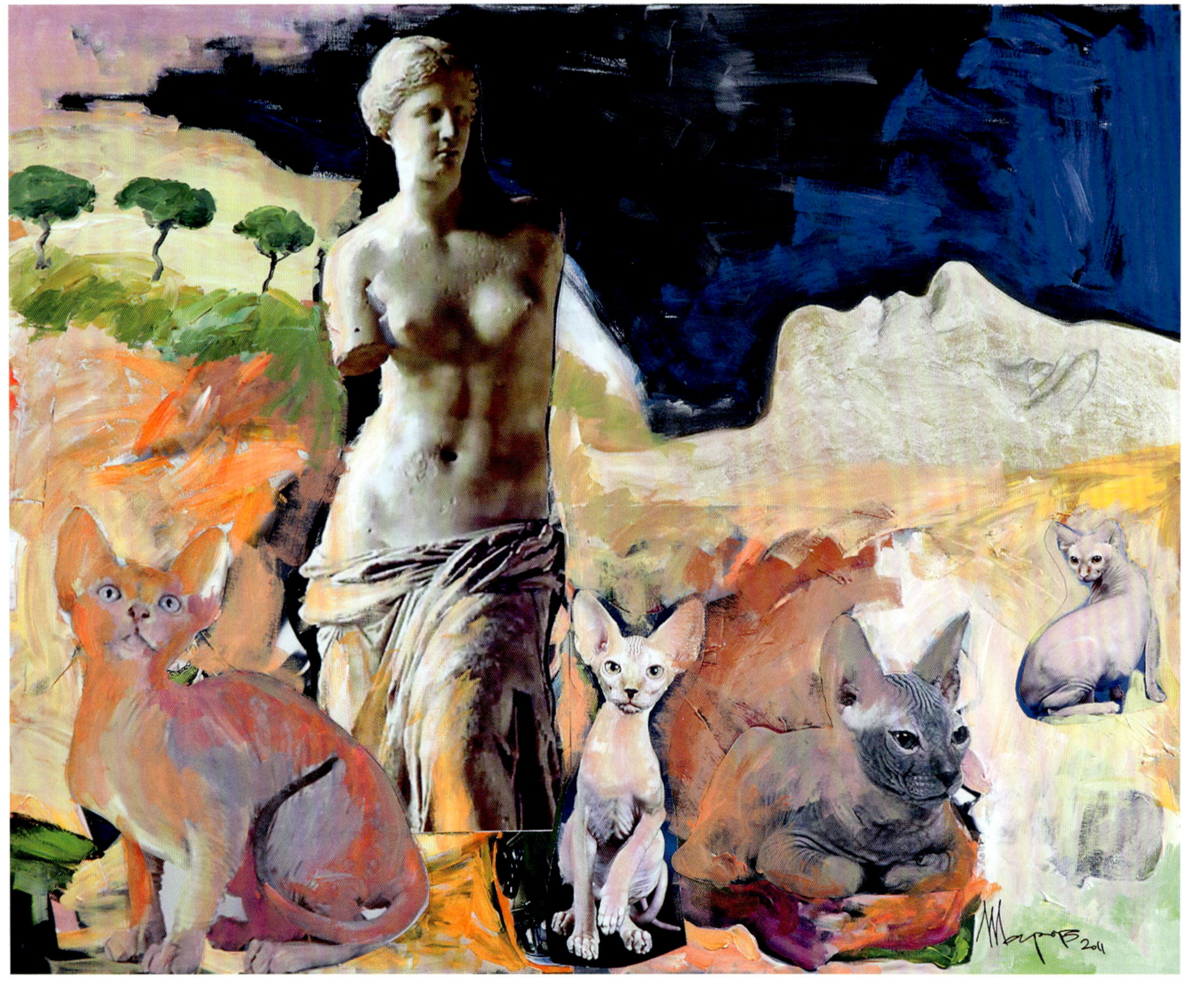

Venus de Milo with Siamese Cats, 2011
acrylic/collage, 150 x 120 cm
V. Klyukin Collection

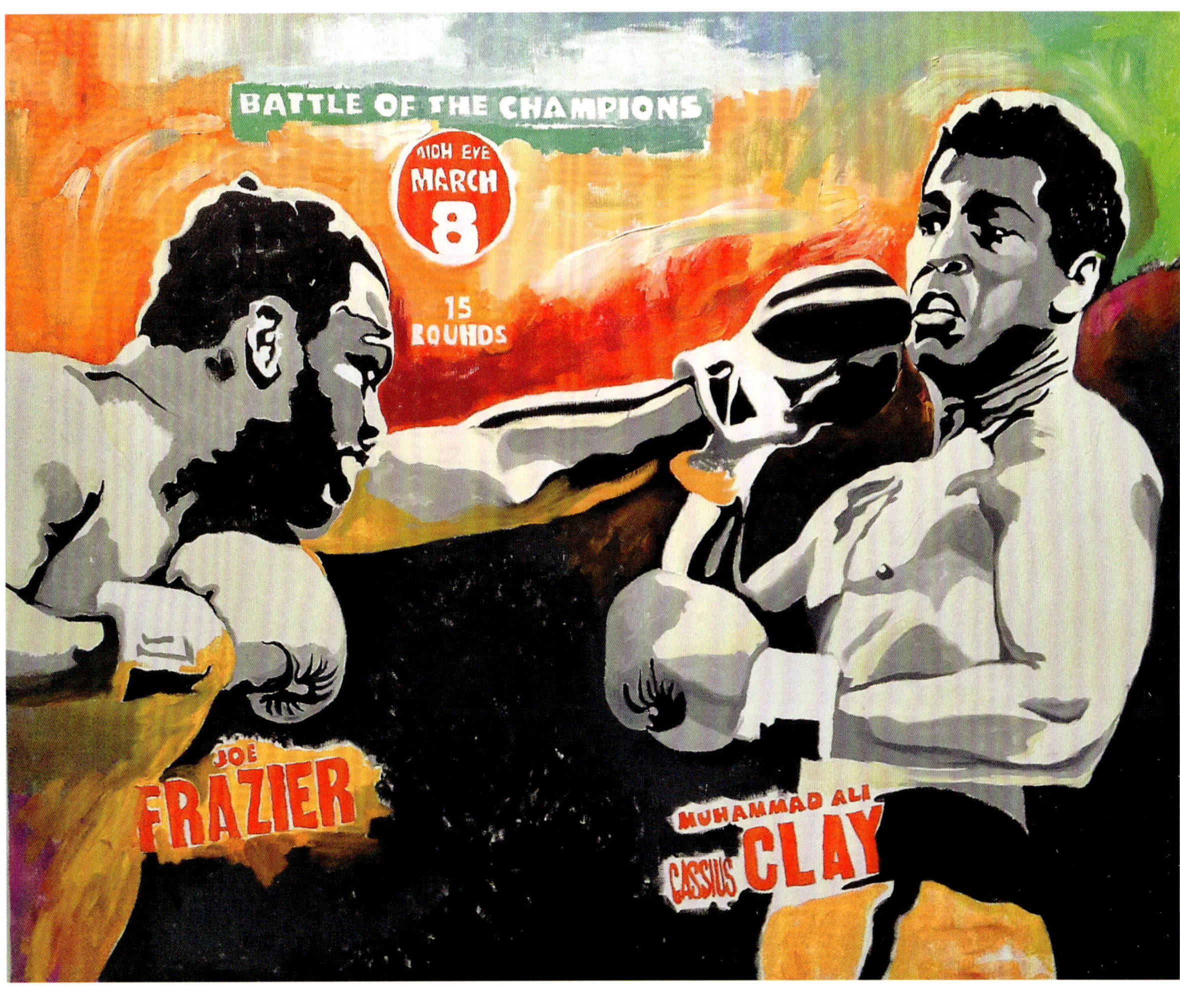

Ali, 2014
oil on canvas, 120 x 150 cm
New York, Salamatina Gallery

But there is more than harmless fun to the versatile Sharov.

In 2005, alongside a Jackson Pollock-like abstraction called *Spring*, he painted two works entitled *The Marriage of Figaro*—with distorted, silhouetted figures like Malaysian shadow puppets.

What better than opera to blend his great loves of theater, fashion and music?

The two works are powerful and enchanting, with something of the Arshile Gorky or Jean Dubuffet about them. Although, stylistically, they proved a dead end, their colorful abstract patterning heralded a new departure in Sharov's œuvre—one that has co-existed with portraiture ever since.

Riding roughshod over the black-and-silver-studded monochrome associated with Punk, Sharov has come to prove himself a supreme colorist: a worthy descendant of Van Gogh, Vlaminck and Van Dongen.

Although this love of color can be traced to his youthful admiration for Korovin, its intensity far exceeds anything produced by Russian Fauves and has more in common with Soutine, Kokoschka and German Expressionism—with echoes of Poland's Sta–nisław Witkiewicz and Hungary's György Kovásznai.

Sharov's recourse to exuberant color can be traced back to his turquoise-and-orange *Red Dior* portrait of 1999, but only became prevalent from 2005, abetted by *Charvin* paints.

These come in 208 colors and were favored by Cézanne. Sharov buys them in Nice during his work-spells in Monaco.

In Soviet times, sighs Sharov, he could not even dream about such paints.

"I didn't even know they existed!"

In 2006 he marked his 40th birthday with a vibrant double-portrait of himself with his wife, featuring a red horse in the background—not another tribute to Petrov-Vodkin, but symbolizing the Fire-horse of the Chinese zodiac (Sharov is a typical Fire-horse: "unconventional and adventurous, suited to careers in art or the media, and able to attract a large following").

In 2007 he produced a series of naïve, anonymous portraits—some resembling tribal art masks or Velasquez head-dresses—set against glowing, single-color grounds of red, lilac, violet or mustard yellow.

Sharov's 2011 version of *The Beatles* (p. 112, top) crossing Abbey Road is even more psychedelic.

The chromatic process culminated in 2012 with

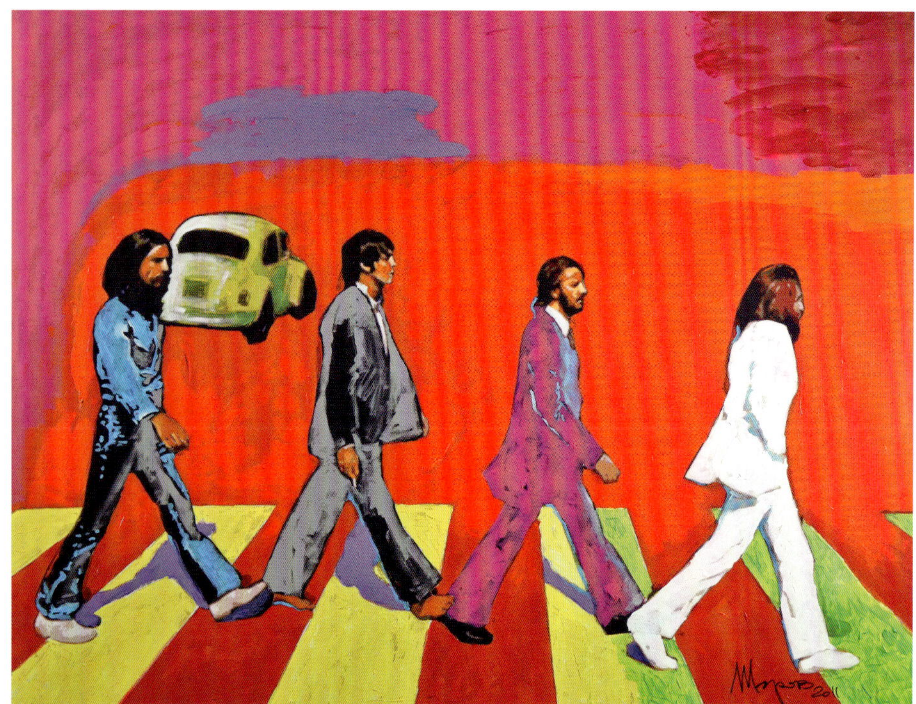

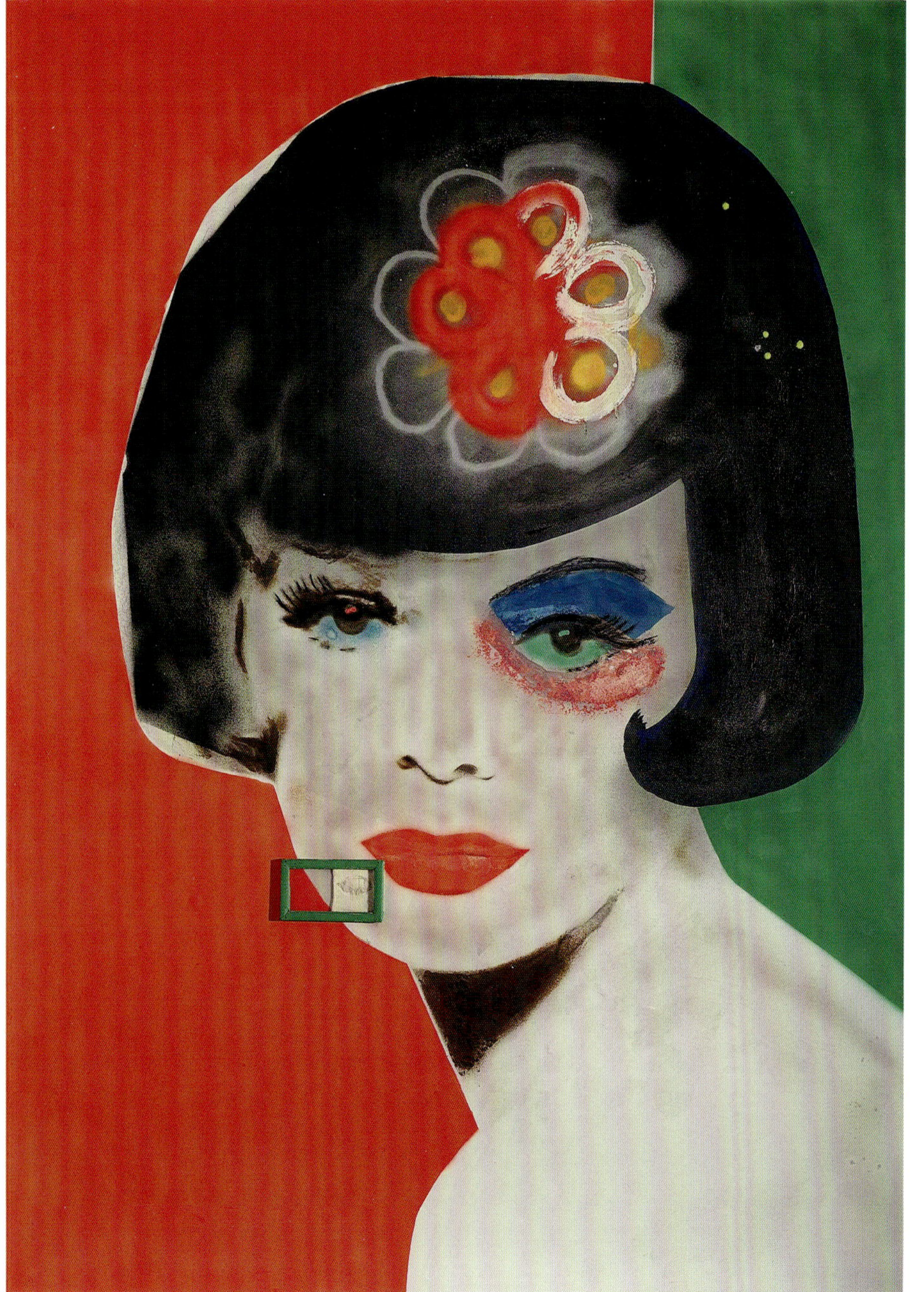

Beatles, 2011
acrylic on canvas, 100 x 120 cm
Property of the artist
Courtesy of the artist and Salamatina
Gallery, New York, Atlanta

Martial Raysse, *L'année dernière à Capri
(Titre Exotique)*, 1962
Private collection

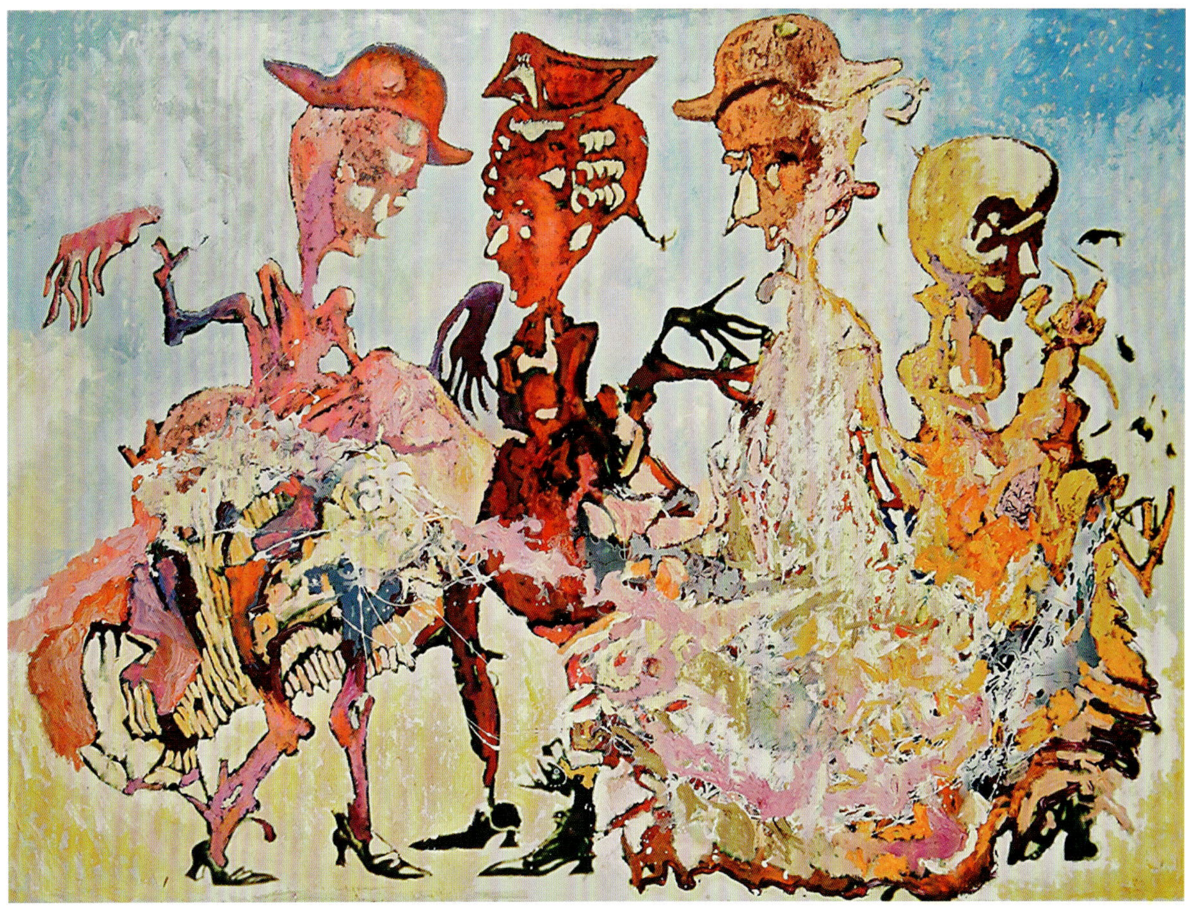

a series of works of unparalleled colour-clash ferocity, attained through riotous collisions: yellow against green, pink against red, turquoise against orange… Their nearest visual equivalent is thermal imaging (heat-sensitive photography), and these works are hot in every sense.

Most feature steamy nudes derived from Modigliani and Ingres, whose *odalisques* are something of a Sharov obsession (as they were for Martial Raysse, with whom Sharov has much in common).

Yet, although Pastiche is a major feature of Sharov's art, it is absent from his most prolific series of works: some eighty still lifes with pears.

These paintings employ different colors and different techniques. The pears invariably emerge from a half-visible bowl, usually in batches of three or four; but one shows a whole bowl with nine pears and a slice of watermelon, while elsewhere the pears stand aligned like skittles, or tower in the background like mountains.

Sharov does not, though, consider himself a still life specialist.

"For me," he reveals, "they're not pears!

They're just color schemes. Just my mood expressed in color!"

The latest outlet for his moods are watercolors. Since Summer 2014 Sharov has been posting them on Facebook.

Some are head studies, others nudes. All betray sublime mastery of light, shadow and the human body. Some are monochrome, others washed through with color whose tingling vibrancy recalls Latvian artist Kristiana Brektes.

Some nudes, grins Sharov intriguingly, will not appear on Facebook "for censorship reasons."

As he nears his half-century, this multifaceted *artiste* is stepping up a gear and continuing to expand his repertoire—pursuing what that prototype Punk Poet Arthur Rimbaud might have called his *élan vers la perfection*.

October 2014

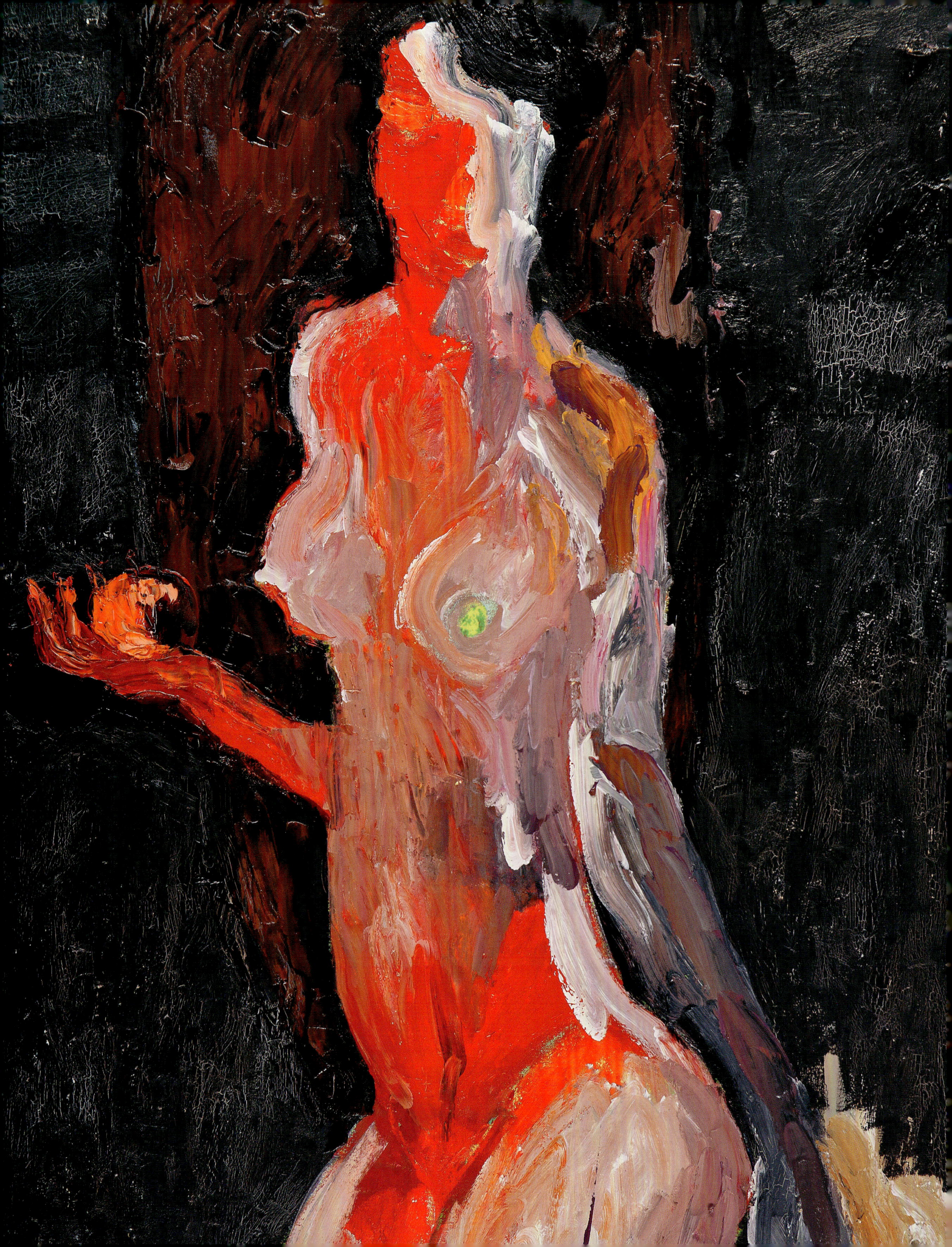

Painting is Color

John Cauman

Nude with Apple, 2012
120 x 80 cm
V. Klyukin Collection

"*P*ainting is color!" declares Andrei Sharov. Freedom—liberation—is the guiding force in Andrei Sharov's life as an artist. Sharov works directly on the canvas, without preparatory sketches. Spontaneity is essential to his method. "I feel the urge to paint, and I paint. I work rather fast. I try to finish a painting without much delay in order to preserve the emotion."

Born in Moscow in 1966, Sharov was raised in a family of the intelligentsia: his father was a physicist, his mother a mathematician. At the age of thirteen, he decided to be an artist: "The decision was immediate and without a second thought. Before that, I didn't even think about it." His parents encouraged his creative pursuits, arranging for his private lessons at their own expense. For the next several years he studied drawing and painting with various artists in their studios.

Andrei Sharov came of age when the punk sensibility—the anti-establishment spirit which had originated in the UK, the US and Australia in the seventies and had affected pop music, fashion, dance, media, and the visual arts—was taking hold in the Soviet Union, particularly among elite, rebellious youth, for whom the official culture seemed stultifying. "What attracted me to the punk sensibility," Sharov recalls, "was the sense of play. I've always tried to live life—to do only what interests me. In my soul, I was always a punk."

Among Andrei Sharov's gifts is his adaptability—his willingness to experiment and explore, without being defeated by fear of failure: "As a painter, I want to be free and separate, just the canvas and myself."

The *Old Courtesan* (2012, pp. 12–13) is a punk takeoff on the established genre of the odalisque. Its prototype is Ingres' *Grande Odalisque* (1814, Paris, Louvre, p. 95), a paradigm of neoclassical beauty. Sharov quotes the Odalisque's reclining three-quarter pose, the arc of her back, the positions of her arms and legs, and even the peacock fan grasped in her right hand—now an ambiguous phallic object in blue-green. Whereas the Odalisque aloofly glances in the direction of the viewer, her face partially submerged in shadow and nearly in profile, the Old Courtesan's grotesque features appear in full three-quarter view; her nostrils, lips and mascaraed eyes, all painted blue-black against ghostly pale flesh tones, project vulnerability and despair, an effect amplified by the red penumbra surrounding her head. The ambiguity of this penumbra—is it a wig? a coiffure?—reinforces the androgynous quality of the face. The effect of anxiety is intensified by the scumbled application of paint in color contrasts of red and green.

Nude Woman in a Red Chair (2012, p. 92) likewise uses as its point of departure, though to very different effect, a masterwork by Ingres—in this instance, *La Grande Baigneuse* (1808, Paris, Louvre, p. 116, right), which holds a canonical place in modernism as the prototype for Man Ray's *Violon d'Ingres* of 1924 (p. 116, left). The inspiration for Sharov's recasting of Ingres' *Baigneuse* is the art of Andy Warhol—in particular, Warhol's celebrity portraits of the seventies; in this case, the "celebrity" is Ingres' masterpiece. Whereas the *Baigneuse* is subtly modeled, restrained in color and seems frozen in time, *Nude Woman in a Red Chair* has the instantaneity of a snapshot or silkscreen image. Geographical and

Man Ray, *Le Violon d'Ingres*,1924
Paris, Musée National d'Art Moderne
Centre Georges Pompidou

Jean-Auguste-Dominique Ingres,
La Grande Baigneuse, 1808
Paris, Musée du Louvre

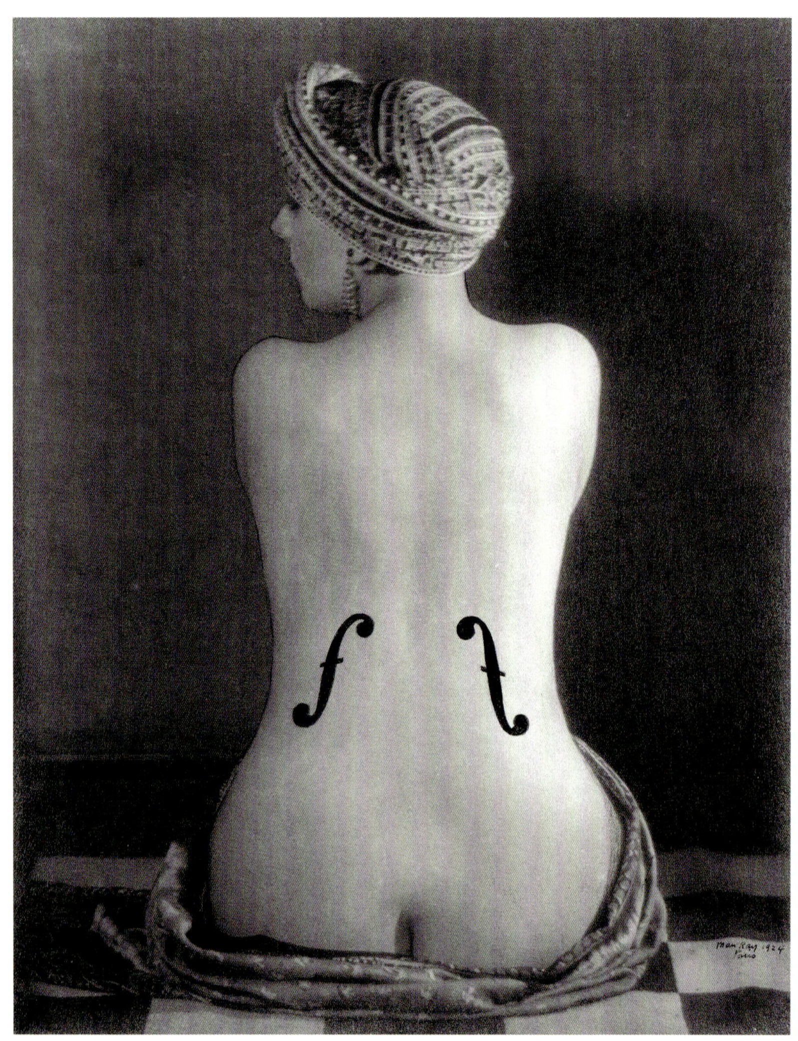

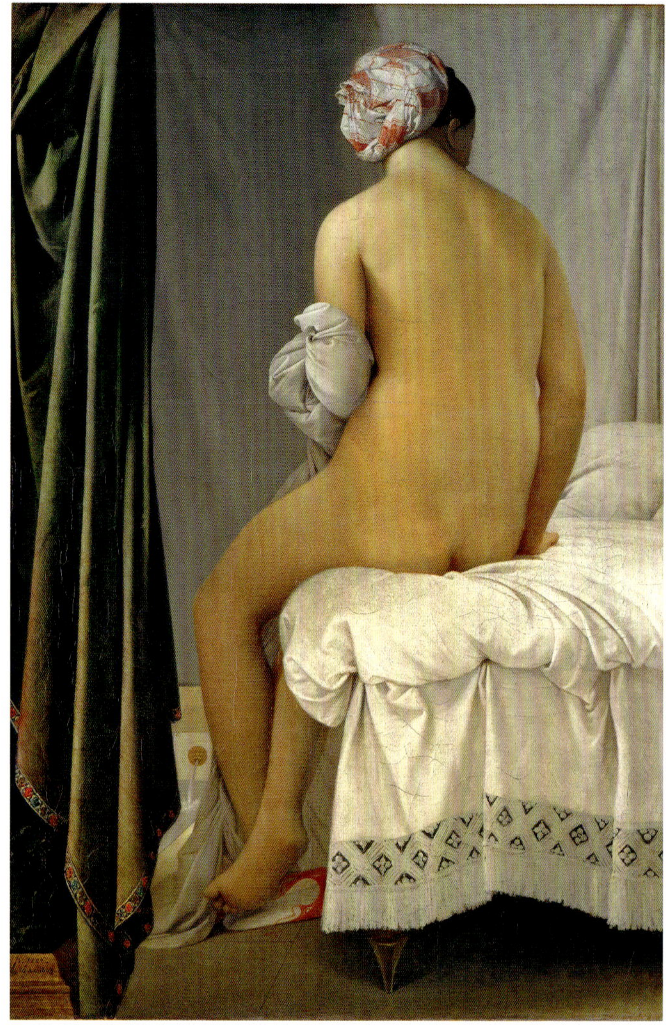

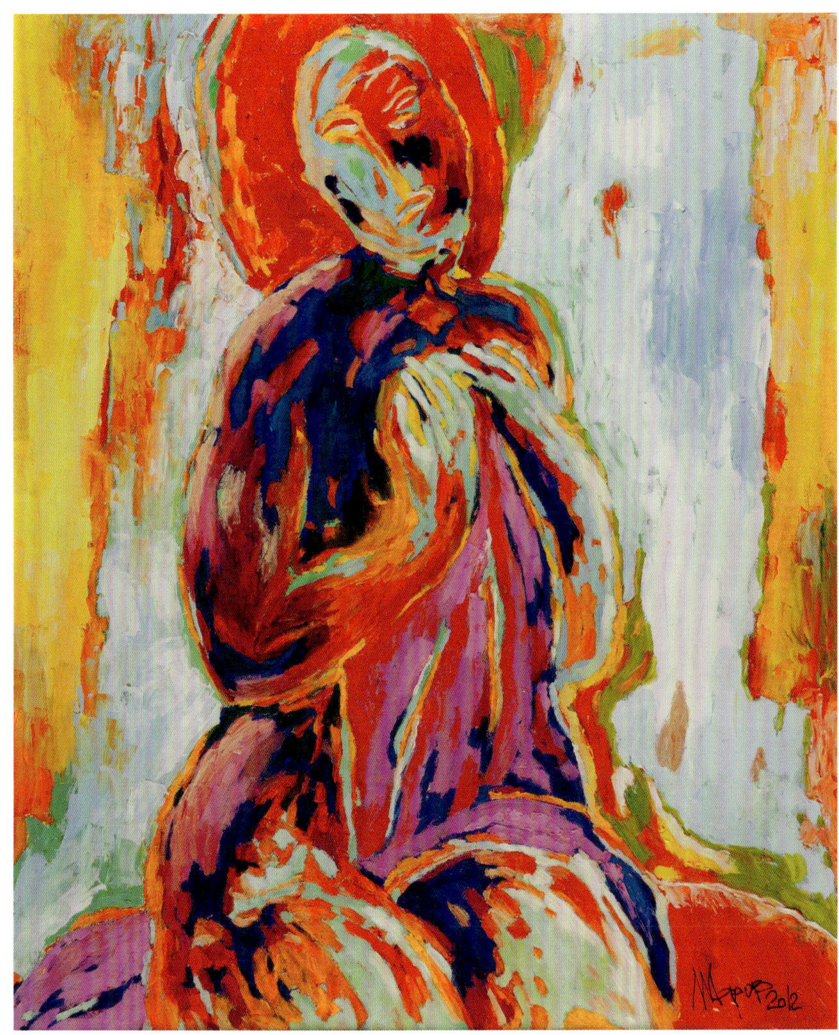

Nude with Towel, 2012
acrylic/oil on canvas, 120 x 100 cm
V. Klyukin Collection

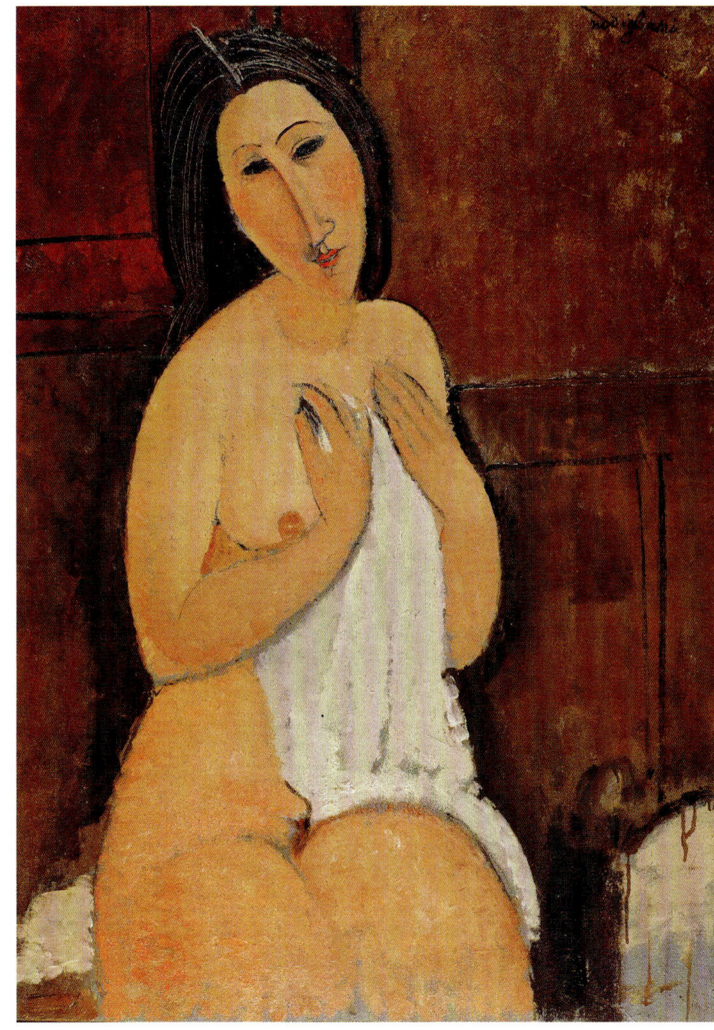

Amedeo Modigliani, *Nu assis
à la chemise*, 1917
Villeneuve d'Ascq, LaM – Lille Métropole
Musée d'art moderne, d'art contemporain
et d'art brut

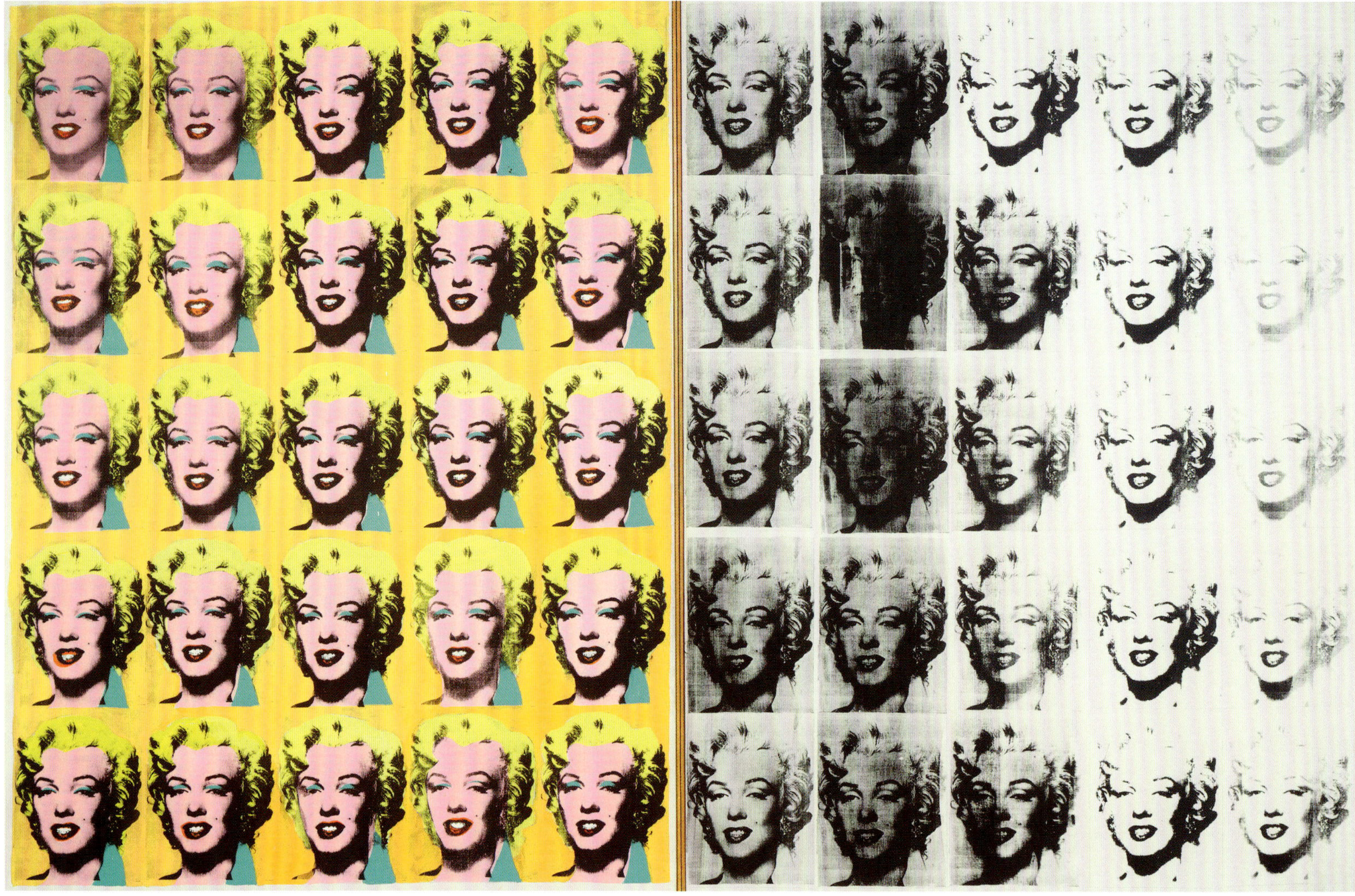

chronological specificities have been excised. Light and shade on the figure are depicted with brilliant hues of red-orange, orange-and-white and violet, set off against the deep red of the chair, in stark contrast to the blue-black shadow that nearly submerges the left contours of the figure in the nocturnal darkness of the room. The sensuality of the subject has its counterpart in the application of paint, lushly applied in both positive and negative space.

Nude with Towel (2012, p. 117, left) has as its template Modigliani's *Nu assis à la chemise* (1917, Villeneuve d'Ascq, LaM – Lille Métropole Musée d'art moderne, d'art contemporain et d'art brut, p. 117, right). Modigliani's original composition is transformed by Sharov's electric color scheme. The figure and her surroundings have become remote in time and space. Excising the naturalistic elements has the effect of emphasizing the *art-nègre* origins of the figure's masklike face. The coiffure, in luminous red with orange highlights, resembles a halo; the *chemise* (nightgown), now a towel, no longer has as its primary purpose the concealment of the figure's nudity—it could be the attribute of a saint. We might be witnessing a transfiguration—if not religious, then psychedelic.

Nude with Apple (2012, p. 114) and *Reclining Nude* (2012) present, in pure form, Sharov's contribution to the genre, his paradigm of the nude. Both are universalized, rather than individualized, and are sensuous in their use of light and color. *Nude with Apple* appears to be an interior, perhaps a boudoir; *Reclining Nude* seems to be set out-of-doors, perhaps on a hillside. Both have primordial elements: the apple is an attribute of Eve, the first woman; the arms of the *Reclining Nude* are gracefully serpentine. Though at first glance both nudes appear to lack specificity of facial features, both may have concealed physiognomies. The red highlights on the standing nude's face suggest a profile at left; subtle highlights on the reclining nude's head imply incipient eyes, nose and mouth. What is notable in both works is the sensuality of the poses, of the application of paint, of the drawing, and of the light and color.

Ultimately, all five of Sharov's recent works considered here seem to defy interpretation, as they convey the freedom, the exhilaration, the sheer joy of their creation.

Andy Warhol, *Marilyn Diptych*, 1962
London, Tate Gallery

Andrei on Theater, Fashion, Rock and Much More

Interview by Agniya Mirgorodskaya

I met with Andrei in his spacious studio in the center of Moscow. It's a separate building with 6-meter high ceilings, situated in Arbat, the historical center of the city. A curious bust in a punk rock style, photographs of famous rock stars, and his paintings' plethora of colors strikes the imagination. All of a sudden, you get the feeling of being in quite an extraordinary place.

A.M. *Andrei, as far as I know, the history of this studio goes way back, and up until now it has been known as a notorious place where famous socialites would gather, is that right?*

A.S. Yes, it's true. This studio is more than 116 years old. It even has a memorial plaque stating that from 1900 until 1932 a famous sculptor, Leonid N. Andreyev, worked here. Back then, before the revolution and after, famous poets, artists and writers would meet here. If only the walls could talk! Many famous artists have also worked here. I became the owner of this studio in 1996. I renovated the place, constructed a set, and installed theatrical light. I wanted to recreate the atmosphere of the *kvartirniks* [Soviet kitchen gatherings] in the 80s. And I succeeded. It became a place where the most interesting people of my generation would gather—literary readings, concerts, weddings, and birthdays all took place here. It became a place where many people felt good and each one brought something unique to the table. Musicians played music; producers organized closed previews on the big screen; and films and videos were shot here. This studio could be converted into anything you wanted.

A.M. *So what famous figures have visited?*
A.S. I happen to know many cultural icons, such as Stephen Friars, Martha Fiennes, Fabio Capella, to name just a few. I got to know many of them through working in theater.

A.M. *What was it like working in that field?*
A.S. Everything in my life has happened by chance; I must be a lucky person. I never planned anything in advance. The only thing I knew was that I wished to be an artist. As I never thought I'd work as a costume designer in fashion or in cinema, making video clips, neither did I realize I'd work in theater. I ended up designing for 47 plays in various Moscow venues. My romance with the form has lasted for 27 years, and continues up until this day. For my designs for the play *Dear Friend* I received a "Chayka", the most prestigious theater award in Russia, while for the play *Celestials* I received a "Tekstura" award for the best set design. Many of my plays have gone on for more than 20 years.

A.M. *Are you still involved in set design and such?*
A.S. I keep receiving offers, but in four years I haven't found anything I'd be interested in yet. Contemporary plays for one–two actors are always a "no". I want a large scale production, like Shakespeare, Tennessee Williams, Chekhov, Muller, Thomas Mann. So that's why I haven't been doing anything theatrical recently. I made a decision to get involved only in something that would absorb me 100%. Now I am fully devoted to making art.

A.M. *In general, what kind of impact has this work had on you?*

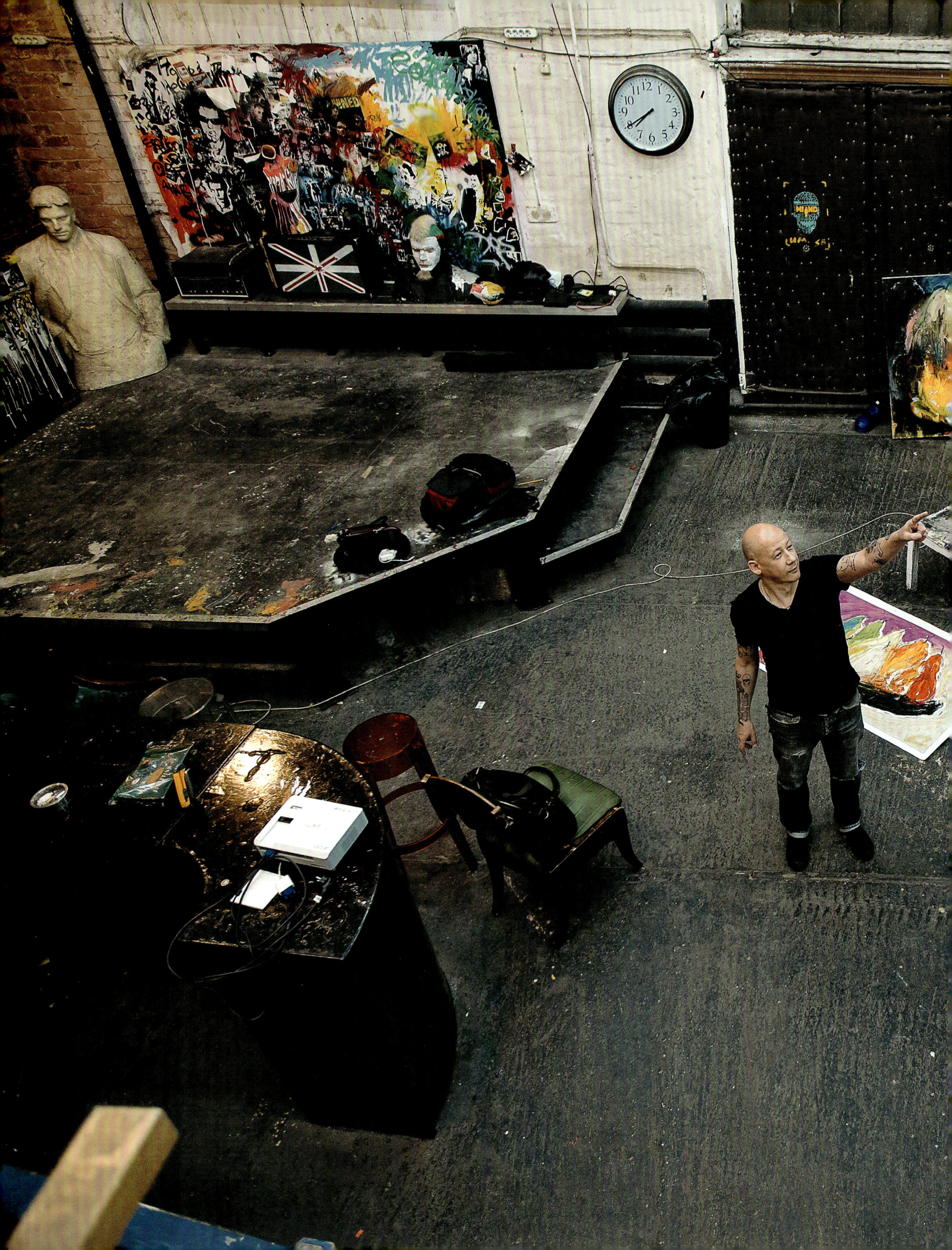

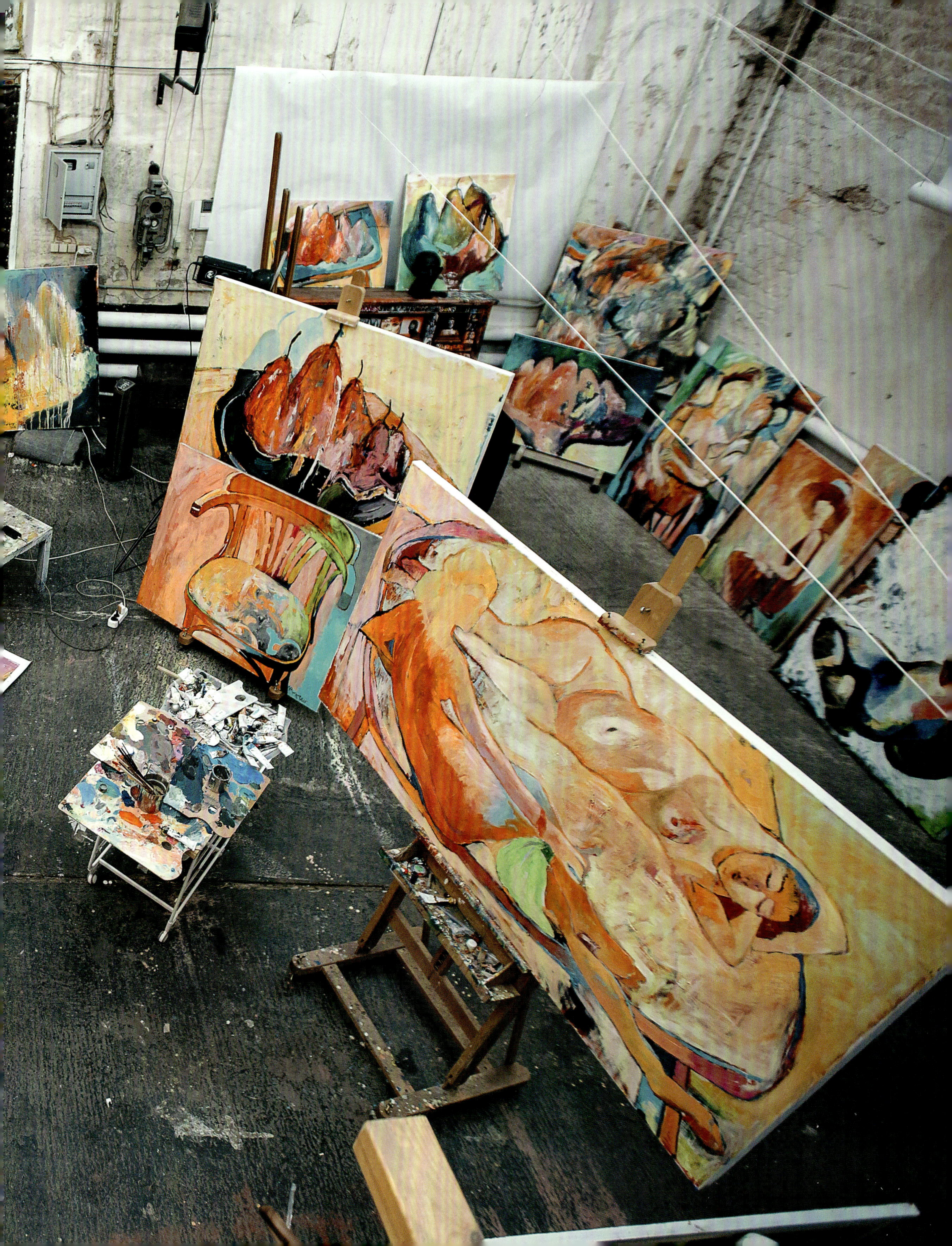

A.S. Theater is a drug. It's a very fascinating world, especially when you're not only a spectator, but directly involved. When you're inside this mysterious country called theater, you get carried away and it's hard to get out. I haven't been taking drugs for more than twenty years now and theater has become mine.

A.M. *Andrei, it's hard not to notice you in the company of rock musicians so widely known all over Russia. As far as I can understand, many of them were your friends and hung out here. I bet it was a great time!*

A.S. The 80s were really fun… the 90s crazy. In the 80s the country was taken over by a rock culture that emerged from the underground. Before everything was happening in the flats there were no nightclubs, no rock clubs and so on. Then suddenly rockers started to gather at stadiums of 60,000 people. These were wild times, and it appeared out of nowhere. As I was studying to be a fashion designer, my fellow musicians started asking me to make costumes for them. Everyone just wanted to look cool.

A.M. *And then punk happened?*

A.S. Yes, punk with its "live fast, die young" philosophy. Many didn't make it to their thirties. Back then it seemed to be a fascinating journey, and we thought this was how you should live your life. Now I believe we were fooling ourselves. Self-delusions and radical views are often present when you're young. I was part of this movement. Thank goodness I've made it to my fifties! I have four beautiful daughters. There came a time when I was ashamed of the fact that I was 28 and still alive. Yes! Morrison and Janis Joplin were no longer around. I was making punk jackets and collecting digital images of punk culture. Jackets were pieces of art in which everything came together: tattoos, Nietzsche philosophy, etc. Back then we only had a vague idea of how it was all supposed to look. Because, of course, we didn't travel a lot. In some way, that was probably a good thing. As I wasn't restrained by any boundaries, I was using my imagination and ended up creating unique objects.

A.M. *You were once a famous fashion designer in Russia. You've been making clothes for celebrities, as well as organizing talked-about catwalks. What was your romance with the world of fashion like?*

A.S. I began to get involved with fashion in 1994, quite by chance. I had been working on a costume made of pins, as a play director asked me to achieve the effect of frozen water. I came up with an idea to connect the pins together, which produced an effect of mercury slowly transforming into metal. The director was extremely pleased. While the performance never happened, the costumes remained, as did numerous sketches. I was working on them day and night; all my hands were swollen and pierced with pins. Nonetheless, I couldn't care less.

In 1992 Andrey Bartenev invited me to take part in a festival called Assembly of the Untamed Fashion, which had been happening in Riga for a few years. Such a thing could only be happening in the 90s. Crazy fashion designers and models would gather together, and for two weeks Riga would turn into a funny farm. No one had a clue what fashion meant back then, so they brought crazy performances. And I also brought my costumes made of pins, as well as dresses made from watches and spoons! This is stating the obvious, but the more weird and unsuited for wearing, the better and cooler the costumes were.

So at first I was doing performances, creating costumes using all sorts of materials: spoons, pins, milk packages, wood, metal, plastic, etc. All this was worn by beautiful women and shown in nightclubs. So fame came to me quite soon. And then in 1996, when I was invited to take part in Moscow Fashion Week, it all became more professional. In only a few years I became one of the five most influential Russian designers, but in 2008 I left fashion for good and haven't been in any fashion shows since.

A.M. *As you mentioned before, since then you've been devoting yourself fully to painting. So let's talk about your paintings, and about your worldview now versus then.*

A.S. I've been painting as long as I can remember. It's true though that for some time it had become a hobby. I could afford to do it entirely for pleasure, without thinking about selling it. Back then, making brave performances felt natural and organic to me. I was young, thirsty for fame, money and success among women. I've gone through a lot since then; it's been a long journey. It's perfectly clear to me that what I'm doing now might be a little bit outdated. But this is what interests me now. It's something that feels natural at this moment of my life.

A.M. *So radical performances don't interest you any longer?*

A.S. As I was involved in creating complex scenography, as well as complicated costumes, I've had enough of it, from back in the 90s, and now it doesn't interest me any more. Now when I see contemporary art installations I feel like I did that 25 years ago.

A.M. *What inspires you today?*

A.S. Women, travels, problems, my daughters. There are eternal themes, and themes that are interesting only in the given moment, only to fade and disappear with time. Fashion is momentary, and there can be nothing eternal in it. After having been involved in that industry for fifteen years I understand that almost none of it will be written into history. I wish to be doing things that reflect my worldview at any given moment. It's okay if it's out of fashion. I've been fashionable for a long time.

One of my eternal themes is nudes. I have a big series of paintings of them. Sometimes I paint from memory, and sometimes I use life models. I like communicating and being around women. I feel quite comfortable in their world. I adore them in general.

A.M. *When one looks at your paintings, you can't help but think that the subject plays a secondary role in your art, and it is rather the emotion and color that are of primary importance. Would it be fair to suggest that?*

A.S. Yes, color for me is the most important thing. Through color I show my attitude toward everything. Emotion is thus important to me. A person either gets it or not. Many of my friends say I can even tell someone to fuck off using color. For example, I've been working on my *Pears* series for a few years now. Here it's not the pears that matter, they're simple and don't demand any philosophical interpretations. Rather, they're more like scales for musicians, in which they become a laboratory for different combinations and interpretations of color. Sometimes this is achieved, other times not. Afterwards, these discoveries are transferred into nudes, or the *Chairs* series.

A.M. *Your color palette tends to be bright. Does that mean you're a positive person?*

A.S. I'm a different person. But when it comes to painting, I only prefer to project my positive energy, in the hope that by doing so I'm making the lives of others at least a little bit brighter.

Maison IRFĒ

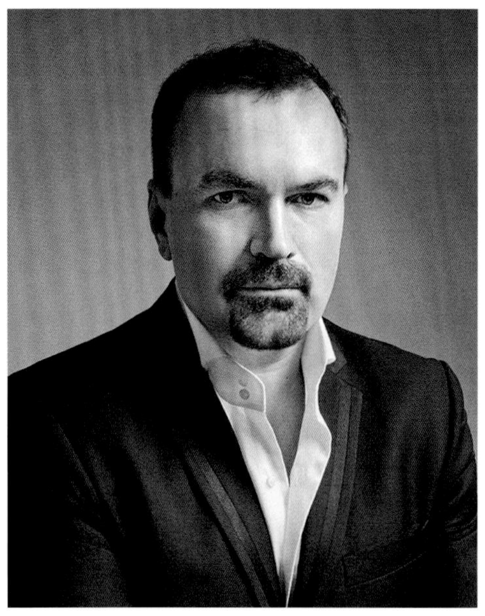 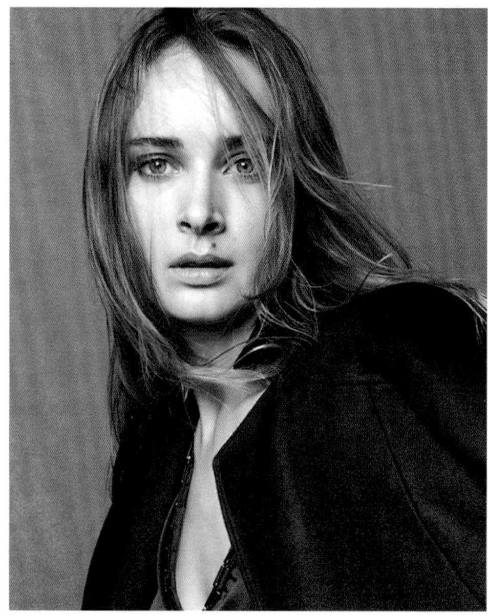

IRFĒ Foundation was established by Maison IRFĒ, Olga Sorokina and Andrey Strukov in 2012,
an institution supporting Russian Art and Culture.
Maison IRFĒ is the first Russian luxury fashion house was founded in Paris by Russian immigrants—
Prince Felix Yousoupoff and his wife Irina Romanova, the niece of the last Russian Tsar Nicholas II.
After a ninety-year break, IRFĒ Fashion House was restored to life by its new owner Olga Sorokina.
The foundation aims expanding the cultural exchange between Russia and other countries,
heritage studies, building up collection of Russian theatrical artists.

Collection of IRFĒ Foundation
The IRFĒ Foundation has one of the greatest theatrical collections. It outnumbers more
than 1,500 designs. There are items from original sketches of costumes and sets,
created by well-known Russian artists. The collection contains works of N. Roerich, N. Goncharova,
A. Benois, M. Larionov, B. Koustodiev, K. Korovin, I. Bilibin and many other outstanding Russian artists.
In 2015 IRFĒ Foundation has published book *Russian Stories – Theatrical designs of IRFĒ Foundation*.

IRFĒ Foundation's special projects
Dance of the Dead Languages, by Vadim Zakharov, presented at the Fifth Moscow Biennale
of Contemporary Art; *The Big Wheel Keeps on Turning*, by Marc Quinn; *Ballerina Dress*,
by Vladimir Glynin.

The IRFĒ Foundation has a long-standing collaboration with great Russian artist Andrei Sharov.
In this book you will find the special art project *Between Art and Fashion*.

IRFE Series, 2016
oil on canvas, 120 x 100 cm
Strukov Collection

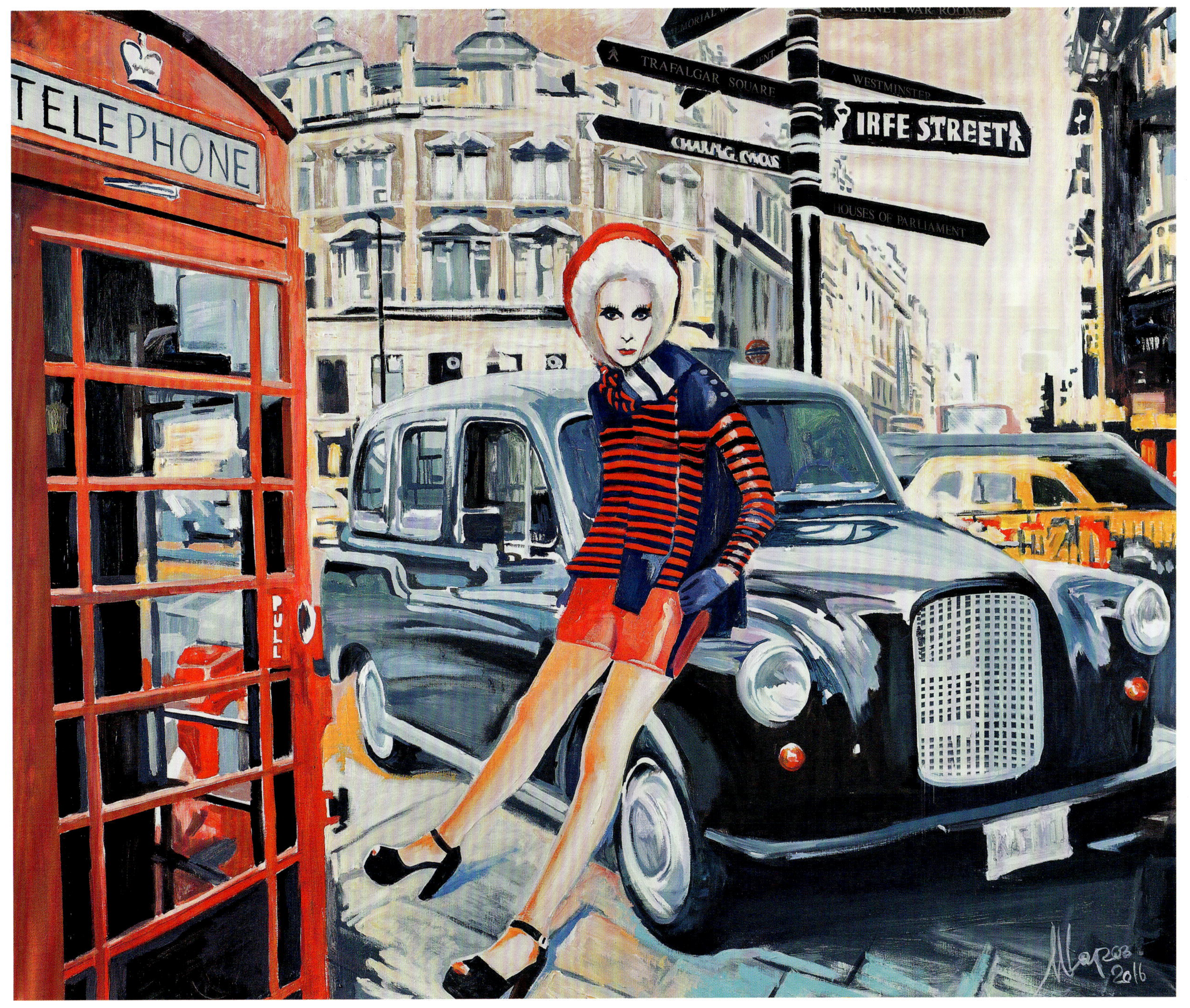

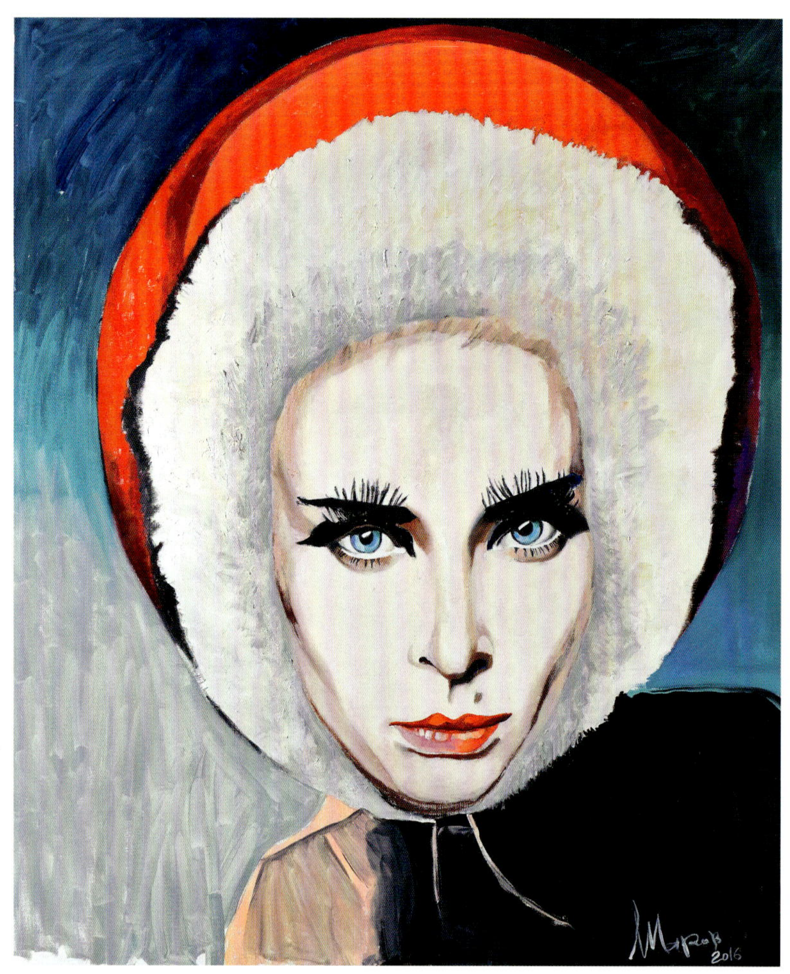

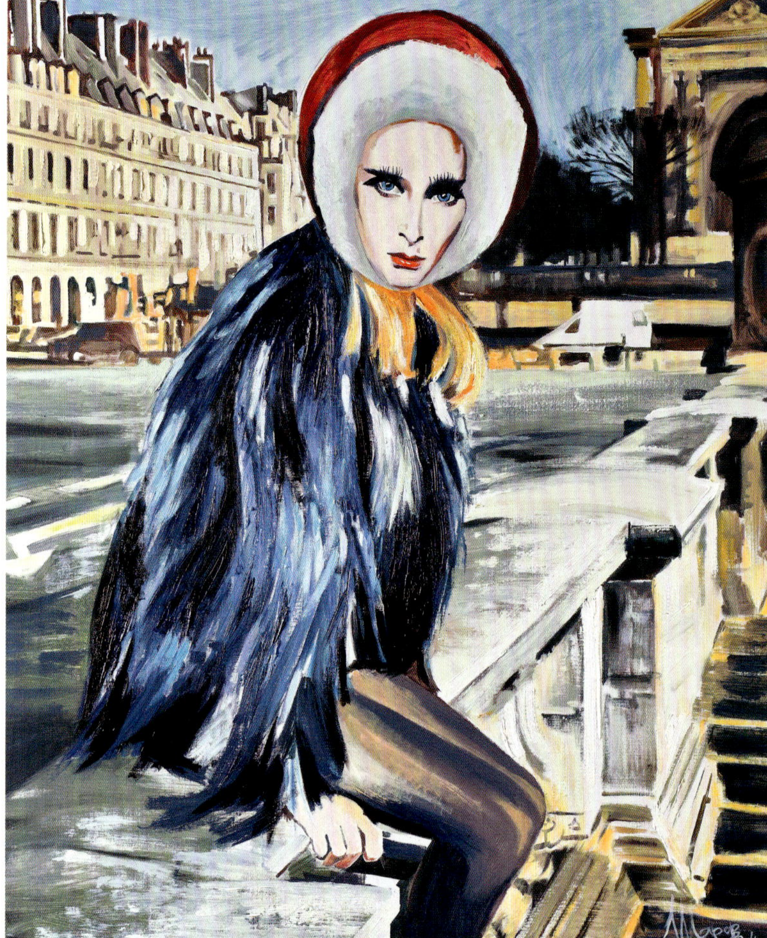

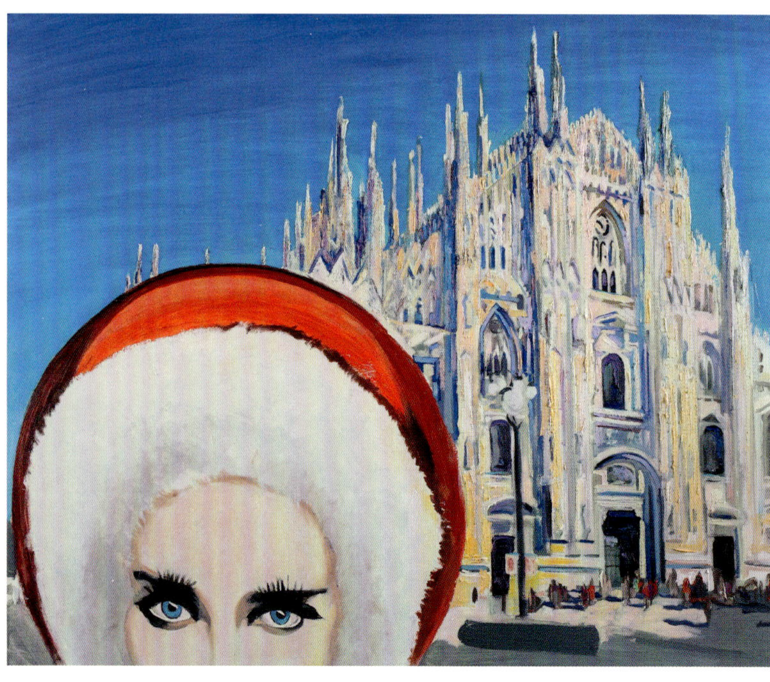

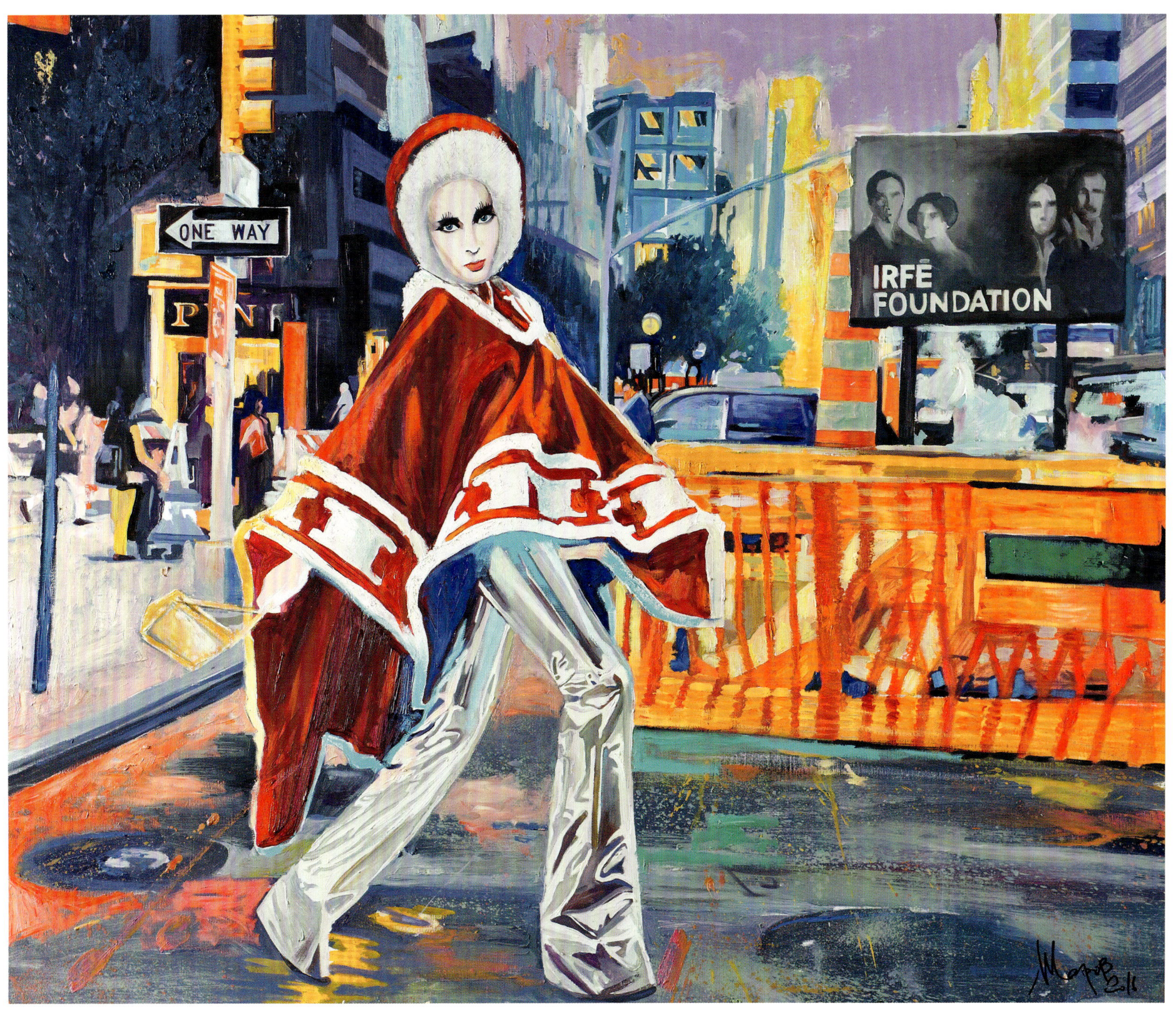

IRFE Series, 2016
oil on canvas, 100 x 120 cm
Strukov Collection

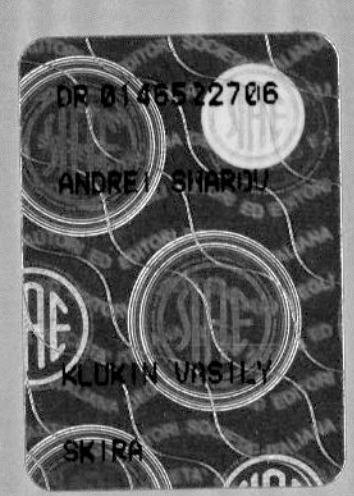
DR 0146522706
ANDREI SHAROV
KLUKIN VASILY
SKIRA